Carol Stream Public Library
616 Hiawatha Drive
Carol Stream, Illinois 60188

The Quest for Absolute Security

The Central Intelligence Agency
The FBI: A Comprehensive Reference Guide
The FBI and American Democracy
Chasing Spies
Civil Rights and Civil Liberties Since 1945
A Culture of Secrecy
J. Edgar Hoover, Sex, and Crime
The FBI: An Annotated Bibliography
From the Secret Files of J. Edgar Hoover
The Boss
Imperial Democracy
Beyond the Hiss Case
The Truman Presidency
Spying on Americans
The Specter
Seeds of Repression
The Yalta Myths

Athan Theoharis

THE QUEST FOR ABSOLUTE SECURITY

*The Failed Relations Among
U.S. Intelligence Agencies*

Ivan R. Dee
Chicago 2007

www.ivanrdee.com

Library of Congress Cataloging-in-Publication Data:
Theoharis, Athan G.
    The quest for absolute security : the failed relations among U.S.
intelligence agencies / Athan Theoharis
        p. cm.
    Includes bibliographical references and index.
    ISBN-13: 978-1-56663-697-1 (cloth : alk. paper)
    ISBN-10: 1-56663-697-3 (cloth : alk. paper)
    1. Intelligence service—United States—History. 2. United States. Federal Bureau of Investigation—History. 3. United States. Central Intelligence Agency—History. 4. Internal security—United States—History.
5. National security—United States—History. I. Title
JF1525.I6T45 2007
327.1273—dc22
                                                      2007014061

To Elizabeth, Chris, Jeanne, George, and Julie,
whose quest for absolute security is both noble and humane

ACKNOWLEDGMENTS

■ I HAVE ACCRUED many debts in the course of researching and writing this book. I wish to thank in particular the following individuals who have shared with me their specialized knowledge of aspects of the CIA's and FBI's history or various files they obtained in the course of their own research: John Stuart Cox, Herbert Mitgang, David Burnham, Steve Aftergood, Kenneth O'Reilly, David Williams, Ellen Schrecker, Melvin Small, John Donovan, Patrick Jung, Cathleen Thom, Christopher Gerard, Stephen Leahy, Susan Dion, John Elliff, Mark Gitenstein, Mike Epstein, Gary May, Seth Rosenfeld, John Henry Faulk, Alger Hiss, William Goodman, Damon Keith, Harrison Salisbury, Don Edwards, Tony Mauro, Anthony Marro, Morton Halperin, Kai Bird, Victor Navasky, Douglas Cassel, Harold Weisberg, M. Wesley Swearingen, David Luce, Richard Criley, Percival Bailey, Kenneth Waltzer, Sigmund Diamond, Steven Rosswurm, Charles Martin, Jon Wiener, John Fuegi, Dan Simoniski, Douglas Charles, Theodore Kornweibel, Sam Walker, Ray Dall'Osto, W. H. Ferry, John Studer, Holbrook Mahn, Allan Witwer, Alex Charns, James Rowen, Laura Kalman, Jessica Wang, Boria Sax, Barton Bernstein, Bruce Craig, Robert Griffith, Timothy Ingram, David Kendall, Ira Shapiro, Lewis Paper, David Thelen, Anna Kasten Nelson, James Dempsey, Michael Warner, John Prados, Kathryn Olmsted, Richard Immerman, Loch Johnson, and Scott Armstrong.

Marquette University has provided invaluable financial support for my research; I particularly thank Jim Marten and Steve

Avella for their efforts to help me develop minimal word-processing skills and particularly Joyce Hunkel who has patiently tutored me on the use of the computer. The Field Foundation, Warsh-Mott Fund, C. S. Fund, Albert Beveridge Award, National Endowment for the Humanities, Webster Woodmansee Fund, and the Fund for Investigative Journalism have provided the financial support essential to defraying the substantial costs of obtaining FBI files under the Freedom of Information Act while the Franklin and Eleanor Roosevelt Institute, the Harry S Truman Institute, and the Lyndon Baines Johnson Foundation have helped fund my research at presidential libraries. I am particularly indebted to the professional staff at the Roosevelt, Truman, Eisenhower, Kennedy, and Johnson presidential libraries and to the FBI's FOI/PA section for their thoughtfulness and helpfulness in assisting my research efforts (and I particularly thank Robert Watson, Susan Rosenfeld, Linda Kloss Colton, and John Fox of the FBI for their help in processing my numerous FOIA requests).

My greatest debt, however, is to Ivan Dee, who urged me to write this book and whose careful editing and pointed queries have immeasurably improved my prose. I have been honored to have worked with (and under) him for so many years.

A. T.

Milwaukee, Wisconsin
May 2007

CONTENTS

The Quest for Absolute Security

INTRODUCTION

■ THE TERRORIST ATTACK of September 11, 2001, traumatized the American public and the U.S. Congress in contrasting ways. It appeared to confirm the nation's vulnerability—yet it seemed clear that it might have been averted. Its impact was heightened soon after by the receipt of anthrax-laced letters by prominent politicians, media employees, and average citizens.

Congress at first responded to the 9/11 attack by expanding federal surveillance authority through the USA Patriot Act. Seven months later Attorney General John Ashcroft changed investigative guidelines for the Federal Bureau of Investigation to put "prevention above all else" and to ensure that FBI investigations would be "proactive" rather than "reactive." These decisions to expand the FBI's surveillance activities commanded widespread support at the time. A new consensus appeared to have emerged—future terrorist attacks must and could be averted by granting the FBI broad and intrusive investigative powers.

But many in Congress and the public seemed to contradict this acceptance of expanded executive power by insisting that the 9/11 attack could have been averted. In this view, officials of the CIA, the Central Intelligence Agency, and the FBI had apparently failed to anticipate an imminent terrorist threat. This concern prompted a joint investigation in June 2002 by the House Permanent Select Committee on Intelligence and the Senate Select

Committee on Intelligence. Because this committee was denied access to all relevant intelligence agency and White House records, as well as the opportunity to interview senior Bush administration officials, Congress in November 2002 authorized a second investigation by a ten-member body, the National Commission on Terrorist Attacks upon the United States, popularly known as the Kean Commission.

When the Joint Committee in July 2003 and the Kean Commission in July 2004 issued their findings, both reports faulted the FBI and the CIA for failing "to focus" on and share relevant information, and failing to assess the "collective significance" of acquired intelligence about "a probable terrorist attack." "Significant pieces of information in the vast stream of data being collected were overlooked," the Joint Committee emphasized; "some were not recognized as potentially significant at the time and therefore not disseminated [to other U.S. intelligence agencies], and some required additional action on the part of foreign governments before a direct connection to the hijackers could have been established." The Joint Committee and the Kean Commission also cited "serious gaps" in the collection capabilities of the two agencies, a "dearth of creative, aggressive analysis" in targeting Osama bin Laden and Al Qaeda, and the lack of a centralized analytic center to ensure that information was fully shared and understood. This they attributed in part to the agencies' differing "missions, legal authorities and cultures."[1]

To rectify these deficiencies, the Joint Committee and the Kean Commission recommended changes to ensure better coordination between the FBI and the CIA through the creation of a more centralized bureaucracy, headed by a director of national intelligence headquartered in the Executive Office of the President.* The in-

---

*These recommendations were not original. They had been advanced as early as 1993 by a host of independent and government commissions. Except for elites interested in intelligence history, they had been ignored.[2]

vestigative bodies differed, however, in their assessment of the FBI's domestic intelligence failure.

The FBI's capabilities had to be strengthened, the Joint Committee concluded, in light of "repeated shortcomings with its current responsibility for domestic intelligence." Congress should "consider," in "consultation" with the Bush administration, "whether the FBI should continue to perform the domestic intelligence functions of the United States Government or whether legislation is necessary to remedy this problem, including the possibility of creating a new agency to perform those functions."

Although it concurred that the FBI's pre-9/11 efforts had been deficient, the Kean Commission rejected this proposed creation of a "new domestic intelligence agency." A director of national intelligence could address this deficiency, commission members concluded, through close supervision and administrative reforms within the FBI to ensure a more "focused" approach. A "specialized and integrated national security workforce" of analysts, linguists, and surveillance specialists should be "recruited, trained, rewarded, and retained to ensure the development of an institutional culture imbued with a deep expertise in intelligence and national security."[3]

Both of these investigative bodies benefited from hindsight—an awareness of what had happened on September 11, 2001. But their reports reflect a poor understanding of the long-term history of limited cooperation among the intelligence agencies and of the FBI's long history of counterintelligence failures.

The FBI's failure to anticipate Al Qaeda's surprise attack was not due to insufficient authority, a lack of aggressiveness, or a "law enforcement" culture. FBI officials had abandoned a strictly law-enforcement approach as early as 1936 when they began to conduct "intelligence" investigations to anticipate espionage, sabotage, or "subversive activities." FBI agents who conducted such investigations had moreover aggressively employed "clearly illegal" investigative techniques, such as break-ins, or "sources illegal in nature," such as wiretaps, bugs, and mail openings. FBI officials had also devised special records procedures to preclude discovery of their illegal and politically motivated practices.[4] Their success in masking their activities enabled them to project a false image of an apolitical law-enforcement agency that did not violate the law, intrude on privacy and First Amendment rights, or engage in partisan politics.

For decades FBI officials had also been "creative and aggressive" and had operated "proactively." Their overriding objective was to contain activists and organizations they considered dangerous, whatever the means. In the process, a culture of lawlessness was created within the ranks of the highly disciplined bureau, based on the premise that the noble goal of curbing internal security threats justified the resort to recognizably illegal means.[*]

When the FBI's abuses of power were first revealed in the mid-1970s, FBI monitoring of "suspicious" activists and organizations and CIA foreign intelligence and counterintelligence activities were briefly circumscribed. But these restrictions were rescinded by President Ronald Reagan. Then, in the 1990s, as a consequence of truck bombings of the World Trade Center in New York and of U.S. embassies in Kenya and Tanzania, terrorism became an FBI priority. The counterterrorist capabilities of all fifty-six FBI field offices were upgraded, and the number of FBI overseas offices focusing on those countries critical to fighting terrorism were increased. Special units were created to address the new terrorist threat. As counterterrorism appropriations increased from $5 billion in 1996 to more than $11 billion in 2000, the budget for the

---

*This mind-set is captured in the response of senior FBI officials upon learning in 1955 that an FBI agent attending a training session had remarked that break-ins were unconstitutional. Briefed on this New York agent's remark, FBI officials immediately suspended the New York office's break-in operations and ordered an investigation to determine whether the agent's "mental outlook might be present" among members of the New York office's break-in squad. Learning that his views were not, the suspension was lifted.[5]

FBI's counterintelligence staff increased by 250 percent and for counterterrorism by 350 percent.*

Despite this expanded authority and a commitment to anticipating terrorism, FBI agents nonetheless failed to uncover the plans of Al Qaeda operatives who entered the United States during the critical months of 2000–2001 to execute the 9/11 attack. Identifying those who *intended* to engage in terrorism proved to be near impossible. Inevitably the FBI had concentrated its investigations on the wrong Middle Eastern alien residents.[6]

If the conclusions of the Kean Commission and the Joint Committee reflected an unwillingness to recognize the inherent limitations of counterintelligence investigations, as well as the pertinent histories of the major U.S. intelligence agencies, so did their assessment of "missed opportunities to thwart the 9/11 plot." These, they decided, derived in part from a lack of full cooperation between the FBI and the CIA, a by-product of "the limitations of the DCI's [Director of Central Intelligence] authority over the direction and priorities of the intelligence community." "Unity of effort" was needed, commission members concluded, and it could be achieved through the appointment of a national intelligence director with the authority to integrate "all sources of information to see the enemy as a whole."[7]

It was true that U.S. intelligence agencies had never fully cooperated. In one particularly serious instance, they had not shared information about Japanese plans and capabilities during the critical months leading to the surprise attack on Pearl Harbor on December 7, 1941.

This ringing failure of cooperation had led Congress to enact the National Security Act in July 1947 to avert future Pearl Harbors, creating two new agencies, a National Security Council

---

*Between April 1998 and September 2001 the CIA doubled the number of its personnel involved in counterterrorism and quintupled its total spending on counterterrorism.

(NSC) and a Central Intelligence Agency. In theory the two agencies would ensure coordination and "a comprehensive program for the future security of the United States." The NSC would "advise the President with respect to the integration of domestic, foreign, and military policies relating to national security so as to enable the military services and other departments and agencies of the Government to cooperate more effectively in matters involving the national security." An independent CIA, operating "under the National Security Council," would provide the broader perspective essential to advancing the president's foreign policy agenda and would do so by "coordinating the intelligence activities of the several Government departments and agencies."[8]

Congress's enactment of the Intelligence Reform and Terrorism Prevention Act in December 2004—implementing the core recommendation of the Joint Committee and the Kean Commission—in effect repeated the 1947 initiative. It created another executive bureaucracy with the objectives of "integrating" and "coordinating." Yet why would the creation of a new layer of bureaucracy, even one headquartered in the Executive Office of the President, produce results different from those achieved—or not achieved— through the 1947 National Security Act?

For this lack of full cooperation was in part the consequence of the scope and indiscriminate character of the FBI's and CIA's collection of intelligence, each agency's reliance on sources of questionable credibility, and each agency's almost obsessive commitment to secrecy. Good practice demanded that unverified or incomplete information *not* be automatically passed to other intelligence agencies. Forwarding all acquired information would not necessarily promote the nation's security interests but might instead compel the recipient agency to pursue useless leads.

No less important, both FBI and CIA officials had often hesitated to share information for fear their secret sources would be compromised. No administrative change can address this underlying "culture of secrecy" problem.

Finally, both the Kean Commission's and the Joint Committee's recommendations ignored the more complex reality of U.S. intelligence agencies cooperating throughout World War II and the cold war years to advance the nation's security interests. Cooperation was not deterred by their different cultures. Their special talents had in fact often been utilized by one another.

Understanding the history of the intelligence agencies and their interrelationships is a key to evaluating recently enacted institutional reforms. This history suggests that a more centralized system and greater surveillance authority carries the risk of politicizing intelligence and once again opening the way to abuses of power.

1 | THE ORIGINS OF U.S. INTELLIGENCE, 1882-1919

■ A CONTINUING CONCERN that has bedeviled U.S. policymakers, since the drafting of the U.S. Constitution in 1787, has been how to create an effective national government and yet ensure that power is not abused and individual liberties undermined. Thus while the history of the United States since 1787 has seen the steady expansion of federal responsibilities, that growth has been episodic, pragmatic in purpose, and uncoordinated. The overriding objective has remained the limitation of federal—and executive—power.

Accordingly the Constitution prescribed, if in vague language, the powers of the president and the executive branch. These were to "conduct" relations with foreign governments, operate as "commander in chief," and "take care that the laws be faithfully executed." In 1789 Congress enacted legislation to enable presidents to meet these defined responsibilities. It did so by creating a Department of State, to maintain official documents and negotiate treaties and trade agreements with foreign governments; a Department of the Treasury, to collect taxes and disburse funds; a Department of War, to raise and maintain an army to defend the nation in the event of a military attack; and an Office of the Attorney General, to represent the federal government in court and, only after 1870, to administer a Department of Justice. In ensuing years Congress created other departments to advance newly perceived national responsibilities, beginning in 1798 with the establishment of the Department of the Navy and extending during the nineteenth and twentieth centuries to the departments of Agriculture, Commerce, Defense,* Education, Energy, Health and Human Services, Homeland Security, Housing and Urban Development, Interior, Labor, Transportation, and Veterans Affairs. Each department's responsibilities were defined by law; in addition their heads were subject to Senate confirmation and depended on congressional approval for appropriations and for legislation to expand their authority.

The nation's explosive growth in territory and productivity during the late nineteenth century, combined with transformative technological advances, gave rise to a complex, urban, industrial society actively involved in international affairs. This growth precipitated a second, distinctive wave of governmental expansion with Congress creating new federal agencies. These independent agencies were not subject, like the departments listed above, to the president; their decisions were to be nonpartisan, based on principles of specialization and professionalism.†

Quite apart from these legislative initiatives, department heads issued executive orders creating agencies with specific responsibilities. These included the Secret Service, to enforce pay, bounty, and counterfeiting laws and to protect the president; an Office of Naval Intelligence, to acquire information about foreign naval capabilities; a Military Information Division, later renamed

---

*The 1947 National Security Act dissolved War and Navy as separate departments, creating a unified Department of Defense.
†These included a Civil Service Commission to ensure a nonpartisan federal work force; an Interstate Commerce Commission to regulate railroad rates; a Federal Reserve Board to supervise federally chartered banks, issue currency, and set interest rates; a Federal Communications Commission to regulate the telephone, telegraph, radio, and television industries; and a Central Intelligence Agency to coordinate intelligence and conduct covert operations.

the Military Intelligence Division, to enable the War Department to plan and anticipate potential military threats to the United States; and a Bureau of Investigation, later renamed the Federal Bureau of Investigation, to promote the prosecution of violators of federal laws. In a departure from this practice, the National Security Agency was established by a secret presidential directive to advance the Defense Department's code-breaking, interception, and communication needs.

This institutional growth ushered in a far more powerful federal government, yet the expansion was unplanned and uncoordinated. Nor did the creation of these departments and agencies reflect a total repudiation of concerns about the dangers of centralized power. A commitment to limited government, and an underlying suspicion of centralized power, explains why the first U.S. intelligence agency was created only in 1882 and why others were later created episodically, with no attempt to ensure they would operate in tandem.

This delay may seem surprising in light of the new nation's vulnerability in 1783, at the time of independence. Then, and in decades to follow, the nation's security was potentially threatened by powerful external and internal adversaries. The British may have formally recognized U.S. independence by the Treaty of Paris of 1783, but they continued to maintain forts in the Ohio Valley in violation of that treaty. Their Canadian colony bordered the United States to the north while the French and Spanish controlled territory to the south and west. These militarily more powerful European states, moreover, could exploit the hostility of Native Americans toward U.S. western territorial expansion.

Native Americans were not the new nation's sole internal threat. The opposition of western Pennsylvanians to the federal taxation of liquor compelled President George Washington in 1794 to send troops to quell the Whiskey Rebellion while Congress in 1798 enacted the Alien and Sedition Acts to suppress sympathizers of the French Revolution of 1789, who seemed willing—in the so-called Citizen Genet affair—to undermine the nation's security. Sectional differences over federal powers, involving the issues of slavery, tariffs, and territorial expansion, ultimately led to civil war in 1861. A continued antipathy toward centralized power, whether of Southerners influenced by the 1867 policy of Military Reconstruction or of labor union leaders who opposed the use of federal troops to suppress the railroad strike of 1877, led Congress in 1878 to enact the Posse Comitatus Act to prohibit the use of federal troops for law-enforcement purposes.

A centralized domestic and foreign intelligence system might have enhanced the federal government's ability to anticipate foreign military threats and preserve domestic order. Until the 1880s that option was rejected. Even then, when the public and Congress tacitly acceded to the creation of rather minuscule naval and military intelligence services by executive order, they remained concerned that such powers could be abused and individual liberties compromised.

The first of these services was established on March 23, 1882. On that date Secretary of the Navy William H. Hunt issued General Order No. 292 creating an Office of Naval Intelligence (ONI) to collect and record such information "as may be useful to the Department in wartime as well as in peace." Hunt wanted to ensure that senior Navy Department officials would have needed intelligence about foreign warships, coastal defenses, and foreign naval operations and resources; data on international trade and merchant vessels; and a secure code for naval communications. His creation of this special office departed from a past practice of relying on naval officers who, by recruiting spies, sought information about recent technological advances or the plans and capabilities of potential and current adversaries. Hunt's 1882 order reflected a new realization that naval modernization and "rehabilitation" demanded officers with this exclusive responsibility.

By the 1880s the need for a rehabilitated navy was seen as essential in meeting the demands of U.S. manufacturers and farmers for greater access to foreign markets. The attainment of this objective, however, was potentially threatened by the major European naval powers' recent imperial expansion in Africa, Asia, and Latin and South America. The European powers had purposely increased their navies to sustain their recently acquired colonies, thereby potentially denying American farmers and manufacturers access to these markets. By documenting the naval superiority of foreign governments, U.S. naval officials hoped to influence Congress and the public to support a stronger navy through a focused intelligence collection system.[1]

This prosaic departmental interest also determined the decision of War Department officials in the fall of 1885 to create the Military Information Division (MID) within the Department's Miscellaneous Branch. Until then, army officers, like their naval counterparts, had collected information about the plans and capabilities of foreign military powers (and Native Americans) as part of their other duties and had done so by recruiting spies or other nonmilitary sources, including contracting for the services of the Pinkerton Detective Agency during the Civil War. Secretary of War William Endicott's onetime request of Brigadier General R. C. Drum, the adjutant general, for information about the armed forces of an unspecified European power was the catalyst to the establishment of a specialized military intelligence service. Unable to answer the secretary's question, Drum on his own initiative appointed a Military Information Division within his office to "gather and file information concerning the military organization of foreign countries in which, for one reason or another, the United States might become interested," to be obtained from "all available sources."

The MID initially consisted of one military officer and a civilian chief supervising two civilian assistants and a messenger, was housed in a one-room office in Washington, and depended for domestic information on National Guard units around the country. Then in 1886 the adjutant general requested chiefs of War Department bureaus and key field commanders to collect and forward to the recently created intelligence office all information of military value—books, maps, and data about the geography, economic resources, and force levels of foreign powers. War Department officials in 1888 also sought congressional funding to station military personnel in the role of attachés abroad. Following congressional approval of this appropriation request, on February 27, 1889, outgoing Secretary of War Endicott assigned military personnel to U.S. legations in London, Paris, and Vienna—and later that year in Berlin and St. Petersburg. Military attachés were to forward to MID headquarters in Washington "all matters of a military or technical character that may be of interest and value to any branch of the War Department and to the service at large." The MID was formally established as a separate division within the adjutant general's office on April 12, 1889, by Endicott's confidential order with the responsibility to obtain and collate "such military data as may be deemed useful and beneficial for the Army at large."[2]

Creation of ONI and MID at the time commanded little public or congressional interest. That was not the case when the Bureau of Investigation was established on June 29, 1908, by executive order of Attorney General Charles Bonaparte. Bonaparte's order was based on the 1870 law creating the Department of Justice, which authorized this new department to "prosecute and detect" violations of federal statutes.

Congress's belated establishment of a Department of Justice marked a rejection of an earlier belief that law enforcement should remain a local and state responsibility. After the defeat of the South in the Civil War, the Republican-led Congress sought to address the legacy of the abolition of slavery through the Thirteenth Amendment by enacting a series of civil rights laws. It drafted the Fourteenth and Fifteenth Amendments, curbing state powers, and instituted a policy of Military Reconstruction of the defeated Southern states. These actions called into question the premise that the federal government should have no law-enforcement role. A consensus had temporarily emerged to endorse a stronger federal role as essential in preventing Southerners from reinstating a system akin to slavery through the so-called Black Codes. By the late 1870s, however, a federal commitment to ensure equal rights for black Southerners was abandoned. Still, many Southern Democrats remained leery of proposals to expand the federal government's powers. Conservative Republicans also shared these antigovernment concerns, stemming from the expansion of federal regulatory powers during the Progressive Era and President Theodore Roosevelt's effective use of the "bully pulpit" of the presidency to pressure Congress to enact legislation regulating corporate business practices.

Following Theodore Roosevelt's ascendancy to the presidency in 1901, Justice Department officials began to enforce more vigorously the Sherman Anti-Trust Act of 1890. The charismatic president concurrently called for greater federal powers to regulate railroad rate practices and the drug and meatpacking industries. And, responding to moralistic demands, Congress enacted legislation regulating prostitution—the so-called Mann Act—and submitted for state ratification the Eighteenth Amendment prohibiting the sale and distribution of alcoholic beverages.

These expanded law-enforcement responsibilities compelled senior Justice Department officials to reassess their operating system. The department had been authorized under the 1870 act to "prosecute and detect" violations of federal statutes. Neither then nor in ensuing decades did senior department officials establish a special investigative division. They saw no need to do so in light of the limited number of federal laws to be enforced and the fact that departmental attorneys could handle most prosecutions. The services of skilled investigators were only rarely required and in those cases could be obtained through the temporary hiring of private detectives, through the Pinkerton Detective Agency, or the Treasury Department's Secret Service agents.

The Pinkerton Agency's controversial role in breaking the 1892 Homestead Strike led Congress in 1893 to prohibit government officials from temporarily hiring private investigators, thereby confining the department's option to the Secret Service. By then skilled investigators had become a more regular departmental interest. Accordingly Attorney General Bonaparte asked Congress to fund an investigative division within the Department of Justice. His 1907 request, however, coincided with a public controversy triggered by revelations, first, that Navy Department officials had used Secret Service agents in investigating the extramarital sexual activities of a naval officer, and, second, that Justice Department officials had relied on Secret Service agents to secure the indictments of two Oregon congressmen, Senator John Mitchell and Representative John Williamson, for land fraud.

Members of Congress cited these publicized uses of Secret Service agents as confirming the threat posed by a "secret police" force to a system of limited constitutional government. Congress not only rejected Bonaparte's 1907 request but in 1908 adopted a rider to the Treasury Department's appropriations prohibiting expenditures for purposes other than enforcing pay, bounty, and counterfeiting laws and protecting the president—the Secret Service's assigned responsibilities. As justification, alarmed members of Congress cited the perils of a "spy system," compared a federal police force with "a general system of spying and espionage of the people such as has prevailed in [tsarist] Russia, in France under the [Napoleonic] Empire, and at one time in Ireland," and suggested that executive officials could employ such an agency "to dig up the private scandals of men." Congressional concerns were further heightened by President Roosevelt's dismissal of their protests over the role of Secret Service agents as an attempt to protect lawbreakers—remarks that tapped into widespread public beliefs that members of Congress were corrupt or corruptible.

The adopted rider in effect foreclosed what had been an informal Justice Department–Secret Service arrangement. In response, on June 29, 1908, with Congress in recess, Bonaparte unilaterally established a special investigative force within the Department of Justice funded through the department's "miscellaneous expense fund." Originally stationed in Washington and staffed by ten former Secret Service agents, the new Bureau of Investigation soon expanded its personnel with agents eventually assigned to field offices in major cities around the country.*

Bonaparte's unilateral action was controversial because it appeared to contravene the spirit and intent of the Congress. After the 1908 elections, a House appropriations subcommittee convened hearings in January 1909 to question the departing attorney general about this decision.

Bonaparte defended his action and at the same time sought to allay the constitutional and abuse-of-power concerns that Congress had raised in 1908. His intent, the attorney general testified, was to further the Justice Department's delegated law-enforcement responsibilities. As attorney general he would personally oversee FBI investigations to ensure that they were confined to violations of federal statutes. These assurances, combined with the small size of the new investigative force stationed in Washington and thus capable of being directly monitored, succeeded in deterring Congress from rescinding his decision. Nonetheless Congress in 1909 adopted a rider to Justice Department appropriations limiting the FBI's authority to the "detection and prosecution of crimes against the United States."[3]

ONI, MID, and FBI had thus been created separately and without any overall plan. But their uncoordinated and bureaucratic independence was of little concern. The public and Congress

---

*Originally known as the Bureau of Investigation, this investigative service was formally renamed the Federal Bureau of Investigation in 1935. I henceforth refer to it under that latter name to avoid confusion.

remained committed to limited government but saw all three agencies as having a narrow mandate, their powers limited by small staffs. By 1917, for example, MID's total headquarters staff, excluding military attachés, consisted of two officers and two clerks; ONI had a staff of eight officers and 18 civilian employees; the FBI, given the recent enactment of federal laws expanding interstate commerce crimes, had a staff of 570 (265 agents and 305 support staff), an increase from 34 in 1909 and 161 in 1914 (122 agents and 39 support staff).

The outbreak of World War I in 1914 and the eventual U.S. military involvement in that conflict in April 1917 immediately changed each of these agencies' international and domestic roles. And for the first time agency officials established informal liaison with their counterparts. These changes were implemented rapidly and without preliminary planning owing to the sudden and unanticipated onset of the evolving crisis.

Despite their tiny staffs, during the years 1914–1917 ONI and MID intelligence-collection capabilities increased as their officials recruited as informers businessmen, journalists, other civilians, and executives in international corporations with offices overseas. In addition, ONI and MID officials enhanced the training and expertise of their own personnel in intelligence analysis.

Initial changes occurred as a by-product of the so-called preparedness campaign of 1915–1916, when the Wilson administration convinced Congress to increase military spending. To ensure the success of this lobbying effort, ONI and MID officials stepped up their efforts to acquire maps and information about the military capabilities of the warring European states and the latest military technology, and prepared surveys of ports and military bases in Europe and in the Western Hemisphere—reflecting contemporary anxieties about German influence and espionage activities in Latin America, Mexico, and the Caribbean.

MID's and ONI's most important growth occurred only after April 1917 when the United States became militarily involved in the ongoing European conflict. By November 1918 MID's staff had increased to 282 officers and 1,159 civilian employees (declining by August 1919 to 88 officers and 143 civilians), and ONI's staff had increased to 42 naval officers, 306 reservists, and 18 civilian clerks (declining by November 1919 to 42 naval and civilian personnel). In contrast, the FBI's growth was relatively slower, increasing to 593 (225 agents and 268 support staff) in 1919 and 630 (301 agents and 329 support staff) in 1920. Senior department officials had assumed that increases in personnel would be temporary, in response to immediate wartime responsibilities. Thus, rather than increase staff, MID, ONI, and FBI officials relied on private citizens for information on perceived domestic threats. Their sources included private detectives, journalists, local police officers, and the co-workers and neighbors of suspected radicals.

This expansion of intelligence activity occurred in an atmosphere of public fear of subversion. As one result, and because the expansion had not been anticipated, Congress and responsible officials in the War, Navy, and Justice departments did not closely supervise the intelligence agencies. The specific initiatives and surveillance targets, ostensibly chosen to promote the nation's security interests in a time of war, were thus determined by the ideological biases of agency officials—anti-radical, anti-labor, anti-Catholic, anti-German, anti-Semitic, anti-Irish, and more generally anti-immigrant.

Indeed, MID officials contacted local FBI agents to obtain FBI reports on "Socialist activities," closely monitored anarchist publications and prominent anarchists (notably Emma Goldman and Alexander Berkman) as well as Sinn Fein and other Irish-American activists (notably James Larkin), prominent pacifists (notably Scott Nearing and Louis Lochner), civil libertarians (notably Roger Baldwin and the fledgling National Civil Liberties Union), and African-American activists and publications (notably William Trotter). ONI officials focused intensively on radical activists, particularly the adherents of the Industrial Workers of the World (IWW) and the Socialist party. Most ONI and MID surveillance activities moreover lacked legal authority, and their policing of labor unions violated the Posse Comitatus Act.

FBI officials also exploited this crisis setting to expand their investigations, though their focus shifted in response to differing prewar and wartime needs. During the 1914–1917 period, FBI investigations centered on alien residents and citizens who were suspected of violating the nation's neutrality laws. FBI agents did uncover information about the attempts of German agents, including consular officers stationed in the United States, to sabotage the shipment of goods from the United States and Canada to Great Britain and France, discovered explosive devices on forty-seven ships bound for Britain and France, and investigated suspicious explosions at a munitions dump on Black Tom Island in New York harbor in July 1916 and at a munitions firm in Kingston, New Jersey, in January 1917. FBI investigations increased dramatically after 1917, focusing on alien residents who could be detained under the 1798 Alien Enemies Act or on citizens suspected of violating the Espionage Act of 1917, the Selective Service Act of 1917, or the Sedition Act of 1918. In addition, under a 1916 rider to Justice Department appropriations, FBI officials conducted investigations at the request of the State Department.* FBI officials also concluded a liaison agreement with a businessmen's group, the American Protective League (APL), headquartered in Chicago.

This liaison program with the APL began in March 1917, the month before Congress declared war on Germany. Under its terms, APL members chauffeured FBI agents and submitted re-

---

*In addition to approving visas, honoring requests for assistance from American tourists and business people overseas, and compiling information about trade and investment opportunities, consular officers collected political intelligence—for example, the plans and contacts of German officials with their American sources.

ports to them about those individuals whom they suspected of violating the conscription, espionage, and sedition laws. Invariably these reports concerned radical political and labor union activists. Attorney General Thomas Gregory endorsed this arrangement with the APL, in part because he opposed "too much machinery" that would be needed if the desired surveillance were to be undertaken solely by FBI personnel.

Under this liaison program more than 200,000 APL members in 1,400 cities and towns spied on suspected "subversives." Working in tandem with FBI agents and local police, APL members went so far as to arrest individuals suspected of violating the Selective Service Act. Their most controversial action involved the mass arrests of suspected "slackers" in New York City in the summer of 1918. In contrast to other APL actions, the "slacker" arrests prompted bitter protests, for those arrested included prominent businessmen who had simply failed to carry their draft cards and who were held in cramped quarters.

MID officers, working in tandem with FBI officials during the war, also solicited APL assistance in monitoring individuals whom they suspected of involvement in industrial sabotage or who applied for overseas duty with service organizations such as the Red Cross, the YMCA, and the Knights of Columbus. APL assistance was intended to promote either the War Department's wartime plant inspection program or the military's responsibilities in France, the latter requiring knowledge about the "character and loyalty" of Americans traveling to that country. By the end of the war, APL members had conducted thirty thousand "character and loyalty" investigations.

World War I presented an unanticipated opportunity for senior department and agency officials to expand ONI's, MID's, and FBI's international and domestic roles. Both ONI and MID officials acted to ensure base security, the loyalty of army and navy personnel, and the security of their communications, and to prevent disruption of military-related industrial production. Their convictions about the "seditious intent" of IWW-led strikes also led ONI and MID officials to create branch offices to investigate and guard plants holding army and navy contracts and to provide intelligence to federal troops that in 1917 and 1918 either broke IWW strikes or detained strikers in the mining and lumber industries. Ethnic Americans were also monitored, owing to MID and ONI officials' suspicions about "disloyalty among Catholic priests and Sinn Fein propaganda."

The quality of the intelligence varied. ONI and MID officials supplemented their information about Germany's military capabilities with contributions provided by their French and British counterparts, having developed an effective relationship. ONI agents also monitored the foreign press and prepared lists of merchant vessels sunk by German submarines. MID, ONI, and FBI officials extensively shared information derived from their domestic investigations and worked closely to contain what they believed to be a serious internal security threat posed by radical activists. Although they met frequently to enhance coordination, officials of all three agencies resisted the establishment of a centralized intelligence system. Their reluctance reflected bureaucratic interests and a mutual disdain for the competence of their counterparts' personnel.

While ONI's and MID's foreign intelligence was not crucial to military victory in World War I, theirs and the FBI's domestic surveillance activities did have a major impact on wartime civil liberties within the United States. One result was the suppression of militant political and labor organizations such as the Socialist party and the IWW.

FBI investigations moved beyond simple law enforcement to political containment. Significantly, of the 2,500 espionage cases that the Justice Department prosecuted in the World War I era, not one involved actual espionage or sabotage. The most notorious case involved the prosecution of the producer of a film on the American Revolution, *The Spirit of '76*. A second involved simultaneous FBI raids in September 1917 on IWW headquarters in Chicago and its offices in Fresno, Seattle, and Spokane, and the seizure of tons of IWW documents. These raids led to the indictments of the union's leaders, who were tried and convicted under the 1917 Espionage Act. The developed evidence, however, documented not that these IWW officials had engaged in espionage or sabotage but that they had in the prewar era denounced a capitalist economic system and contended that capitalism led to imperialist wars (recorded in IWW pamphlets and correspondence). Other essentially political cases involved the conviction of leaders of the Socialist party, notably Charles Schenck, the party's executive secretary, for publishing a pamphlet opposing conscription, and Eugene Debs, the party's presidential candidate, for a speech he gave in Canton, Ohio, opposing the war as imperialistic. FBI agents also conducted intimidating interviews of pacifists, German-American and Irish-American activists, Lutheran ministers, and others who criticized the Wilson administration's foreign and internal security policies. FBI agents warned these dissidents to desist from their "seditious" views, lectured them about proper "Americanism," and advised that their continued "disloyal" speech could lead to prosecution. These tactics differed only in method from those of MID and ONI officials who worked closely with the wartime Committee on Public Information—the so-called Creel Committee—to promote a domestic propaganda campaign of 100 percent Americanism. It included the censorship of books, periodicals, lectures, and the foreign-language press.

The armistice of November 1918, formally halting military combat, did not end FBI surveillance. In fact FBI agents now expanded their monitoring of radical activists as a consequence of the Bolshevik Revolution of November 1917 and the emergence of a fledgling Communist movement in the United States. To address this new threat, Attorney General A. Mitchell Palmer on August 1, 1919, created a special Radical Division, later renamed the General Intelligence Division (GID), to collate all FBI information about radical activists. By 1920 more than 200,000 files had been amassed on radical activists and organizations, on the role of radicals in the 1919 and 1920 steel and coal strikes, on suspect domestic newspapers and periodicals, and on more than 500 foreign-language newspapers—to keep up with "radical propaganda." The subjects of these files included the settlement-house reformer and pacifist Jane Addams, the anti-war Senator Robert LaFollette, the militant black nationalist and founder of the Universal Negro Improvement Association Marcus Garvey, the Irish nationalist Eamon De Valera, the Hearst press and the *Chicago Tribune* (owing to their pro-Irish and anti-British stances), and editors of black newspapers and periodicals who were suspected of "exciting the negro element of this country to riot and to the committing of outrages of all sorts."[4]

After the war ONI, MID, and FBI officials encountered different pressures and opportunities. Because the public and Congress were not fully aware of the scope and targets of the three agencies—and those that were known seemed to be responsive to a perceived wartime German threat—there was no consensus to support either continued postwar surveillance or a more centralized intelligence system. Nonetheless their wartime experiences emboldened ONI, MID, and FBI officials to monitor a new internal security threat posed by pacifists, ethnics, and radical activists. Their commitment to this continuing campaign had mixed results. Some of their initiatives had to be aborted after negative publicity that prompted public and congressional condemnation on states' rights grounds. Other initiatives succeeded because of their congruence with the ethno-religious and anti-labor prejudices of the 1920s that led to the postwar resurgence of the Ku Klux Klan, the enactment of discriminatory immigration legislation in 1921 and 1924, and the suppression of the labor movement. In the confrontation with labor, federal troops were used to defeat strikes in the steel and coal industries in 1919 and 1920, a sweeping court injunction halted the 1922 railroad strike, and the Supreme Court handed down anti-labor rulings in the *Hitchman*, *Duplex*, and *Tri-City* cases of 1917 and 1921. As they entered the 1920s, all three agencies searched for a new role in the postwar years.

2 | A PERIOD OF TRANSITION, 1919–1936

■ THE ARMISTICE of November 1918 marked the end of military operations in World War I and raised the question of the U.S. role in a vastly changed postwar world. To President Woodrow Wilson, American assistance in defeating Germany and Austria-Hungary offered the opportunity to create a "new world order" wherein disputes among nations would be resolved through diplomacy. Central to Wilson's policy was the creation of a permanent collective security system, the League of Nations. The president seemed to have achieved this objective through the treaty he helped negotiate at the Versailles peace conference. But the victory proved to be short-lived as the Senate, under the leadership of Henry Cabot Lodge, the Republican chairman of the Senate Foreign Relations Committee, twice voted to reject ratification. Unqualified ratification, Lodge argued, would compromise national sovereignty and Congress's exclusive power to declare war.

Ironically the Wilson administration's success in 1917–1918 in discrediting public opposition to the war as disloyal had promoted an intolerant, nationalistic climate. Lodge and conservative Republicans capitalized on it, first to defeat ratification and then to gain control of Congress and the presidency in the 1920 elections. The resurgent conservatism of the so-called New Era specifically tapped into popular concerns about wartime centralization of power in the executive branch and thereby affected the postwar status of the intelligence agencies.

This narrow nationalism and opposition to international commitments lent support for limitations on naval armaments, incorporated in the Washington Naval Conference negotiations of 1921–1922, and the outlawing of war, incorporated in the Kellogg-Briand Pact of 1928. Then the stock market crash of October 1929, ushering in the Great Depression, further intensified anti-militarist and nationalist sentiments. As one by-product, in 1934 Congress initiated hearings into the role of munition makers in undermining neutrality and promoting unnecessary military conflict. The so-called Nye Committee soon extended this inquiry to the role of bankers and secret presidential diplomacy.

This radically changed political climate challenged the leadership of ONI, MID, and FBI. On the one hand, narrow nationalism and anti-militarism, combined with fiscal conservatism, strengthened demands to limit military spending. On the other hand, a newly strengthened conservatism of ethnic politics and limited government in the 1920s, and then a growing public tolerance for radical ideas in the 1930s, undercut the rationale for surveillance of suspect subversives. New Era policymakers instead identified internal security threats in ethno-religious terms, exemplified in the revival of the Ku Klux Klan and the enactment of the National Origins Act of 1924 which limited immigration. These nativist prejudices did not long remain dominant: the crisis of the Great Depression lent support instead for New Deal policies to address economic and social injustice.

ONI, MID, and FBI officials did not fully adapt to this changing political reality. Throughout the 1920s and 1930s they continued to monitor radical and liberal activists, convinced that the nation confronted a new internal security threat, whether it was a product of the Bolshevik Revolution of 1917 or the anti-militarism of women activists, pacifists, and civil libertarians.

Thus MID officials sought to sustain the agency's expanded intelligence role in the face of popular and congressional indifference. During World War I they had been able to capitalize on wartime concerns as Congress increased funding for intelligence operations to prevent the disruption of military production. Recognizing that Congress would not continue such funding levels, Secretary of War Newton Baker in 1919 reduced MID personnel from 1,000 to 274. The numbers were further reduced to 234 in 1920, to 75 by 1930, and to 70 by 1934.

This retrenchment constituted MID officials' specific dilemma given their alarm over the postwar increase in labor strikes in 1919–1920 and the outbreak of race riots in twenty-six American cities in 1920. MID officials viewed these developments from an intolerant, anti-radical perspective. Radicals, one MID officer concluded, intended "to excite the interest and emotions of the masses of people." Another MID officer added that radicals were "90% Jewish," and still another decried the "sinister . . . agitators [who sought] to create a state of chaos out of which would spring a revolution" in the United States.

Anticipating the need for military action to curb a revolutionary threat that was not "transitory" but "a permanent feature to be reckoned with," MID officials in 1919 drafted a contingency plan, code-named War Plans White, to identify potentially dangerous radical activists and groups. No revolution materialized. For one, the labor movement never recovered from its defeat in the strikes of 1919–1920; the Communist party, a tiny minority, was devastated by the Palmer Raids of 1920; African Americans became victims of a revived Ku Klux Klan; and Congress in 1921 and 1924 enacted ethnic quota legislation that discriminated against Eastern and Southern Europeans and virtually halted immigration from Europe.

By October 1921, then, Secretary of War John Weeks rescinded War Plans White, concluding that monitoring civilians was properly the responsibility of the FBI. Even the head of MID worried that "The suspicion of [MID] gum-shoe work is doing the Army much harm."

Unwilling to abandon domestic surveillance yet recognizing that the libertarian character of postwar conservatism made funding for continued surveillance unlikely, MID officials first sought to continue their wartime arrangement with the American Protective League. Attorney General Thomas Gregory's 1918 order disbanding the FBI-APL relationship—upon which MID had relied—had apparently foreclosed this option. But MID chief Marlborough Churchill responded by directly seeking APL's assistance. Until 1924 APL members sometimes volunteered or honored specific MID requests for information about radical activities. At the same time MID officials established informal liaison relationships with the recently formed American Legion, conservative businessmen, and sympathetic reporters.

MID's most valued source, nonetheless, remained the FBI. Both agencies continued after 1919 to share information each had uncovered about targeted labor union, civil liberties, women's, and pacifist activists. This informal relationship, however, suffered a serious blow when Attorney General Harlan Fiske Stone in May 1924 barred the FBI from monitoring political activities. Thus, when in April 1925 MID director James Reeves requested FBI assistance to reactivate the War Department's secret Emergency Plans White (the successor to the discontinued War Plans White contingency plan), FBI director J. Edgar Hoover replied that the FBI no longer routinely investigated radicals. Despite this formal break, FBI and MID officials continued to share information on radical activities, including the participation of suspected Communists in the veterans' 1932 Bonus March on Washington.

Given the decimation suffered by radical movements—notably the Socialist and Communist parties and the IWW—in the years after 1917, MID surveillance activities in the 1920s concentrated on moderate and respectable organizations, especially peace and civil liberties organizations such as the American Civil Liberties Union and the Women's International League for Peace and Freedom.

Women activists, disillusioned by the results of U.S. participation in World War I and convinced that war was the inevitable result of an arms race, after 1920 assumed a primary role in the opposition to military spending and a militaristic foreign policy. Specifically they and civil liberties activists demanded curbs on the Reserve Officers Training Corps (ROTC). Indeed, progressive legislators in Wisconsin enacted legislation in 1923 making participation in ROTC voluntary at the University of Wisconsin. MID officials were particularly alarmed by the influence of these seemingly respectable subversives.

MID surveillance activities intensified in the aftermath of the stock market crash of October 1929 and the onset of the Great Depression. The severity of the economic downturn had led many Americans to question a capitalist economic system; their antipathy toward corporate influence prompted some to tolerate, even endorse radical demands for far-reaching economic change. MID officials responded by monitoring individuals and groups as varied as youth employed under the Civilian Conservation Corps and veterans who organized the Bonus March. One MID official concluded that the Bonus Marchers had been funded by subversive business corporations, singling out the motion picture studio Metro-Goldwyn-Mayer. "Metro-Goldwyn-Mayer," an MID officer warned, "is known to be 100 per cent Jewish as to controlling personnel, and . . . high officers of this corporation are in politics. An unconfirmed rumor circulated many months ago, stated that agents of the U.S.S.R. had contacted motion picture companies in California, and contributed to some of them with a view to insuring propaganda and support of U.S.S.R. policies."

Recognizing the risks inherent in MID's monitoring of political activists, as early as 1919, MID director Churchill had counseled "against letting [MID surveillance] activities be known."

MID agents were urged not to go "on record" when recruiting volunteers from conservative organizations or citizens for "assistance." Secrecy was imperative, Churchill emphasized, to forestall the subjects of MID surveillance and their allies in the media and Congress from learning about this recruitment and surveillance: "They would come down on us and exert pressure on the White House."

For the most part MID officials succeeded in precluding public awareness of their surveillance activities—an ignorance that extended even to the secretary of war. In at least one instance, this independence proved to be counterproductive. When they were convinced that the campaign of women pacifists against chemical warfare threatened the national interest, MID officials in 1923 asked the War Department's Chemical Warfare Service for help in discrediting these women activists. MID officials then prepared and publicly circulated a chart linking prominent women activists with alleged radical groups, implying that they were either Communists or doing the work of the Communists, and that the "activities of all women's societies and many church societies may be regarded with suspicion." The identified women activists immediately protested this aspersion on their loyalty and denounced this confirmed example of MID domestic surveillance. An embarrassed secretary of war thereupon ordered the destruction of the notorious chart, denying it had been prepared by the War Department. Following on the secretary's order, the deputy adjutant general reaffirmed earlier War Department orders prohibiting MID monitoring of civilians.[1]

ONI's situation paralleled that of MID. ONI officials were also forced to reduce their postwar staff, from 364 to 42 by July 1920. Congressional funding for ONI operations in fact never exceeded $150,000 throughout the 1920s and 1930s. Nonetheless ONI officials could briefly tap a secret, unexpended wartime appropriation of $450,000, so they were not reconciled to this forced retrenchment. They sought to offset the cutback in personnel by continuing their wartime liaison with the FBI, each agency sharing information about suspect subversives. ONI officials also relied on the FBI to compile lists of foreign-born employees at defense plants and to provide the fingerprints of individuals working on defense contracts. They also obtained permission for their personnel to attend the FBI National Police Academy—later renamed the FBI National Academy—to study the latest scientific technology and law enforcement methods.

Like MID, ONI officials also recruited private citizens as informers. These included journalists—for example the *Cleveland News* editor Dan Hanna—prominent businessmen, retired naval officers, and professors of naval science employed on college campuses. Later, with the sharp upsurge in pacifist activities on college campuses in the 1930s, ONI director Hayne Ellis recruited sympathetic faculty at Yale, Harvard, Georgia Tech, Northwestern, and several West Coast universities to spy on "ultra pacifist" students and faculty at their universities. Ellis even directed ONI officers to develop programs to counteract the historian Charles A. Beard's anti-war book *The Navy: Defense or Portent*, as well as "insidious propaganda of a similar nature with which pacifist organizations are flooding the country."

These ONI efforts reflected a conviction that, as in wartime, the nation continued to confront a serious internal security threat. An imminent Communist revolution, seemingly confirmed by the 1919–1920 labor strikes, required "immediate and radical steps in its suppression." In addition, ONI officials feared, the anarchists Alexander Berkman and Emma Goldman intended to launch a nationwide terrorist operation that would "surpass anything that ever happened in this country." By the mid-1920s, however, ONI officials had concluded that the major internal security threat came from the ACLU, liberal Christians, pacifists, and anti-war groups such as the National Council for the Prevention of War, the National Federation of Churches, and the Women's International League for Peace and Freedom.

To counter this threat, ONI officials were not content simply to monitor "subversive" activists but sought to counter what they perceived to be "the ignorance of the public, even the educated classes at what the navy stands for." They worried that the public might warm to anti-militarist and civil liberties arguments and acted aggressively to offset publications, movies, plays, and literature that promoted these ideas. One such effort, for example, was designed to ensure "a correct understanding" of the 1922 Washington Naval Conference treaty limiting naval armament. Articulating this equation of liberal ideas with subversion, ONI director William Puleston concluded, based on reports of ONI agents' monitoring a Philadelphia education conference, that Communists had infiltrated this conference "to interest teachers in the United States of Communist teachings."

In their quest for information to rebut the navy's anti-military and pacifist critics, ONI officers broke into the New York office of the U.S. Communist party, the Japanese consulate in New York, the New York office of the Japanese Imperial Railway, and bank and business offices in New York and on the West Coast. They had hoped to confirm a link between the navy's domestic critics and the Soviet and Japanese governments. A similar concern about the Nye Committee hearings of 1934–1937 led to ONI monitoring of this congressional committee and its staff director Stephen Raushenbush. After reviewing the reports of this surveillance, ONI director William Puleston starkly warned Assistant Secretary of the Navy Henry Roosevelt in February 1935 that "*the Nye investigation is Communist inspired and Pacifist operated and that the Munitions Investigation is merely a smoke screen under the cover of which the minds of the people of the United States may be poisoned against the National Defense and that Mr. Raushenbush was purposely placed where he is by subversive activities.*" (The italics are Puleston's.)

In contrast to MID, the scope of ONI surveillance operations and ONI officials' ability to foreclose public or congressional awareness of their use of illegal investigative techniques was apparently known to senior White House officials—an awareness indirectly confirmed by a 1930 request of President Herbert Hoover.

The president had learned that Democratic political operatives had developed derogatory information about himself and his administration. To "know what the contents of the mysterious [Democratic party] documents are," Hoover turned to the ONI's New York office, whose skilled operatives had successfully carried out the New York break-ins noted above. ONI officers Glen Howell and Robert Peterkin then broke into the Democratic party office in New York City. The break-in team's findings were immediately relayed to President Hoover, though nothing was discovered as the office was vacant at the time. To prevent discovery of this partisan operation, all records relating to it were sealed with specific instructions "in no case should they ever be supplied to the National Archives or any other agency to which the general public has access."[2]

Much like their ONI and MID counterparts, FBI officials were committed to sustaining their political surveillance activities after the war. Wartime internal security concerns combined with the legal authority of the espionage and sedition laws of 1917 and 1918 had undercut the libertarian and states' rights concerns voiced at the time of the FBI's creation in 1908. In wartime the public and Congress had tolerated FBI surveillance of radical activists and anti-war critics as a legitimate law-enforcement initiative to prosecute disloyal individuals and organizations. The end of the war, however, halted the FBI's authority to continue such investigations.

FBI officials were not reconciled to this loss of legal authority. In 1919–1920 they devised a strategy designed to convince Congress to enact peacetime sedition legislation that would authorize continued surveillance of radical and "subversive" activists. The brainchild of J. Edgar Hoover, head of the recently established

General Intelligence Division, and Anthony Caminetti, the head of the Immigration Bureau, this plan entailed the launching of dragnet raids to enforce a 1918 immigration law that authorized the deportation of alien residents who were members of revolutionary organizations such as the Communist and Communist Labor parties. FBI and Immigration Bureau officials had complementary objectives in planning this operation. For Hoover, the publicity generated by the arrests of thousands of alien radicals could highlight the magnitude of a continuing revolutionary threat. For Caminetti, the raids could expedite the deportation of alien radicals. Detainees subject to deportation would normally have the right to legal counsel, who invariably advised their clients not to volunteer information about their political beliefs. Under Hoover's and Caminetti's plan, the January 2, 1920, raids relied on telegraphic rather than individual warrants to ensure the desired large numbers of detainees and further "facilitate the making of arrests." In addition, FBI agents, who had successfully infiltrated these two parties, arranged that FBI branch offices in thirty-three cities made simultaneous raids on January 2. Detainees were then denied the right to counsel.

The strategy at first succeeded brilliantly. Six thousand to ten thousand were arrested with accompanying publicity. The *New York Times*, for example, headlined its story "Revolution Smashed," with the reporter extolling the "clarity, resolute will and fruitful intelligence" of those who had planned the raid. The editor of the law journal *Bench and Bar* also captured this sense of an aborted revolution in acclaiming, "The need for repression is great, and the time for repression is now," while the *Washington Post* observed, "There is no time to waste on hairsplitting over infringement of liberty."

This positive response quickly evaporated. Further revelations provoked a powerful backlash. The catalyst was Assistant Secretary of Labor Louis Post. Responsible for issuing deportation orders, Post grew concerned over the methods employed in conducting the raids and the deportation hearings. His discovery of the use of telegraphic warrants and the denial to the detainees of the right to counsel eventually led him to authorize the deportation of only 556 of those arrested.

Post's rulings challenged Attorney General A. Mitchell Palmer, who had immediately sought to exploit the initially favorable publicity to advance his candidacy for the 1920 Democratic presidential nomination. For the assistant secretary's actions in effect minimized the severity of the crisis and implicitly questioned the methods employed during the raids. A frustrated attorney general responded by publicly criticizing Post while his allies in Congress demanded the assistant secretary's impeachment.

Post, however, used the impeachment hearings to dramatize the abusive methods that had been employed during the raids—the FBI's lack of authority to enforce immigration laws, the initial arrests of both alien residents and citizens, and the violation of Labor Department rules governing the right to counsel. Then, in 1921, Congress convened hearings into the raids and cited numerous examples of the "continued violation of [the] Constitution and breaking of . . . Laws by the Department of Justice." The effect of both congressional proceedings was to revive prewar libertarian and anti-statist concerns and to reframe the issue as one of abuse of power and political demagoguery. As a result, Palmer's presidential ambitions were quashed. More important, Congress refused to enact peacetime sedition legislation, instead repealing the 1918 Sedition Act in 1921.

Denied the legal authority to monitor "subversive" individuals and organizations, FBI officials now sought alternative ways to utilize the acquired information. They shared information about "subversive" activists with ONI and MID, and in some cases with the State Department and the Customs Bureau. They also worked behind the scenes to circulate to corporate executives information about labor union organizing and strike activities, and to Michigan state police officials about a meeting of Communist activists in Bridgman, Michigan, in an unsuccessful attempt to convict Communist leaders Charles Ruthenberg and William Foster under the state's anarchist and syndicalist laws. FBI information efforts were more successful in helping New York and Arizona authorities obtain convictions under state laws. As part of a broader program to influence public opinion, FBI officials leaked information about radical activities to the conservative American Defense Society, the National Civic Federation, and the journalist Richard Whitney, who was preparing a series of articles for publication in the *Boston Evening Transcript*.

FBI officials also acted more aggressively to discredit their own critics. Thus, upon learning of a critical report on the FBI's role in the conduct of the Palmer Raids, written by Harvard law professors Zechariah Chafee and Felix Frankfurter, FBI officials ordered a "discreet and thorough" investigation of these critics, as well as of Assistant Secretary of Labor Louis Post and of federal judge George Anderson, who had issued a scathing ruling criticizing FBI procedures. Derogatory information about Chafee was then leaked to a sympathetic member of Harvard University's board of trustees in an attempt to effect his dismissal from the law faculty. Evidence of Frankfurter's "communist propaganda activities" was relayed to Undersecretary of State William Hurley.

For the most part FBI officials succeeded in precluding discovery of their surveillance and dissemination activities. One exception involved their brazen actions in 1923 in the so-called Teapot Dome affair.

During World War I the U.S. government had acquired valuable oil reserves in Teapot Dome, Wyoming, and Elk Hill, California, for naval supply purposes. When the end of the war eliminated the need for these reserves, Secretary of the Interior Albert Fall granted leasing rights to businessmen Edward Doheny and Henry Sinclair. Because the interior secretary had done so without competitive bidding, the Senate in 1923 launched an investigation of this decision in response to demands by Senators Thomas Walsh and Burton K. Wheeler.

The Senate investigation at first centered on Fall's leasing decision but soon shifted to Attorney General Harry Daugherty's quashing of a Justice Department investigation into the matter. Another issue soon surfaced with the disclosure that FBI agents had investigated Walsh and Wheeler after their questioning of Fall's decision and had unsuccessfully sought to have Wheeler convicted on trumped-up charges of influence peddling. In an even more dramatic revelation, FBI agents were disclosed to have broken into and wiretapped the offices and opened the mail not only of Senators Walsh and Wheeler but of Senators Robert M. LaFollette, Thaddeus Caraway, and William Borah, and Congressmen Roy Woodruff and Oscar Keller. President Calvin Coolidge promptly fired Daugherty for his refusal to cooperate with the Senate investigation. By then the FBI had become the subject of sharp criticism, with some observers questioning whether a federal police force inevitably undermined a system of limited government and privacy rights.

Moving quickly to staunch this scandal, Attorney General Harlan Fiske Stone, Daugherty's successor, fired FBI director William Burns and implemented a series of changes to prevent FBI abuses of power. The GID was dissolved, wiretapping was banned, and stricter standards for FBI appointments were established to avoid political influence and enhance the professionalism of FBI agents. "A secret police may become a menace to free government and free institutions because it carries with it the possibility of abuses of power which are not always quickly understood," Stone warned. To avert that possibility he prohibited FBI investigations of "political or other opinions of individuals" and permitted investigations "only with their conduct and then only with such conduct as is forbidden by the laws of the United States."

Stone's restrictive orders, however, had limited consequences. J. Edgar Hoover, Burns's successor as FBI director, did institute stricter personnel standards for FBI employees. These included the close monitoring of FBI agents' personal and official conduct and their handling of investigations. But Hoover encouraged FBI agents to continue monitoring personal and political conduct, and acted to foreclose discovery of actions that contravened prevailing anti-statist concerns and the attorney general's ban.

The astute FBI director first sought to refurbish the FBI's tarnished reputation by exploiting current moralistic concerns: he created a special Obscene File for FBI agents' reports involving pornography investigations. Any information acquired during these investigations was to be submitted to FBI headquarters in envelopes marked "OBSCENE" and was then to be separately maintained. This reporting procedure had two purposes: first, to limit access by FBI agents to such information, fearing their "undue curiosity about such filth," and, second, to create a centralized depository that could promote future prosecutions given the "potential publicity value." Agents were also to brief FBI headquarters before any arrest to ensure wide publicity. The FBI director emphasized the threat posed by such literature to "school children and adults with perverted minds" and in promoting "local vice" and "racial agitation."

FBI investigations of political organizations such as the liberal American Civil Liberties Union and the radical American Communist party, moreover, did not stop. They were merely scaled back and conducted far more discreetly. The principal reason for this cutback derived not from legal sanctions but from reduced appropriations, which required Hoover to contract FBI personnel strength. Sixty-two employees were dismissed in 1924, and five of the FBI's fifty-three field offices were closed.* The FBI director offset this reduction in staff by soliciting the assistance

---

*FBI personnel declined from 1,127 in 1920 (579 agents and 548 support staff) to 657 in 1924 (441 agents and 216 support staff) and thereafter stabilized, reaching 821 in 1932 (388 agents and 433 support staff).

of conservative activists and organizations, such as the American Legion and the American Defense Council, and local and state police officers who were encouraged to continue volunteering information about suspect political activities. Hoover always counseled volunteers that because the reported information confirmed no violation of a federal statute, no FBI investigation could be initiated, but they should continue to forward such information. FBI agents also directly monitored press reports about radical activists and organizations and disguised their own surveillance activities by claiming that reported information had been provided by a "confidential informant" or a "very reliable and confidential informant." In at least one known instance, FBI agents in 1929 broke into the ACLU's New York office to photocopy the organization's records.

FBI officials had few opportunities in the late 1920s and early 1930s to act on this accumulated personal and political information, beyond highly publicized pornography or Mann Act prosecutions. The few known instances involved requests from the Herbert Hoover administration. In seeming contravention of his libertarian views and antipathy toward an expanded federal role, President Hoover sought FBI assistance to discredit his administration's increasingly effective critics. The President's key aides, Lawrence Richey, Walter Newton, and Theodore Joslin, for example, requested FBI reports on organizations that had attacked the president, ranging from the conservative Sentinels of the Republic and the Navy League of the United States to the liberal ACLU and the National Association for the Advancement of Colored People (NAACP). In addition, FBI officials furnished the White House with derogatory information about the World War I veterans who organized and participated in the 1932 Bonus March. In one case in October 1931, FBI officials willingly honored a White House request to investigate George Menhinick, editor of a financial newsletter who had sharply criticized President Hoover's economic policies. FBI agents conducted an intimidating interview of Menhinick, eventually reporting back that he was "scared" and likely would not "resume the dissemination of any information concerning the banks or other financial institutions."[3]

For the most part, the anti-statist and libertarian politics of the 1920s and early 1930s forced ONI, MID, and FBI officials to operate in the shadows. Their continued monitoring was crimped by limited budgets, forcing them to rely on conservative activists for information. And they had few opportunities to act on their accumulated information. In those exceptional cases when they acted carelessly or too boldly—notably the Palmer Raids, the FBI's investigation of members of Congress demanding an investigation of the Teapot Dome scandal, and MID's attempt to link women peace activists with subversion—their actions backfired, leading senior administration officials to prohibit future surveillance. Ironically, the only formal limitations that restricted these agencies' intelligence activities were imposed by senior administration officials. Members of Congress never moved beyond expressions of outrage to prescribe by statute the permissible authority of the intelligence agencies. The most significant executive restriction on the agencies' operations imposed in the 1920s involved MID foreign intelligence and counterintelligence operations.

MID's role had expanded substantially during World War I. The new responsibilities led to the agency's reorganization with the creation of a number of specialized branches, one of them a Codes and Ciphers section. In June 1917 Herbert Yardley was recruited to head that section's Cryptographic Bureau. Owing to his acquired expertise in codes and ciphers, Yardley's talents led to the breaking of intercepted German coded messages. Seeking to enhance his skills further, Yardley traveled to France and England in 1918, first to consult with those nations' more experienced code experts and then to assist the U.S. delegation at the Versailles peace conference—having been assigned to safeguard

U.S. communications and decipher those of other delegations at the conference.

MID officials remained convinced after the end of the war of the value of a code-breaking and code-making capability. This assessment was shared by War and State department officials, who agreed in 1919 to jointly fund a postwar cipher bureau, known colloquially as the American Black Chamber and headquartered in New York City. The decision to locate this bureau in New York was necessitated by Congress's ban on the expenditure of State Department funds for such a project in Washington, D.C. New York had the additional advantage of minimizing the possibility of foreign governments discovering that the United States sought to intercept and decipher telegraphic messages.

State Department officials, through a negotiated agreement with the Western Union Telegraph Company and the Postal Telegraph Company, acquired and forwarded to the Black Chamber the diplomatic messages of certain foreign governments, notably those of Europe, Latin America, and Japan. Analysts in this bureau eventually deciphered the messages of European and Latin American governments. Their main priority, and greatest success, however, involved the Japanese code, a success that proved invaluable for the U.S. delegation at the Washington Naval Conference of 1921–1922 in providing insights into Japanese negotiating strategy.

The Black Chamber's total budget for 1919, when it was established, was only $100,000, 60 percent of which was paid by the War Department and 40 percent by the State Department. Congressional budgetary restraints halved the Chamber's budget by 1924, with further reductions in 1929 to $25,000, of which the State Department paid $15,000. These budgetary cutbacks forced the Chamber after 1927 to concentrate almost exclusively on Japanese communications.

Despite its successes, the Black Chamber was dissolved in 1929. The reason, however, was not budgetary but the appointment of Henry L. Stimson as secretary of state. Briefed in May 1919 about this interception program, Stimson immediately ordered its termination, affirming that "Gentlemen do not read each other's mail." Stimson's elimination of State Department funding necessitated the closing of the New York office of the Black Chamber on October 31, 1929, and the transference of its files and personnel to the army's Signal Corps.[4]

3 | THE ORIGINS OF THE NATIONAL SECURITY STATE, 1936–1945: Part I, Domestic Intelligence

■ THE CRISIS of the Great Depression ushered in fundamental changes in the roles of the federal government and the presidency, provoking a divisive debate over governmental power. Franklin Roosevelt won election to the presidency in 1932 by capitalizing on public repudiation of the Herbert Hoover administration and its principles of limited government. He interpreted this success as a mandate for an ambitious economic recovery program. His New Deal approach to shaping a legislative agenda and expanding the federal government's role in the life of the nation heightened concerns in some quarters about privacy rights and federal intrusion on states' powers. Many prominent conservatives condemned Roosevelt's use of the media as demagogic and his specific initiatives as undermining traditional relationships between government and the private sector. They responded similarly to his later foreign policy initiatives of the mid- to late 1930s. A powerful anti-presidential sentiment at the time, fueled by the Nye Committee hearings of

1934–1937, with attendant concerns that Wilson's unneutral policies had led to unnecessary American involvement in World War I, commanded broad public support. Roosevelt's controversial attempt at Supreme Court "packing" in 1937 heightened these concerns.

This antipathy threatened Roosevelt's foreign policy agenda. By the late 1930s the president was challenging the belief that the United States could and should avoid involvement in European and Asian affairs. He sought to rally public support for a more interventionist U.S. role in order to curb Axis expansion in Europe and the Far East. His efforts accelerated after the German invasion of Poland in September 1939, and by 1941 he succeeded in forging a popular consensus for U.S. involvement.

Predating this new consensus, the president turned to the U.S. intelligence community to address what he saw as potentially serious internal security and foreign intelligence threats from Nazi Germany and the Soviet Union. The United States would have to help curb these nation's expansionist objectives, Roosevelt concluded. Yet, given the initially skeptical popular mood, preventive measures would have to be taken secretly. The president feared that Germany and the Soviet Union, as subversive powers, would attempt to exploit ideologically sympathetic fascist and Communist movements in the United States and in Latin America—just as the leaders of both countries had done in Europe in the mid-1930s. Furthermore the devastating economic crisis of the Great Depression and the resulting public disillusionment with democracy and capitalism had appeared to offer an unparalleled opportunity for greater fascist and Communist influence.

But reliance on the U.S. intelligence community could be politically risky, given still-powerful beliefs about limited government. This risk was particularly acute since the president's plans included abandoning a law-enforcement approach to internal security. He wanted one that went beyond dealing with espionage and sabotage to include efforts to influence public opinion within the United States and Latin America, specifically the opposition to a more interventionist U.S. foreign policy.

In contrast to later cold war presidents, Roosevelt could not count on the support of conservatives to expand the role of the U.S. intelligence agencies. Conservatives' suspicions of presidential and federal powers had led them, for example, to view the FBI as a New Deal bureaucracy and to decry Director Hoover's efforts of the mid-1930s to publicize the FBI's successes in its war on notorious gangsters as demagogic and potentially dangerous. The voice of Midwestern conservatism and isolationism, the *Chicago Tribune*, displayed this mind-set in a debunking profile on Hoover written by its Washington bureau chief Walter Trohan and published in the *Tribune*'s June 21, 1936, Sunday magazine. Trohan depicted the FBI as a New Deal bureaucracy and its director as a publicity-seeking demagogue particularly skilled "in the political arena—his position alone bespeaks that. Further, the number of southerners in the ranks of G-men, a movement which took place shortly before the New Deal came into office and at a time . . . when Democratic senators and representatives were preparing for the committee chairmanships they now hold, gives evidence that the director knows how to court favor."[1]

Sensitive to these political realities, President Roosevelt relied on secret directives to expand the FBI's investigative authority. His first, tentative step occurred at a conference at the White House on May 8, 1934. At this meeting Roosevelt asked FBI director Hoover to conduct "a very careful and searching investigation" into whether the German embassy and German consulates "may have" a connection with the American fascist movement. Hoover responded by ordering an investigation of the "activities of the Nazi groups with particular reference to the anti-racial and any anti-American activities having any possible connection with official representatives of the German government in the United States." This was to be an intelligence investigation—in other words, noncriminal in that it had no law-enforcement purpose—

with reports "at specific intervals" forwarded to Attorney General Homer Cummings for delivery to the president.[2]

This onetime investigation resulted in no prosecutions under federal espionage or sabotage laws. But it was not predicated on a looser "probable cause" standard, as was the case in the contemporaneous FBI investigation of a suspected German espionage ring headed by Guenther Rumrich. In that case, Customs Bureau officials in 1935 had stumbled onto a spy ring that had been operating in New York City since 1927. MID and FBI agents were then brought into this investigation that led to the arrests in 1938 of four German Americans. Fourteen other participants escaped arrest by fleeing to Germany. The four were indicted and convicted for attempting to relay sensitive information to Germany about U.S. military technology and ship movements in the port of New York. The arrests and subsequent trial received extensive news coverage and even led to a movie. More important, they prompted President Roosevelt to consider the U.S. intelligence community's capability to prevent future espionage operations.[3]

The Rumrich case became the catalyst to decisions for improved coordination of U.S. intelligence operations. It reinforced the concerns of Secretary of War George Dern, who two years earlier had called for action to anticipate and contain "subversive" activities. At that time Dern had specifically recommended the establishment of a "civilian" service "to prevent foreign espionage in the United States and to collect information so that in case of an emergency any persons intending to cripple our war effort by means of espionage or sabotage may be taken into custody." FBI director Hoover immediately endorsed Dern's recommendation and urged Attorney General Cummings to reestablish the World War I GID to "conduct appropriate investigations into so-called subversive activities"—a broader standard than the one used in Roosevelt's singular 1934 initiative. Cummings, however, did not even brief President Roosevelt on Dern's recommendation.[4]

In both 1934 and January 1936 the attorney general had been directly involved in discussions about the FBI's role beyond law enforcement. This was not the case, however, in August 1936 when FBI director Hoover met alone with President Roosevelt at the White House.

In inviting Hoover, Roosevelt aimed to "discuss the question of subversive activities in the United States, particularly Fascism and Communism." The FBI director had earlier briefed the president about a proposed right-wing military coup,* and at this meeting he specifically alerted Roosevelt to "Communist activities in this country." Hoover described in detail how Communists sought to control three key labor unions, the International Longshoremen's and Warehousemen's, the United Mine Workers, and the Newspaper Guild. He emphasized that through their control of these unions Communists "would be able at any time to paralyze the country." He further described Communist activities "within Government service, particularly in the National Labor Relations Board, and that the Soviet Comintern had instructed American Communists to vote for Roosevelt in the 1936 presidential elections." When the president then expressed an interest in "obtaining a broad picture of the general movement and its activities as may affect the economic and political life of the country," Hoover observed that no federal agency currently collected such information but that under a 1916 appropriation the FBI could "investigate matters referred to it by the Department of State." Roosevelt endorsed this proposal and scheduled a meeting the next day with Hoover and Secretary of State Cordell Hull to secure this "formal request."

At this next meeting Roosevelt conveyed to Hull his concern about "Communist activities in this country, as well as Fascist ac-

---

*An American Legion official had approached retired General Smedley Butler in 1934 to lead a military coup to force changes in the Roosevelt administration's domestic policies.[5]

tivities." "There had been certain indications," Roosevelt observed, that Soviet consul Constantine Oumansky "was a leading figure in some of the activities in this country, so consequently it was a matter which fell within the scope of foreign affairs over which the State Department has a right to require an inquiry." Hull, the president continued, could request an FBI investigation under a 1916 appropriations statute. When the secretary of state asked whether this should be done "in writing," Roosevelt demurred, fearing a leak. The authorization would be oral. Roosevelt further directed Hoover to discuss this matter and its implementation with the attorney general.[6]

Hoover acted immediately, but without first briefing Attorney General Cummings. Appropriate instructions were issued to FBI personnel on August 28, 1936, on the proposed intelligence investigation. Its "general classifications" confirm the breadth of this ongoing inquiry. Those to be targeted included: "Maritime industry, Government affairs, steel industry, general strike activities, Armed Forces, educational institutions, general activities—Communist and affiliated Organizations, Fascisti, anti-Fascisti movements, and adherents in organized Labor organizations." FBI agents were to obtain information from "all possible sources" but could initiate no inquiry without first obtaining "specific authorization" from FBI headquarters. Belatedly on September 10—misleadingly dating his meeting with the president as having occurred on September 1—Hoover briefed Cummings on this secret presidential directive. Cummings approved the initiative, adding that the FBI should coordinate its investigation with MID, ONI, and the State Department, but "in a most discreet and confidential manner."[7]

Roosevelt's, Hull's, and Cummings's concerns for secrecy, like those of senior FBI officials, stemmed from the realization that this FBI investigation would include political and labor activities. Such investigations had been conducted by FBI, ONI, and MID during the World War I years, ostensibly under wartime legislation. While such surveillance continued during the 1920s and 1930s, FBI, ONI, and MID actions had not been authorized by presidents or senior department officials. Roosevelt's oral directive of August 1936 accordingly marked a major turning point for U.S. intelligence agencies, the more so since the FBI's intelligence investigations were to be ongoing. They were initiated at a time of prevailing sentiment against the president and against intervention in foreign conflicts among the minority Republican leadership in Congress and conservative media commentators and reporters.

The 1938 disclosure of a German-directed espionage ring had also prompted an internal reassessment of the FBI's counterespionage role. FBI director Hoover thus briefed Attorney General Cummings in October of that year on the "close and coordinated plan of cooperation" between the FBI, ONI, and MID, and the results of the FBI's ongoing intelligence investigations. Such investigations should be expanded, Hoover underlined, and could be "covered" under "present provisions" of the 1916 statute authorizing FBI investigations when requested by the State Department "of matters which do not in themselves constitute a specific violation of a Federal Criminal Statute, such as subversive activities." "The utmost degree of secrecy" was needed, Hoover cautioned, "to avoid criticism or objections which might be raised to such an expansion by either ill-informed persons or persons having some ulterior motive." "Special legislation" to authorize intelligence investigations should not be sought, the FBI director added, as this "would draw attention to the fact that it was proposed to develop a special counter-espionage drive of any great magnitude." Attorney General Cummings and President Roosevelt concurred with this strategy; the president instead proposed increasing FBI, MID, and ONI appropriations.[8]

This shift in the focus of FBI operations, and the independence by which they were conducted, inadvertently became an issue in 1941 when Attorney General Robert Jackson drafted rules to govern future departmental and agency requests for FBI investigations. The proposed guidelines assumed that FBI investigations were limited to violations of federal statutes. Hoover responded that these strictures were cumbersome, "make ineffective any work the Bureau might attempt to do," and could curb the FBI's ability to meet a serious subversive threat. The FBI director then specifically emphasized the "difference between 'investigative' and 'intelligence' activity":

> Investigative activity, such as is conducted when there is a specific violation of a Criminal Statute involved, always presupposes an overt act and is proceeded upon with the very definite intention of developing facts and information that will enable prosecution under such legislation. Intelligence activity is predicated upon an entirely different premise. Much of the activity indulged in by Communists and subversive elements does not, in its original stage, involve an overt act or a violation of a specific statute. These subversive groups direct their attention to the dissemination of propaganda and to the boring from within process, much of which is not a violation of a Federal Statute at the time it is indulged in, but which may become a very definite violation of law in the event of the declaration of war or of the declaration of a national emergency.

Jackson responded by affirming that he had not intended "to restrict or alter in any manner the internal operations of the F.B.I. . . . or its *right* to proceed in all the fields in which it has been operating."[9]

Having obtained presidential authorization to investigate "subversive" activities, FBI officials soon encountered a major obstacle. It was a consequence of the claimed legal rationale for investigation, which required an initial State Department request. State Department officials, intent on meeting their supervisory responsibility, in early 1939 instituted a cumbersome committee system whereby the undersecretary of state would oversee FBI,

MID, ONI, and Treasury Department investigations of subversives. The undersecretary would request and then, on receipt of results, decide which agency should continue to handle a specific investigation. Under this plan, FBI, MID, and ONI would handle the bulk of such referrals. Resentful of State's claimed supervisory authority and intent to make his own determination of when an investigation should be initiated, FBI director Hoover protested the process to Attorney General Jackson. This committee system should "be abandoned," Hoover asserted, and no agency beyond the FBI, MID, and ONI should be allowed to conduct "espionage, counter-espionage and sabotage cases." This would "centralize" all intelligence investigations in the FBI, enabling it to "continue work in this field with continued intensity." President Roosevelt endorsed Hoover's proposal, issuing a "confidential" directive on June 26, 1939, specifying that the FBI, MID, and ONI would "control" and "handle" "all espionage, counterespionage and sabotage investigations." The heads of these three agencies would "coordinate their activities," and no other federal agency would be permitted to investigate such matters.[10]

Roosevelt's secret directive in effect reflected his indifference to the scheme proposed as the legal authority for FBI intelligence investigations. Because the intent was not to prosecute, the scope and purpose of these investigations would remain unknown. Political considerations made such secrecy imperative, for Roosevelt's directive was issued at a time of heightened tensions in Europe but before the outbreak of World War II in September 1939. Anticipating that the United States might become involved in an imminent European war, FBI, MID, and ONI officials deliberated how best to coordinate their investigations and avert duplication.

Initiating these deliberations in 1940, officials of the three agencies reached agreement to delimit their responsibilities and ensure more effective liaison. The FBI was to be primarily responsible for handling "all investigations involving allegations" that U.S. citizens and alien residents might be involved in espionage, sabotage, and subversive activities. It would also conduct surveys of those industries "considered of essential interest to the War and Navy Departments," and would "keep in close touch with the activities and developments of Un-American groups, whose activities are aimed to frustrate or interfere with the national defense program." MID and ONI were barred from investigating "cases where the persons involved were civilians"; their investigations were to be confined to military personnel and military installations. The FBI, however, would share any acquired information relating to MID's and ONI's missions and responsibilities. To ensure needed cooperation, FBI, MID, and ONI "liaison officers" would "maintain contact with each other" and exchange information at weekly conferences.[11]

This arrangement did not definitively resolve the delimitation matter as MID officials continued to investigate subversive activities. FBI director Hoover moved quickly to forestall such actions, and in October 1940 directly raised with the White House his concern over MID's establishment of "undercover" offices in several states. Then in November 1940 he convinced Attorney General Jackson to authorize an FBI liaison program with the American Legion, in this case to deter American Legion officials from effecting an arrangement with MID.* By 1941, with the increasing possibility of U.S. military involvement in World War II, Hoover and Jackson solicited President Roosevelt's support to nip in the bud what they feared might be an MID attempt "in event of war" to "supersede the F.B.I. in dealing with subversive activities."[13]

---

*This program radically expanded FBI surveillance capabilities. During World War II, FBI agents successfully recruited approximately 60,000 legionnaires from that organization's 11,700 nationwide branches to monitor American residents of German, Italian, French, and Russian descent employed in defense industries. FBI agents later turned some of the more reliable Legion recruits into Confidential National Defense Informants (that is, informers who were paid and directly controlled by the FBI).[12]

President Roosevelt's broad authorization, and the delimitation agreements governing FBI, MID, and ONI investigations, radically expanded the role of the U.S. intelligence agencies. These changes minimized bureaucratic conflict and, equally important, possible discovery of the scope and purpose of the agencies' surveillance activities. The arrangement ensured the FBI's primacy in domestic surveillance. The outbreak of World War II, however, intensified Roosevelt's concerns about the "subversive" threat posed by American fascists and Communists. He now decided to expand further the FBI's surveillance capabilities.

Congress in 1934 had enacted legislation banning wiretapping. In 1937 and 1939 the Supreme Court had ruled—in two separate cases of *Nardone v. U.S.*—that this ban applied to federal agents, and that any indictment based on evidence obtained from an illegal wiretap would require dismissal of the case. Roosevelt found this ruling troubling, for he was now convinced that wiretapping was an invaluable investigative tool in addressing perceived internal security threats. Privately concluding that the 1934 law and the Court's ruling applied only to *criminal* investigations, in May 1940 he issued a secret directive authorizing FBI wiretapping during "national defense" investigations whose purpose was to anticipate espionage or sabotage, not prosecute spies or saboteurs. But FBI wiretaps would first have to be reviewed and approved by the attorney general "after investigation of the need in each case," with such taps "conducted to a minimum" and limited "insofar as possible to aliens."

Unwilling to challenge the president's interpretation of the law and the Court's rulings, but fearful that this practice might become public, Attorney General Jackson decided not to maintain records of his approval of such FBI requests. Wiretap authorization records would be "maintained" only in FBI director Hoover's office. Jackson's decision, and his further failure to institute rules requiring the regular reauthorization of approved taps, effectively negated his and future attorneys general's oversight of FBI wiretapping operations. Attorneys general could learn of ongoing FBI wiretaps only if the FBI director informed them, could not determine whether the original "national defense" justification had been met, and further could not discover whether FBI officials on their own had authorized other taps. Some FBI taps continued for decades while others were installed by FBI officials without consulting the attorney general.[14]

The Roosevelt administration's reliance on secrecy and its commitment to expanding FBI investigative authority also had the unanticipated consequence of inviting FBI officials to act independently in their use not only of wiretaps but of other illegal investigative techniques. Roosevelt's secret May 1940 order applied only to FBI wiretapping, and attempted to circumvent Congress's legislative ban and the Supreme Court's rulings. But while wiretaps would provide access to sensitive communications, microphones—bugs—could be even more valuable, intercepting in-room conversations. The installation of bugs, however, would require trespass, in violation of the Fourth Amendment.

Rather than seeking another presidential directive or notifying the attorney general of their intent to commit trespass, in 1940 FBI officials began authorizing bugs on their own. At the same time the FBI director, recognizing the riskiness of this practice, in 1942 instituted a special records procedure called Do Not File. Before any break-in could be attempted—the FBI's phrase was "black bag job"—the head of an FBI field office, the special agent in charge (SAC), had to request approval from senior FBI officials at headquarters. Requests were to justify the value of the installation and describe the safeguards that would be adopted to preclude discovery. This authorization requirement meant that written records would be created. Normally such records would then be serialized and indexed in the FBI's central records system when received at FBI headquarters. To finesse this problem, SACs were to caption their requests "Do Not File." On receipt at FBI headquarters, Do Not File memoranda would not be placed in the FBI's central records system but instead would be routed to the FBI director's office. This ensured that no retrievable, official record would be created. The genius of this procedure was that it would enable FBI officials to respond truthfully to any future congressional subpoena or court-ordered discovery motion and affirm that the FBI's "central records system" contained no record of an illegal activity. Break-ins, moreover, were conducted by specially selected and trained agents who understood the need to preclude discovery. Before a planned break-in, three to five agents would case an intended target to identify possible problems. The actual break-in would then be conducted by a squad of eight to ten agents, with each agent performing a separate task— monitoring the subject or neighbors, guarding an entrance, photographing documents, returning the photographed documents to their original location.[15]

Pushing further, FBI officials, again on their own, instituted another program in 1940 code-named Z-Coverage, whereby they arranged to open mail addressed to Soviet and Axis embassies in Washington. This program, later expanded to these nations' consulates in New York City and to the embassies of the Axis-aligned governments of Spain, Portugal, and France, sought to "detect" individuals who might be involved in espionage or who "might be illegal agents." Discontinued with the end of World War II, the program was reinstated in the early 1950s when it was directed at the Soviet Union and other Communist-bloc countries. It was finally discontinued in 1966.[16]

Armed with this broad authority, and no longer subject to strict media, congressional, or judicial oversight, FBI officials could concentrate their investigations on individuals and organizations they believed posed a serious internal security threat. Their obvious targets included "diplomatic representatives" monitored at "the sanction of the State Department."[17] In the course of these investigations, FBI agents, at minimum, broke into the French, Swedish, Spanish, and Chilean embassies in Washington (and also in Latin America*) to photograph code books, ciphers, enciphering keys and deciphering tables, cipher tapes, instructions for the use of Swedish cipher machines, copies of telegram messages, and decodes of German radio messages. This valuable intelligence was immediately forwarded to MID and ONI to assist in their codebreaking and counterespionage operations.[18] FBI officials, again dating from at least 1940, also wiretapped the German, Italian, Japanese, and Soviet embassies in Washington[19] as well as the headquarters of the American Communist party and prominent Communist party activists, including Steve Nelson, Alexander Bittelman, Boris Morros, Jean Tatlock, Haakon Chevalier, William Dieterle, and James Miller.[20]

Given their political definition of subversive threats, FBI officials also authorized wiretaps and bugs of hundreds of radical labor union and civil rights organizations and their leaders. The targets included the NAACP, the March on Washington Movement, the Alabama People's Education Association Congress, the Congress on Industrial Organization Council, the CIO Maritime Committee, the National Maritime Union, the United Automobile Workers, and the United Mine Workers. Considering that the United States was allied with the Soviet Union against the Axis powers during World War II, only six pro-fascist organizations were tapped during the years 1940–1941 while taps on "Fascist and Italian matters" were discontinued in June 1941 and on "Nazi and German matters" in December 1941.[21]

Although break-in memoranda were to have been regularly destroyed under the Do Not File procedure, some inexplicably escaped destruction, including those filed in office files of FBI assistant directors Louis Nichols and D. Milton Ladd and of the head of the FBI's New York office. These extant records confirm

---

*In June 1940 President Roosevelt assigned to the FBI responsibility for conducting "foreign intelligence" in Latin America. This program is discussed in the next chapter.

that FBI break-in targets during World War II included, at minimum, the Soviet Government Purchasing Commission (and an unsuccessful break-in attempt of the Soviet consulate in New York), the American Youth Congress, the American Mobilization Committee, the Washington Committee for Democratic Action, Russian War Relief, the League of American Writers, the American Slav Congress, the Council for a Democratic Germany, the Joint Anti-Fascist Refugee Committee, Carol King, Bertolt Brecht, Ruth Berlau, Leonard Frank, Erwin Piscator, Ludwig Renn, the Independent Citizens Committee of the Arts, Sciences and Professions, Veterans of the Abraham Lincoln Brigade, the Negro Labor Victory Committee, the Nationalist Party of Puerto Rico, and the International Workers Order.[22]

The expansion of FBI investigative authority and the administrative changes that ensured the FBI's primacy in internal security investigations did not necessarily promote the nation's security interests. Four case studies of FBI counterespionage operations confirm this, with two confirming that the failure to anticipate and prevent espionage was due neither to the lack of legal authority nor to a lack of cooperation among the U.S. intelligence agencies. These cases instead underscore the difficulty of *anticipating* espionage. The FBI's failures were the consequence of FBI officials' essentially political conceptions of potential security threats.

The first case involved the June 1941 arrests of a thirty-three-member German espionage ring headed by Frederick Duquesne. The occasion for this success was not FBI intelligence investigations but good luck—the defection of William Sebold. An American citizen of German descent, Sebold had traveled to Germany in February 1939 to visit relatives. During this visit, agents of the German espionage service, Abwehr, pressured him to spy on Germany's behalf. Fearful that refusing to honor this request could endanger his relatives, Sebold agreed. On his return to the United

States in June 1940, however, Sebold advised the FBI of Abwehr's plan. FBI officials thereupon devised a sting operation, helping him establish a short-wave radio transmitter station in Centerpoint, Long Island. Through this facility, Sebold received from other recruited German agents information they had obtained about U.S. defense plants, military equipment, and the sailing dates of U.S. cargo ships. FBI agents screened this information before Sebold's transmittal to limit its damage, though their principal objective was to identify those whom Abwehr had recruited to spy on behalf of Germany. This operation was suspended after a year with the arrest of the identified spies.[23]

The second case appeared to be an even more dramatic FBI success: the apprehension in June 1942 of two four-member German sabotage teams that had landed in Amagansett, Long Island, and Jacksonville, Florida, earlier that month. The teams' objective was to sabotage U.S. transportation and industrial plants along the East Coast, an aluminum plant in Tennessee, and locks on the Ohio River. FBI agents' apprehension of the saboteurs was again the product of good fortune—in this case the defection of George Dasch, a member of the four-man team that had landed in Amagansett. Shortly after this team landed, its members were discovered by a Coast Guard officer, John Cullen, who was patrolling the area. The four Germans claimed to be fishermen and bribed Cullen to do nothing. But Cullen immediately reported the incident to his superiors. Coast Guard agents combed the area the next day and discovered the uniforms and equipment that the four had buried on the beach. They promptly informed the FBI of this discovery. At the same time Dasch, who feared that his four-man team would be discovered, approached the FBI, described the purpose of the mission, and identified and provided the cover names and U.S. contacts of the other members of the Amagansett team and of the second four-member team that had landed in Florida. Within a week after the landings, FBI officials announced the capture of the eight prospective saboteurs. Press coverage extolled this dramatic FBI success.[24]

In contrast to these publicized FBI windfalls, the two other cases, though not known to the public at the time, involved FBI failures to uncover Soviet espionage activities.

In 1943 FBI officials first became aware of a planned Soviet espionage operation through a wiretap of the headquarters of the American Communist party in New York. FBI officials had learned in late 1942 that the head of the party, Earl Browder, had advised party operative Steve Nelson of a "sensitive" assignment. Thus forewarned, FBI agents bugged Nelson's residence in Oakland, California. This bug first intercepted Nelson's March 29, 1943, meeting with Joseph Weinberg, a physicist employed at the University of California–Berkeley Radiation Laboratory. At this meeting Weinberg briefed Nelson about a "highly secret" experimental project that the Radiation Laboratory was conducting, work that was about to be moved to Los Alamos, New Mexico. Through their physical surveillance of Nelson, FBI agents on April 6, 1943, uncovered Nelson's meeting with Peter Ivanov, a Soviet consular official in San Francisco. The agents concluded that Nelson had then given Ivanov the information he had acquired from Weinberg about this sensitive U.S. program to develop the atomic bomb.

The FBI's bug of Nelson's residence moreover recorded his second meeting on April 7, 1943, with Vassili Zubilin, third secretary of the Soviet embassy in Washington, D.C. Zubilin had then given Nelson a large sum of money—the bug recorded their joking about the amount—to place "Communist Party members and Comintern agents in industries engaged in secret war production for the United States Government so that information could be obtained for transmittal to the Soviet Union." This advance intelligence was supplemented by FBI director Hoover's receipt in August 1943 of an anonymous letter, written in Russian and postmarked Washington, D.C., which identified Zubilin and a number of other Soviet officials* as spies.[25]

FBI officials immediately inaugurated two highly sensitive programs: CINRAD (Communist Infiltration of the Radiation Laboratory) and COMRAP (Comintern Apparatus). These were separate programs governed by the FBI's quite different responsibilities.

Under the recently concluded delimitation agreements, security at the Radiation Laboratory and at Los Alamos was MID's exclusive responsibility since both facilities were involved in the production of military weapons. Thus, should FBI agents uncover any relevant information, it was to be passed to MID. In addition, the FBI would conduct specific investigations requested by MID. Because of this bureaucratic division of labor, FBI director Hoover rejected a subsequent recommendation of FBI assistant director Conroy to consolidate the CINRAD and COMRAP investigations in light of the sensitive "confidential data" that FBI agents had uncovered relating to the Radiation Laboratory and Los Alamos. MID was responsible for CINRAD, Hoover noted; the FBI's COMRAP investigation, in contrast, was "broader in scope and is being conducted without any jurisdictional limitations imposed by the Military Intelligence Service." This bureaucratic division of responsibilities even led MID officials to reject an FBI recommendation that they "alert" ONI to the CINRAD investigation. Such a briefing, the head of the FBI's San Francisco field office believed, would ensure that ONI would act vigorously to protect its "own confidential projects," an action that ONI "would not otherwise take."[26]

---

*Those identified were Soviet consular officials Gregory Kheifets and Pavel Klarin, Amtorg employees Semen Semenov and Leonard Kvasnikov, Soviet embassy employees Vassili Dolgov and Vassili Mironov, and Soviet Government Purchasing Commission officials Andrei Schevchenko and Serghi Lukianov. The writer also identified two American Communists, Boris Morros and Earl Browder, as working with these Soviet officials to furnish "important information about the U.S.A."

FBI officials did immediately brief MID officials about the intercepted Nelson-Weinberg meeting of March 29 and the plan to place Communist party members in the Radiation Laboratory to obtain information for "transmission to U.S.S.R." Weinberg and Nelson, FBI officials further reported, had also criticized J. Robert Oppenheimer as no longer sympathetic to Communist interests. At the time, employees of the Radiation Laboratory, including Oppenheimer, were already the subjects of MID surveillance, with MID officers being particularly suspicious of their labor organizing activities. Senior MID officers had also uncovered Oppenheimer's past Communist associations and had then opposed his Los Alamos appointment on security grounds. General Leslie Groves, head of the Manhattan Project to produce the atomic bomb, had rejected this recommendation in September 1942 when he placed the prominent physicist in charge of the project.

MID officials nonetheless remained concerned about Oppenheimer and other physicists employed at the Radiation Laboratory. Based on the Weinberg-Nelson report, MID officer Colonel Boris Pash acted to address this security problem: Weinberg was later assigned to an army post in Alaska and David Bohn, another identified Communist, was denied clearance to work at Los Alamos.

FBI officials continued to brief MID officials about their subsequent discoveries under the CINRAD and COMRAP investigations, including Oppenheimer's meeting in September 1943 with Jean Tatlock, his former mistress. Based on this report, Pash urged Groves to fire Oppenheimer as head of the Los Alamos project. Groves again rejected this recommendation as he valued the scientist's administrative and scientific abilities.[27]

While FBI and MID officials wrongly suspected Oppenheimer's loyalty, they failed to identify the Communist activists employed at Los Alamos who in 1944–1945 did engage in atomic espionage on behalf of the Soviet Union—David Greenglass, recruited by his brother-in-law Julius Rosenberg, and Theodore Hall, recruited by his friend Saville Sax.* Neither FBI nor MID agents uncovered the participation of these two men in atomic espionage in 1944–1945, or the roles of their recruiters. The FBI, however, was not primarily responsible for this failure since clearance of Los Alamos employees was MID's responsibility. FBI agents could learn of current or prospective Los Alamos employees only if briefed by MID and could initiate investigations only in response to specific MID referrals. Their direct knowledge involved only information they might have developed in the course of their own intelligence investigations.

MID's background and ongoing investigations of Hall raise questions about this agency's thoroughness and diligence. For one, its background investigation of Hall was at best perfunctory, consisting primarily of interviews with his associates and former professors who attested to his brilliance and loyalty. Its monitoring of Hall once he was employed at Los Alamos at minimum led to the interception of one of his letters to Sax (and Sax's reply) and revealed that in the fall of 1944 he had visited his own family in New York, at which time he had met Sax, a friend from college. This correspondence contained critical comments on Soviet and Communist activities from a radical perspective. But neither these letters nor Hall's visit to New York apparently raised any red flags for MID security officers.[29]

From the 1930s FBI agents had intensively monitored the activities of American Communists and had compiled massive files

---

*At least two other Los Alamos employees also became Soviet spies—Klaus Fuchs and a code-named PERS. Fuchs was a British citizen assigned to Los Alamos. Having successfully deciphered intercepted Soviet consular messages under the code-named VENONA project, in 1949–1950 military intelligence agents belatedly learned of Fuchs's, Greenglass's, Rosenberg's, Hall's, and Sax's witting participation in atomic espionage. Their success was due in part to helpful FBI assistance in identifying individuals whose identities were concealed through cover names. FBI and MID officials, however, were unable to identify the individual disguised under the cover name PERS.[28]

on both prominent party leaders and party functionaries. As one result they had uncovered the Browder-Nelson initiative in late 1942 and then the Nelson-Weinberg and Nelson-Zubilin meetings of March/April 1943. In the COMRAP investigation prompted by the Nelson-Zubilin meeting, FBI agents focused on prominent Communist officials. The core assumption was that monitoring them would lead to the identification of those who agreed to spy on behalf of the Soviet Union. At minimum, this focus on prominent Communists missed Greenglass, Rosenberg, Hall, and Sax, who were not directly recruited but instead had independently volunteered to spy. For example, when Hall briefed Sax about the Manhattan Project during his visit to New York in October 1944, his friend had then urged him to contact the Soviets and Sax agreed to volunteer as a courier for Hall's subsequent reports to the Soviets.[30]

This same failure was repeated in the FBI's massive COMRAP investigation, which lasted two years. It would seem to have had the advantage of being able to concentrate on specifically identified individuals rather than indiscriminately monitoring all Soviet officials stationed in the United States and all American Communists. From their monitoring of Nelson and Zubilin, FBI agents uncovered their contacts with other possible suspects, whom they then investigated. Overall forty-six individuals were intensively investigated. These suspects were physically monitored, and FBI agents used wiretaps, bugs, break-ins, and mail openings in their surveillance. This investigation, however, failed to uncover evidence of espionage activities. An FBI report summarizing COMRAP's results instead confirmed that FBI agents had discovered only that American Communists endorsed Soviet foreign policy, supported radical political and economic change, sought to influence popular perceptions of the Soviet Union, and recruited others to join the Communist party. This December 1944 summary of what the agent described as a "vast, illegal and conspiratorial Russian-controlled and dominated International Communist Organization, Comintern Apparatus," reported the targeted subjects as having sought to "influence" the American public to accept Soviet foreign policy, to distribute "pro-Russian propaganda," to operate an "illegal courier system, based on American Communist seamen," to promote "Soviet Russia's goal of world domination," to collect "political information of value" for the Soviet Union, and to have Communists infiltrate U.S. government agencies to "secure information of value" for the American Communist party and ensure that other Communists would obtain federal employment.[31]

That FBI officials did not uncover Soviet or American Communist involvement in espionage is further documented by the reports that FBI director Hoover regularly sent to the Roosevelt White House. Hoover had initially briefed the White House in May 1943 about the discovery of the Zubilin-Nelson meeting and had then assured the president that "steps" were being taken to "identify" all members of this Comintern apparatus "as well as agents of the apparatus" in various war industries. Hoover submitted no follow-up report on the COMRAP investigation, however, though he did report periodically on the activities of Browder, Nelson, and Soviet officials in addition to quarterly briefings captioned "General Intelligence Survey in the United States." These various reports described only Soviet and Communist political activities—for example, that Soviet officials were concerned about the activities of Americans of Baltic descent, were interested in the deportation proceedings involving labor union leader Harry Bridges, and were concerned about U.S. development of high-octane gasoline. The FBI director's reports on Browder and Nelson described their political activities while the quarterly surveys on FBI espionage and counterespionage operations cited no instance of Soviet espionage, only that American Communists sought to recruit new members, promote Soviet foreign policy, and were involved in civil rights and labor organizing.[32]

Why were FBI agents unable to uncover Soviet espionage activities during World War II? FBI officials did have hard evidence, in advance, that identified Soviet officials and American Communist leaders who intended to recruit Communist activists to spy. This evidence had sparked the CINRAD and COMRAP investigations. But neither investigation uncovered either the atomic espionage activities of Fuchs, Greenglass, Rosenberg, Hall, and Sax or the information that two Washington-based spy rings, headed by Nathan Gregory Silvermaster and Victor Perlo, had obtained technical and other sensitive classified information from Communists employed in various federal agencies, which was then delivered by courier to Soviet consular officials in New York City. These failures were obviously not due to legal prohibitions against wiretaps, bugs, break-ins, or mail openings that limited the FBI's ability to uncover Soviet espionage since FBI agents employed these techniques extensively.

FBI agents' failure to uncover these Soviet espionage operations was due in part to precautions adopted by Soviet officials to preclude discovery of their actions. Soviet agents anticipated that they were being monitored by the FBI. They could not risk discovery of their willingness to spy on a military ally, an action that not only was treacherous but could affect Soviet security interests. The U.S.-Soviet alliance might have been one of convenience, not shared interests, but the Soviet Union nonetheless depended on continued U.S. Lend-Lease assistance and the establishment of a Second Front to draw German troops away from occupied Soviet territory. As well-trained professionals, Soviet agents acted to ensure that their American recruits were reliable and trustworthy, that these recruits were trained in the craft of "conspiracy" and would meet "only with reliable undercover contacts" of the American Communist party who the FBI would not suspect were involved in espionage. Embassy and consular staff were directed not to use "real surnames of recruits" and to limit knowledge of their work by other Soviet staff on a need-to-know basis. Safeguards were adopted to counteract anticipated FBI wiretapping and bugging, and automobiles were used to arrange secret meetings in order to frustrate FBI physical surveillance. Meetings were discontinued or suspended when it was suspected that they were being monitored by the FBI.[33]

The fourth instance of a problematical FBI counterespionage operation involved the Soviet defector Victor Kravchenko. Soviet officials' response to the April 1944 defection of Kravchenko, a Soviet military officer stationed in the United States as a member of the Soviet Government Purchasing Commission (the Soviet agency that coordinated Lend-Lease shipments to the Soviet Union), confirms their interest in averting discovery of their espionage activities. Soviet agents were deeply troubled when they learned of Kravchenko's defection and then of his public allegations of Soviet untrustworthiness, espionage, and expansionist objectives. They responded publicly by minimizing his defection, describing him as a low-level employee. Privately, however, they pressured U.S. officials to deport him on the grounds that he was a military defector. Caught off guard, Soviet intelligence officers meanwhile conducted an intensive investigation into how Kravchenko had been able to defect, a concern that ultimately led to Zubilin's recall from the embassy in Washington to Moscow in October 1944. Soviet officials also aggressively sought to discover where Kravchenko was residing after his public defection (he had gone into hiding) through sources they had developed in the American Trotskyite community. It is unclear if their purpose was to assassinate him or pressure him to recant.

FBI officials had advance knowledge of Kravchenko's intent to defect, having learned of his plan as early as February 1944. Because of the potential impact of this defection on U.S.-Soviet relations, FBI director Hoover first sought and obtained carte blanche from President Roosevelt and Attorney General Francis Biddle to "proceed with the Kravchenko case as the Bureau desires." FBI agents were then authorized to meet Kravchenko in the month before his April 3 defection, at which time they learned he was willing to provide information about Soviet espionage activities in the United States and the "organization and plans of the NKVD," the predecessor to the KGB, the Soviet security police. In return Kravchenko demanded personal protection, including transportation to a safe hiding place, a gun, and changed identity, and financial support—"no monetary worries for about a year and a half." But senior FBI officials did not attempt to exploit this opportunity to acquire insights into Soviet espionage operations and plans. FBI director Hoover and senior FBI officials instead worried that Kravchenko "may be an agent" of the NKVD and that his defection and proposed cooperation might be "part of a NKVD scheme to check on the Bureau's activities and attempt to lay some predication for possible embarrassment of the Bureau." Acting on the FBI director's orders, dating from March 1944 and continuing through 1945, FBI agents closely monitored Kravchenko and his contacts in the American Russian and Trotskyite communities, an impressive list of militant anti-Stalinists that included David Dallin, Isaac Don Levine, Charles Malamuth, Eugene Lyons, Max Eastman, Sol Levitas, and William Chamberlain. Alerted to the possibility of a "double tail"—that the NKVD might be following those who followed Kravchenko—FBI agents also extensively wiretapped Kravchenko's various residences, opened his mail, wiretapped and opened the mail of Dallin and Malamuth, and reviewed FBI wiretap logs on Soviet officials and the Soviet embassy.[34]

FBI agents' failure to uncover Soviet espionage operations was also due to their focus on the wrong American Communists. For example, in the COMRAP investigation they had concentrated on prominent American Communists (Nelson, Browder, Alexander Bittelman, Joseph Freeman, Louise Bransten) but not those Communist functionaries (Hall, Sax, Greenglass, Julius Rosenberg) who were actually engaging in espionage. They even missed an opportunity to uncover an ongoing Soviet espionage operation.

FBI officials first learned of this particular operation in November 1945 after the defection of Elizabeth Bentley, who since 1943 had served as a courier for information acquired by Communists employed in various wartime federal agencies for transmittal to Soviet intelligence agents in New York. Based on Bentley's testimony, FBI officials immediately launched an intensive investigation in 1945–1946. They were unable, however, to confirm Bentley's account—in this case because Soviet officials had immediately been alerted to Bentley's defection and to the FBI's investigation by another of their spies, Kim Philby, who at the time served as British liaison to U.S. intelligence.[35]

FBI agents could have uncovered this espionage operation a year earlier. In October 1944 FBI agents monitoring one of the COMRAP suspects, Louise Bransten, learned of her meetings in Washington with Nathan Silvermaster, the head of one of the two spy rings, and Charles Flato, a participant in this spying operation. Silvermaster at the time was the subject of an FBI Hatch Act investigation, authorizing the dismissal of an employee who was a member of the Communist party. The Bransten meeting, however, prompted a rather perfunctory investigation of Silvermaster and Flato but did not lead to their being targeted under COMRAP. FBI agents merely uncovered Silvermaster's and Flato's involvement in radical politics and labor union activities.[36]

The COMRAP and Kravchenko investigations indirectly underline the key reason for FBI counterespionage failures: the difficulty of anticipating future conduct. FBI officials invariably focused on individuals whose political activism commanded their attention. FBI intelligence investigations were predicated on preconceptions about involvement in labor union and civil rights activities and attempts to influence public policy. The specific subjects of some of the FBI's most intensive investigations of the World War II era highlight this phenomenon of political profiling.

FBI agents, particularly during the critical years 1939 through December 1941—that is, from the German invasion of Poland through direct U.S. military involvement—closely monitored the "subversive" press made up of isolationist and pro-fascist newspapers and periodicals. The subjects included such mainstream conservative newspapers as the *Chicago Tribune*, the *Washington Times-Herald*, and the *New York Daily News*, and their reporters, columnists, and editors (*Chicago Tribune* reporter Stanley Johnston, *Washington Times-Herald* gossip columnist Inga Arvad, and *New York Daily News* editor and publisher Joseph Patterson). FBI officials even intercepted a telegram from *Chicago Tribune* publisher Robert McCormick to reporter Arthur Hennings. The acquired information was shared with the Roosevelt White House, which welcomed this intelligence about its press adversaries and even pressured the Justice Department to prosecute "seditious publications." None of these suspected subversives was indicted, though the Justice Department did conduct a content analysis of editorials published by the *Chicago Tribune*, the *New York Daily News*, and the *New York Journal American* "in terms of consistency and contradictions of manifest statements with respect to 16 major Nazi radio themes."[37]

Reflecting this ideological definition of subversive threats, FBI officials on their own initiative in 1942, and without briefing the president or the attorney general, launched a massive investigation of Communist "infiltration and control of the motion picture industry," code-named COMPIC. It endured until January 1956, when FBI officials concluded that Communist influence in Hollywood was "practically nonexistent at the present time." The initial impetus for this investigation was a concern that Communist-influenced films could shape public opinion—as one FBI official darkly commented, such influence was "potentially the most dangerous from the standpoint of their propaganda and financial value to the [Communist] Party." The probe intensified in 1943 as the result of FBI director Hoover's concern over the release of films that year that were either militantly anti-fascist— *For Whom the Bell Tolls*, based on Ernest Hemingway's novel—

or pro-Soviet—*Mission to Moscow*, based on the memoirs of former U.S. ambassador to the Soviet Union Joseph Davies.

Through extensive use of break-ins and wiretaps, FBI agents identified Communists employed in the film industry and then linked them with the production of specific films. These films, ironically, accorded with the current U.S. policy of alignment with the Soviet Union against the Axis powers. In any event, the subjects of this investigation were not individuals who had access to classified military or diplomatic information. FBI officials had strayed beyond this reasonable counterintelligence purpose with their concerns about the ability of Communists to influence the popular culture. Indeed, FBI officials lamented that Communists were attempting to "get complete control of the motion picture business and use it for propaganda purposes," to "recruit" others employed in the film industry to join the Communist party, to "spread propaganda within and without [Hollywood] unions to create sympathy for the Soviet Union and their system of government," or to make movies "which glorify the Soviet Union and create sympathy for the Communist cause" or delineate "the Negro race in most favorable terms as part of the general line of the Communist Party."[38]

More important, the COMPIC investigation was not an atypical FBI intelligence operation. Similar ideological concerns underpinned another FBI investigation, in this case of German émigré writers who had fled Nazi Germany during the 1930s to seek asylum in the United States and who then wrote books or film and theater scripts. FBI officials' interest in these talented writers— Bertolt Brecht, Thomas Mann, Heinrich Mann, Billy Wilder, Berthold Viertel, Anna Seghers, Ruth Berlau, Leonhard Frank, Erwin Piscator, and Lion Feuchtwanger—stemmed from their radical politics, including their lobbying for economic and political change in postwar Germany. As in the COMRAP and COMPIC investigations, FBI agents extensively employed wiretaps, bugs, break-ins, and mail openings.[39]

The same ideological concerns were behind another massive investigation initiated in June 1942 and lasting until 1945. Code-named RACON, this secret inquiry centered on "racial conditions in the United States" and sought to determine "foreign-inspired agitation among American Negroes," both Axis and Communist. The premise was that those individuals, and even the African-American press, who challenged the racial status quo threatened the nation's security. FBI officials decried this "anti-American ideology" as confirming "foreign influence" and were particularly troubled by the upsurge in 1943 of race riots in Los Angeles, Detroit, and Philadelphia. No evidence of Axis or fascist espionage or sabotage was ever uncovered. Nonetheless an FBI analyst concluded that "there have been subversive forces at work among American Negroes causing unrest and dissatisfaction." Such agitation, this analyst contended, was promoted by Germany, Japan, and American Communists. He recommended a "program of education" to counter the extremism of radical black and militant white supremacists.[40]

The RACON survey produced an ancillary, if seemingly perverse, consequence. In the course of conducting their survey of "foreign inspired agitation among Negroes in the country," FBI agents in the Savannah and Birmingham field offices learned about "other causes of agitation," specifically rumors circulated by Southern white supremacists "concerning the formation of Eleanor or Eleanor Roosevelt Clubs among the Negroes." A Birmingham agent reported one "attempt" to form such clubs "by a strange white man and a large Negro organizer" who sought to organize "female domestics" on the "slogan" of "A White Woman in the Kitchen by Christmas." A Savannah agent reported similar incidents—"Negro maids allegedly demanding their own terms of working and at the same time stating they were members of an Eleanor Roosevelt Club." FBI director Hoover took these reports seriously and ordered an investigation. Reporting the preliminary results of this inquiry, FBI assistant director D. Milton

Ladd affirmed that such clubs were "an actual fact" and had been "started at Washington [and] spread out like a fan to other sectors." Ladd conceded, however, that the FBI's "many inquiries" had uncovered no "specific information" that such clubs existed but that a further investigation would be conducted.[41]

FBI officials' concerns about the rumored Eleanor Roosevelt Clubs were not simply a by-product of the RACON investigation. They had long suspected Mrs. Roosevelt's subversive views and associations, though they hesitated to monitor the First Lady directly—that would have been too risky. Records maintained by FBI director Hoover and FBI assistant director Louis Nichols in their secret office files, while not necessarily reflecting the totality of their efforts, confirm that senior FBI officials suspected her personal character and loyalty.

One such operation involved an FBI break-in of January 1942 into the New York headquarters of the American Youth Congress (AYC). FBI agents conducted this break-in the month after the Pearl Harbor attack, at a time when this radical youth organization had shifted from opposing to supporting U.S. involvement in World War II. As one result, agents discovered and photographed Mrs. Roosevelt's extensive correspondence with AYC officials, which they then immediately forwarded to FBI director Hoover. He responded by ordering his aides to analyze and prepare a report on this intercepted correspondence.[42]

The First Lady's political activities remained an ongoing interest of the FBI director. FBI agents had also uncovered Mrs. Roosevelt's active involvement in a debate among student delegates attending a December 1942 meeting of the International Student Association over wartime and postwar diplomacy. They immediately alerted the FBI director to Mrs. Roosevelt's adherence to "a Great Power line," and specifically her behind-the-scenes pressuring of student delegations from the Baltic states not to raise questions about their country's postwar status. Hoover found Mrs. Roosevelt's actions "nauseating."[43]

The FBI director's concerns about the First Lady's politics were shared by MID officials. Before drafting the 1940 delimitation agreement barring MID from conducting domestic surveillance, in April 1939 MID officials established a special Counterintelligence Corps (CIC), ostensibly to monitor military personnel and military installations. MID officials nonetheless interpreted this mandate broadly as they remained committed to curbing "subversive activities." One of the CIC's investigations, of a recent army draftee, Joseph Lash, uncovered his relationship with Mrs. Roosevelt.

Lash was a radical activist who had developed a personal friendship with Mrs. Roosevelt through his leadership of youth organizations in the 1930s. In 1939 he had diverged from the First Lady over the president's interventionist foreign policy. After the Pearl Harbor attack, however, Lash volunteered for military service and was assigned as a trainee to Chanute Field near Urbana, Illinois. Owing to his preinduction radical activities, MID agents continued to monitor him, and in 1943 they intercepted his correspondence and telephone conversations with Mrs. Roosevelt and with Trude Pratt, Lash's future wife who was in the process of obtaining a divorce from her first husband. Learning of Lash's plans, CIC agents then monitored his weekend visits with Mrs. Roosevelt in nearby Urbana on March 5–7, 1943, and with Trude Pratt on March 12–14. When they monitored Lash's weekend visit with Trude Pratt, however, CIC agents also bugged their hotel room, recording their sexual activities over this weekend. And, during their absence, CIC agents entered the hotel room to photograph Pratt's and Lash's personal papers. Agents later monitored Lash's visit with Mrs. Roosevelt at Chicago's Blackstone Hotel on March 27–28.

In December 1943 Edward Kibler, MID's liaison to the FBI, briefed his FBI counterpart on a particularly sensitive matter. Kibler claimed that "powerful elements within or near the War Department" had dismembered the CIC and had ordered the destruction of all records pertaining to CIC's domestic surveillance activities. Kibler attributed this decision to the discovery by White House aide Harry Hopkins that a CIC unit had bugged Mrs. Roosevelt's hotel room in Chicago and had then uncovered her involvement in a sexual affair with Joseph Lash. President Roosevelt had been informed of this affair, Kibler went on, and in the presence of his wife and a military officer had demanded that "anyone who knew about this case should be immediately relieved of his duties and sent to the South Pacific for action against the Japanese until they were killed." According to Kibler, Lash had been sent "within ten hours" to an overseas combat post, and John Bissell, head of MID, had been blacklisted from promotion to lieutenant general. Kibler then offered his FBI counterpart, George Burton, CIC's surveillance records of this investigation—which should already have been destroyed.

FBI officials welcomed the offer of these records. Because of their sensitivity—they involved the First Lady, and the FBI's acceptance violated General George C. Marshall's record-destruction order—these and related follow-up records were maintained in FBI director Hoover's and FBI assistant director Nichols's secret office files.

FBI officials uncritically accepted Kibler's account of an affair between Lash and Mrs. Roosevelt, and of President Roosevelt's personal action. In fact the MID official's story was erroneous on all counts, perhaps because Kibler hoped that FBI officials would accept it. (The tapes recorded only Lash's sexual activities with Trude Pratt, and the papers his correspondence with Mrs. Roosevelt and Pratt.) The CIC had not been disbanded, only the unit that had monitored Mrs. Roosevelt. This unit had indeed been dissolved in response to Mrs. Roosevelt's discovery that MID agents had monitored her during her stay in Chicago on March 27–28, having been briefed by employees at the Blackstone Hotel upon her departure. The First Lady, who consistently rejected Secret Service protection, protested to

Hopkins what she considered an invasion of her privacy. This led to General Marshall's order to dissolve the CIC unit. Its members were not sent to the Pacific to be killed—indeed, the head of the unit later held a highly sensitive counterintelligence assignment; Bissell was not denied a promotion; Lash was not sent to a combat post in the Pacific "within ten hours" but to a noncombat weather station in the Pacific in late April. MID officials moreover had effected Lash's transfer, having interpreted his intercepted correspondence with Mrs. Roosevelt as confirming "a gigantic conspiracy participated by not only [Lash] but also by E.R. [Eleanor Roosevelt], [Vice President] Henry Wallace, [Treasury Secretary Henry] Morgenthau, etc." Eager to "get [Lash] another assignment" and to stymie Mrs. Roosevelt's efforts to ensure his promotion, MID officials devised a plan to achieve these objectives. Having learned that Lash planned to meet Trude Pratt in Chicago over the weekend of April 3, MID officers intended to alert the Chicago police to arrest him "on a morals charge" (Pratt being a married woman), "in such a manner that there would be no publicity" of MID's role and with "sufficient publicity that E.R. would not care to intervene in the matter." This plan was never implemented, initially because Lash was unable to meet Pratt that weekend and then because, owing to Mrs. Roosevelt's protest, General Marshall dissolved this CIC unit.

FBI officials' possession of the Lash materials and of the Do Not File memo recording Kibler's briefing of FBI liaison George Burton at first posed a crisis, then an opportunity. Resentful over the loss of the Lash materials, in 1949 and 1950 MID officials circumspectly circulated a rumor in Washington about an affair between Lash and Mrs. Roosevelt, adding that the FBI had records documenting this affair. Conservative activists immediately contacted FBI assistant director Louis Nichols for confirmation, as part of their general effort to discredit the Roosevelt

New Deal—these included requests from Frank Waldrop, editor of the *Washington Times-Herald*, in 1949 and from Republican Senator Arthur Watkins in 1950. Waldrop's and Watkins's requests posed a dilemma for senior FBI officials since the incumbent president, Harry Truman, was a loyal New Deal Democrat. Eager to deny that they possessed any such records, FBI officials first ensured that the secretaries in Nichols's and Hoover's office would not contradict them, and then advised Waldrop and Watkins that the "FBI files do not contain any such information." This denial was technically truthful as the records were not maintained in the FBI's central records system.

Only with Dwight Eisenhower's election to the presidency in 1952 did FBI officials see an opportunity to exploit this misinformation about Mrs. Roosevelt. The first occasion occurred in January 1953. George Murphy and Francis Alstock, high-level Republican campaign operatives, had scheduled a meeting with FBI assistant director Nichols to discuss future FBI–White House relations and the priorities of the newly elected Republican administration. During this meeting Murphy and Alstock remarked that President-elect Eisenhower had "a thorough distrust, distaste and dislike for Eleanor [Roosevelt] and told [Secretary of State–designate John Foster] Dulles several times to get her out of the picture" as U.S. ambassador to the United Nations. Nichols responded by reporting on Mrs. Roosevelt's alleged affair with Lash, to which Alstock commented that once she was replaced as a UN delegate "she would become the object of any Congressional investigation, but that sooner or later there was going to be an investigation of her affair with Joe Lash." Mrs. Roosevelt was not retained as a U.S. delegate; President Eisenhower nominated Mary Lord as her replacement. Nonetheless the hoped-for congressional investigation never materialized. Then, in February 1954, Nichols urged Hoover to brief President Eisenhower on the Lash affair. As justification he noted that "Joe

Lash is a friend of [*New York Post* editor] Jimmy Weschler and the last word I had was that Joe Lash was working for the *New York Post* which has been exceedingly critical of the President as well as of us."[44]

In 1959 this willingness to besmirch the Eisenhower administration's (and the FBI's) press critics was repeated. On this occasion Attorney General William Rogers requested a detailed report on the homosexual activities of the syndicated columnist Joseph Alsop. The attorney general's request had been prompted by a general concern within the Eisenhower administration over Alsop's recent columns criticizing Eisenhower's fiscal conservatism as being responsible for an alleged "missile gap" between the United States and the Soviet Union. He intended to share the requested information with senior administration officials, Rogers advised Hoover, but would not be responsible should the information be further disseminated. In fact, one recipient, Joint Chiefs of Staff chairman Nathan Twining, having concluded that Alsop could not be "trusted," contended that the administration had the "obligation to let some of the [newspaper] publishers [of Alsop's column] know of this incident"—Alsop had been compromised in 1957 in a homosexual tryst in Moscow. If not General Twining, at least President Eisenhower and White House press secretary James Hagerty are known to have circulated this information about Alsop's "moral character," with Hagerty pointedly describing Alsop as a "fag" to a journalist during the missile-gap controversy and threatening to "lift his White House pass."[45]

The crisis of World War II and President Roosevelt's concerns about fascist and Communist activities led to the unprecedented expansion of the FBI's power and the emergence of a more centralized domestic intelligence system. While the president's purpose may have been to promote the nation's security, his initiatives had unintended long-term consequences. Because FBI intelligence investigations concentrated on political activists and not on spies and saboteurs, FBI officials did not uncover Soviet espionage operations. Further, the Eleanor Roosevelt and Joseph Alsop cases underline the effects of the FBI's ability to acquire derogatory personal and political information, whether in helping the White House discredit an influential political adversary or promoting the political and bureaucratic agendas of the powerful FBI director.

4 | THE ORIGINS OF THE NATIONAL SECURITY STATE, 1940-1945: Part II, Foreign Intelligence

■ NAZI GERMANY's expansionism in the late 1930s, and then the onset of World War II in September 1939, posed a critical dilemma for the Roosevelt administration. Nazi leaders had been willing to risk war with Great Britain and France to achieve their objectives—and thus welcomed a neutral United States. German agents, moreover, had successfully exploited the shared ideology of native fascist movements to subvert the established governments of Austria and Spain in 1938 and 1939 and to effect a quick French surrender in June 1940.

President Roosevelt perceived these German actions as threatening American economic and strategic interests and responded by pursuing a two-pronged strategy. First, he publicly sought to strengthen the U.S. military and to develop support for a more active U.S. international role in deterring Germany. Then, after U.S. military involvement in 1941 he sought to help mount guerrilla warfare and encourage internal resistance in Axis-occupied areas. In Latin America, an area of long-term U.S. interest, Roosevelt confronted a different situation. There, powerful anti-Yankee sentiments and the appeal of native fascist movements offered an opportunity for expanded German influence. To meet that threat, Roosevelt sought to promote greater cooperation among the existing U.S. intelligence agencies and to create new agencies having enhanced foreign intelligence and counterintelligence capabilities.

In the two years after 1939 Roosevelt rallied support for increased military appropriations and a non-neutral foreign policy by couching his proposed initiatives in defensive terms—designed to deter German aggression without direct U.S. military involvement in the European war. Political constraints, however, at first hindered his counterintelligence plans. Roosevelt therefore embarked on a series of institutional changes in 1940–1941 to expand U.S. intelligence capabilities, some by secret directives and others through informal liaison arrangements. His ad hoc and episodic initiatives resulted in a jerry-built system that impeded centralized coordination and invited continued bureaucratic rivalry. Nonetheless by 1945 a better-coordinated and expanded foreign intelligence system evolved, one that enhanced Roosevelt's ability to wage war, anticipate international crises, and act unilaterally to promote his conception of U.S. strategic interests.

Either because these institutional changes were secretly instituted, or because public directives were justified as war-related, no permanent national security system was created. The legacy of World War II, then, was at best a precedent for future institutional changes. The demonstrated value of Roosevelt's initiatives virtually ensured that future presidents would seek to sustain and build upon his creation of a more effective intelligence system while intelligence officials would seek to prevent the postwar loss of their newly won influence and independence.

Changes in the foreign intelligence arena at first grew out of Roosevelt's concerns over German influence in the Western

Hemisphere—namely, that German agents would seek both to recruit spies and saboteurs in the United States and to exploit Latin American nationalist movements. After 1941, once the United States entered the war, the president aimed to reverse Axis control of occupied countries. Roosevelt was willing to act decisively and, more important, to ignore established rules and procedures. His underlying motivation, beyond countering German influence, was to minimize the public's discovery of his actions. He wanted no divisive debate that might subvert his efforts to rally support for a greater interventionist U.S. role. Fully aware of the political risks involved in any initiative to expand the nation's foreign intelligence and counterintelligence roles at a time when the United States was formally neutral, Roosevelt consistently resorted to independent and secret actions. His initial move was to rely on personal agents who held no official governmental position, were personally loyal, and did not depend on a public salary. At the same time he issued both secret and public directives.

Roosevelt's interest in secrecy at first led him to tap a wide circle of wealthy friends. Cornelius Vanderbilt III was one such recruit. A wealthy socialite and syndicated columnist, and a supporter of the New Deal, Vanderbilt nonetheless retained close ties with wealthy anti–New Deal activists and could exploit his position as a widely traveled private citizen. This enabled him to monitor right-wing opposition to Roosevelt's known foreign policy initiatives. Dating at least from 1941, Vanderbilt "served in a confidential capacity in the Federal Bureau of Investigation by order of the President." "From time to time" he reported on the activities of U.S. military officers, political appointees, and prominent socialites whom he suspected of intending to subvert the president's foreign and domestic policies. As a private citizen he was not subject to congressional oversight; at the same time his direct access to the White House enhanced his standing with senior FBI officials. And as a newspaper columnist he could travel around the United States, Cuba, Mexico, and British Columbia without suggesting that he was monitoring military and civilian facilities.[1]

President Roosevelt meanwhile asked another journalist, John Franklin Carter, to prepare a series of reports on international developments. In this case Carter's private operation was financed through the president's emergency fund, though his findings were to be coordinated with Assistant Secretary of State Adolf Berle. Carter eventually recruited a staff of eleven and successfully exploited his personal contacts with the National Broadcasting System's radio network and with foreign correspondents, refugees, scholars, and international businessmen. His reports, ultimately numbering 660, assessed fifth-column activities in Martinique, the suspect loyalty of Japanese residents on the West Coast and Hawaii, the threat of a Nazi fifth column, European industrial conditions, and more generally matters relating to "national defense."[2]

Roosevelt's most problematic personal recruit was Vincent Astor, his wealthy Hudson Valley neighbor. Astor was recruited because of the advantages he offered to the ambitious yet secretive president. Personally loyal but also a managing director of the Western Union telegraph company, with excellent contacts in Wall Street banking and journalism, Astor could obtain valuable intelligence about German and Soviet financial dealings, communications, and plans. Through Western Union he could view Axis cable messages and through Chase National Bank the banking transactions of Amtorg, the Soviet export agency—all the while avoiding suspicions of the president's involvement. Astor's close family and personal ties with British intelligence officers also helped establish an informal liaison relationship with British intelligence during the crucial years 1940–1941, when the United States was officially neutral and when a formal relationship would have provoked a bitter congressional and public debate. Roosevelt informally appointed Astor his personal liaison to the special joint committee—composed of representatives from FBI, ONI, MID, and the State Department—that Assistant Secretary of State Berle established in June 1940 to coordinate U.S. intelligence operations. In March 1941 the president formally appointed Astor area controller for the port of New York. In both his informal and formal roles, as Roosevelt's personal representative Astor could act to improve cooperation among U.S. intelligence agencies. His official responsibility as area controller, for example, included mediating "conflicts or potential conflicts" among ONI, MID, FBI, and State Department officials relating to "subversive (sabotage or espionage) activities" in the New York area. The various agencies were to "consult" with Astor before making "any new contacts" in the area, which was a center for commercial, passenger, and mail traffic to Latin America and therefore crucial to monitoring German intelligence agents. These agency officials were further required to brief Astor on "all contacts" they had made since their last report. In addition, Astor's ownership of the St. Regis Hotel in New York offered a secret locale for members of the joint committee to meet outside Washington, minimizing the possible discovery of their potentially most controversial action, their liaison with British intelligence.[3]

Astor's informal and formal assignments exemplified Roosevelt's penchant for ad hoc responses to expand and coordinate intelligence operations. A second, if more significant, initiative involved his secret decision of June 1940 to assign responsibility for foreign intelligence operations in Latin America to the FBI. The president turned to the FBI not because he was dissatisfied with the State Department's intelligence-gathering abilities but because he wanted to move beyond diplomacy and use covert action to counteract German influence. Under Roosevelt's secret directive of June 24, 1940, responsibility for "foreign intelligence" would be divided among the FBI, ONI, and MID, with the FBI "responsible for foreign intelligence work in the Western Hemisphere on the request of the State Department," and ONI and

MID responsible for "covering the rest of the world as and when necessity arises."

FBI director Hoover immediately established a Special Intelligence Service (SIS). Three hundred sixty agents were eventually employed in SIS and were stationed in Mexico, Peru, Chile, Uruguay, Venezuela, Argentina, and Brazil, under cover as consular officers, business consultants, or employees of major U.S. corporations. Liaisons were established between SIS and the U.S. Border Patrol, the Royal Canadian Mounted Police, and British agents operating under cover in the British Purchasing Commission or the office of the British Security Coordinator.* SIS agents were to obtain "economic, political, industrial, financial" and subversive-activities information, particularly about "movements, organizations and individuals whose activities are prejudicial to the interests of the United States." British intelligence agents, who operated on American soil as well as from bases in Bermuda and Canada, relayed the fruits of their investigations to the FBI. FBI agents would then report to ONI and MID any relevant information they obtained on their own or from their British and Canadian counterparts. This relationship was particularly sensitive, making secrecy imperative. After all, U.S. agents in a time of U.S. neutrality were working in tandem with agents of a foreign power then at war with Germany.

In June 1940, moreover, State Department officials sought the FBI's assistance to conduct inspections of the U.S. embassy staffs in Madrid, Berlin, and Moscow. Five specially selected agents with language skills eventually identified security deficiencies at these embassies.

Under Berle's June 1940 order, FBI, ONI, MID, and State Department representatives met periodically in New York to exchange information and identify future needs and responsibilities.

---

*William Stephenson served as British Security Coordinator, heading a staff of British intelligence agents with headquarters in New York City.

But Astor's presence, whether as Roosevelt's personal liaison or as area coordinator, did not resolve an ongoing problem of coordination and bureaucratic rivalry. For one, neither senior MID nor ONI officials were resigned to playing second fiddle to the FBI in the Western Hemisphere; their own military responsibilities, they concluded, required them to acquire information independently. Thus the various meetings of the joint committee, whether held in Hoover's Washington office or in New York, never achieved close cooperation. Neither Berle nor Astor had the supervisory or budgetary authority essential for clear lines of authority or the oversight required to set priorities and allocate responsibilities. And despite his status as Roosevelt's personal representative, Astor did not have the administrative ability or expertise to manage a difficult situation.[4]

By late May 1941 President Roosevelt had decided to abandon his reliance on personal representatives: this informal system had failed to advance his policy interests. The president thereafter relied on newly created institutions to ensure a more centralized system. The final catalyst in this decision ironically derived from Vincent Astor's inept handling of the Kermit Roosevelt affair, a matter having little to do with security.

In March 1941 Belle Roosevelt, the wife of Kermit Roosevelt— President Roosevelt's distant cousin and the son of former President Theodore Roosevelt—sought a meeting with the president. Her reason for seeking this "urgent" appointment, she told him, was her concern about her husband's health. Belle Roosevelt disclosed that her husband was having an affair with a masseuse, Herta Peters, had contracted a venereal disease, and needed to be hospitalized. Requesting the president's assistance in locating her missing husband, she said she hoped to break up this affair and avert a possible public "scandal." Presidential secretary Grace Tully thereupon informed Astor of the president's desire that Kermit Roosevelt be located. Following a joint committee meeting in New York, Astor asked Thomas Donegan, the FBI's liaison to the joint committee, to have the FBI locate Kermit Roosevelt. When the FBI director was later briefed about this request—Astor having failed to go through channels—he ordered the head of the FBI's New York office to abort the investigation. The FBI could not risk the possible discovery that it was investigating a relative of the president, Hoover emphasized, and could do so only if directly asked by the president. Learning of Hoover's decision, Astor asked Tully to inform Hoover of the president's interest, at the same time conveying his anger over Hoover's action in delaying FBI assistance to the head of the FBI's New York office, Percy Foxworth. Astor added ominously that he might seek to have Hoover replaced as FBI director.

Astor's impolitic action confirmed one liability of the president's reliance on amateurs to oversee intelligence operations. Astor's threat to fire Hoover was hollow and had the unintended consequence of rendering the president vulnerable to the astute FBI bureaucrat. The denouement came in a follow-up telephone conversation between Hoover and Astor. The FBI director began by criticizing Astor's inept handling of this matter, remarking how Astor's direct approach increased the risk that the FBI's conduct of a personal investigation could become known. Hoover continued by pointing out that he had conducted similar operations in the past, relying not on field agents but on special, certifiably reliable squads. He then acknowledged his awareness of Astor's threat to have himself fired, and threatened to resign. An abject Astor apologized profusely, cognizant that he had placed the White House in a most difficult position since Hoover's resignation would reveal that the president had intended to use the FBI for a personal matter. Kermit Roosevelt was nonetheless located and entered a hospital for treatment. The White House then sought to sever Kermit Roosevelt's relation with Herta Peters by the subterfuge of offering him an assignment of a special mission to East Africa.[5]

Hoover had never intended to resign. He purposefully exploited this opportunity to enhance his standing, having become deeply concerned about a broader initiative the president was considering. Roosevelt wanted better coordination among the intelligence agencies through the creation of a special office, which would be headed by William Donovan, a prominent Republican and Wall Street lawyer. Donovan was a nemesis of the FBI director dating from his stint as Hoover's supervisor while assistant attorney general in the Coolidge administration. Hoover had learned of the proposal to create a coordinating office and in May 1941 had discussed this prospect with the heads of ONI and MID. He had then relayed their joint opposition to White House aide Edwin Watson over the "designation of a coordinator for the three intelligence services." There was "no need" for the proposed coordinator to "supervise" the actions of the FBI, ONI, and MID, Hoover wrote, given the current "complete coordination and cooperation" among the three agencies. Any differences among them had already been "eliminated" by the June 1940 delimitation agreement. The proposed coordination, the FBI director further argued, would create a "cumbersome and complicated" system which would undermine their efforts, "especially in the increased temper of war," and would cause "serious detriment to the National Service, while offering only negligible advantages." Privately MID officials denounced the proposed coordinating agency as "very disadvantageous, if not calamitous." It would intrude on their ability to collect and evaluate "all military information which we now gather from foreign countries."[6]

But FBI, ONI, and MID opposition failed to dissuade Roosevelt. On July 11, 1941, the president established an Office of Coordinator of Information (COI) by executive order. This new office would "collect," "analyze," and "correlate" information "which may bear upon national security," issue publications designated "propaganda," and provide "such supplementary activities as may facilitate the securing of information important for national security not now available to the Government." Creation of COI, and Donovan's appointment as its head, marked a decided improvement over Roosevelt's personal and informal system. Donovan, however, had not been granted supervisory and budgetary authority over FBI, MID, ONI, and State, for the president had hesitated to create a centralized intelligence system and had bowed to bureaucratic realities. His reluctance grew out of an unwillingness to provoke a congressional and public debate over executive power at a time of U.S. neutrality while war raged in Europe and Asia.

Donovan, moreover, had astutely anticipated Hoover's opposition, recognizing the potentially disruptive role the FBI director could play. Thus, before the formal announcement of his appointment, Donovan sought to meet with Hoover to allay "any fears" he might have about the new arrangement. Denied an appointment with the FBI director, Donovan met instead with FBI assistant director Edward Tamm. He had not sought this new position, Donovan assured Tamm, and had accepted only "upon the President's promise" to allow him to eventually "handle troops if he would set up the coordinating agency." The new office, Donovan continued, would "not in any way . . . interfere with the function of the Bureau, ONI, and Military Intelligence." It would be confined to the "economic field" and would simply coordinate information provided by the existing intelligence agencies, though in certain instances it might request specific information from them. COI would be a service agency, "a laundry" through which the reports of the existing agencies "would be ironed out and distributed" to interested parties. Donovan added that he would establish an advisory group to help shape "policies for the coordinating agency," and the FBI would be represented in it. President Roosevelt also acted to ensure Hoover's full cooperation by appointing his son, James Roosevelt, as liaison between COI and the FBI. The FBI chief would "assist and cooperate" with Donovan, he promised, "in carrying out the duties assigned to them by the President."

Despite this pledge, Hoover ordered FBI agents to monitor the activities of both COI and Donovan, including Donovan's staff appointments, and to compile critical radio and press commentary about this new agency. FBI officials also worked behind the scenes with favored reporters to promote a contrast between the FBI's experience and expertise in "the handling of intelligence work" and COI's "untrained and untested" and "inexperienced" personnel.[7]

Because of his limited authority, the COI director proved unable to effect full coordination or curb internecine feuds in the pursuit of foreign intelligence and counterintelligence. But the changed circumstances of U.S. military involvement in World War II after the Japanese attack on Pearl Harbor caused Roosevelt to revisit his informal decision assigning the FBI responsibility for foreign intelligence operations in the Western Hemisphere. Deciding to refine this informal system, on December 23, 1941, he issued a directive vesting "all responsibility" for such intelligence work in the FBI. The agency would coordinate its activities with British, Canadian, and Mexican intelligence services; all other U.S. intelligence agencies were to "clear directly" with the FBI any intelligence work in the Western Hemisphere. MID, ONI, COI, and State were urged to meet to "straighten out this whole program" and were to recommend any changes essential to preventing interference with any work they were already conducting in the area.[8]

Military developments after December 1941 in time led President Roosevelt to reassess the adequacy of the intelligence system. He soon concluded that further institutional changes were needed to enhance the nation's ability to acquire better political intelligence or support native-led resistance movements worldwide. Thus on June 13, 1942, he issued an executive order establishing a new intelligence agency, the Office of Strategic Services (OSS), at the same time dissolving COI. William Donovan was appointed by the president to head OSS and would operate under the "direction and supervision" of the Joint Chiefs of Staff. OSS would collect and analyze "strategic information" and "plan and operate such special services as may be directed." Roosevelt's order furthermore transferred COI's propaganda activities to the newly established Office of War Information and barred OSS from any intelligence or counterintelligence role in the Western Hemisphere, which remained the FBI's primary responsibility. OSS eventually acquired a large staff—reaching thirty thousand by 1945 in contrast to COI's thirteen hundred—with specialized divisions for Research, Special Operations, Counterespionage, and Morale (covert propaganda). More important, as an agent of the Joint Chiefs established under the president's commander-in-chief powers, OSS transcended the narrow bureaucratic orientation of MID, ONI, FBI, and State. This relationship, and OSS's temporary wartime role, had the further advantage of averting public or congressional opposition based on concerns about expanding presidential powers—an important factor in Congress's willingness to exempt much of its spending from normal accounting requirements.[9]

Wartime needs also enabled Roosevelt to institute another important change, again of limited duration because it was a wartime measure. On December 8, 1941, the President had first asked FBI director Hoover to lead "all censorship arrangements" concerning international mail, telephone, telegraph, and radio communications. This appointment was temporary, to enable the various interested agencies and departments having responsibilities over such communications—the Post Office, the Federal Communications Commission, the State and Treasury departments, ONI, MID, and FBI—to study how best to coordinate wartime censorship. Based on the recommendations of these officials, on December 19 Roosevelt appointed Byron Price as director of censorship with the authority to coordinate the review of all international communications to and from the United States. Congress legalized this wartime censorship program in 1942.[10]

Because of the immediate needs posed by the War, and without any well-formulated plan, U.S. intelligence agencies experienced an unprecedented explosion in their capabilities as a consequence of their growth in personnel and the creation of OSS and the FBI's SIS. These changes created a sprawling bureaucracy, not a centralized system. Bureaucratic interests and politics continued to affect cooperation and coordination. The heads of FBI, ONI, and MID continued to resist efforts to circumscribe their authority and succeeded in avoiding direction by the OSS.

FBI agents might not have had prior experience or expertise in foreign intelligence and counterintelligence, but in the years 1940–1945 FBI's SIS successfully contained German espionage operations in Latin America. Working closely with State, MID, and ONI, and in some cases with foreign police forces, FBI agents exposed 832 German espionage agents and assisted local police in convicting 336. They also shut down 24 clandestine radio stations that German agents had used to communicate with Berlin or with other agents stationed in Latin America.[11]

OSS's record was even more impressive. OSS analysts provided the president and the nation's military leaders with valuable intelligence about political, military, and economic conditions in the European and Asian theaters and worked closely with resistance movements in Axis-occupied areas of Europe and Asia. Their alignment with and support for resistance movements promoted the sabotage of Axis supply lines and helped undermine Axis occupation governments. Their covert propaganda damaged the morale of Axis collaborators and encouraged popular resistance in Axis-occupied and Axis-aligned states.[12]

Still, the lack of a centralized system obliged U.S. intelligence officials to rely on the willing assistance of their counterparts. This informal aid often proved to be valuable. In 1944, for example, OSS officers sought and obtained access to the FBI's massive Obscene File, which included pornographic literature, in order to "combat" the actions of Japanese officials who were circulating "obscene photographs" of American girls throughout the Far East to "create the impression of loose morals on the part of Americans." OSS officers were granted access to "similar material" the FBI had acquired about Japanese girls, which was then used in OSS counterpropaganda activities.[13]

COI and then OSS agents were not willing to seek FBI help in all cases. At times they preferred to act on their own, including the use of illegal investigative techniques during sensitive operations within the United States—even though ostensibly they were barred from operating in domestic matters and in the Western Hemisphere. As part of COI's efforts to obtain information about the plans of Axis-aligned or sympathetic powers, in early 1942 COI officer Donald Downes broke into the Washington embassies of Vichy France, Portugal, and Turkey. After he was transferred to Mexico City, Downes led a COI break-in squad as part of an assignment to obtain information about Japanese subversive activities there. Downes's activities in Mexico City, however, soon became known to FBI officials, who protested to COI director Donovan about this violation of the FBI's exclusive jurisdiction in Latin America. Donovan responded by falsely denying that Downes was a COI employee, and the incident ended without further ado. Transferred back to Washington, Downes led COI break-ins of the Spanish embassy in July, August, and September 1942, and again in October 1942 as an OSS employee. Downes's objective then was to obtain information about Spanish codes that might prove helpful to code-breakers. Having learned of Downes's actions in the course of their own surveillance, FBI agents subverted his October break-in by sounding a siren, forcing the OSS operative to flee. FBI officials then privately raised this jurisdictional matter with Donovan, who agreed that henceforth OSS would rely on the FBI for all future embassy break-ins.[14]

This pledge was not honored. In February 1945 an OSS analyst, upon reading an article on Thailand published in the January

26, 1945, issue of *Amerasia*, a journal of Far Eastern affairs, discovered that it was an almost verbatim account of a classified report he had written. Seeking to identify the source of this obvious leak of classified information, OSS agents broke into the Washington office of *Amerasia* and discovered thousands of classified OSS, ONI, and State Department documents. This find was immediately reported to the FBI, which launched its own investigation. FBI agents now broke into the *Amerasia* office and the private residence of one of the suspects, and wiretapped its editor and other identified suspects. Because of the illegal methods that had been employed first by OSS and then by FBI agents, the Justice Department's attempt to prosecute the six individuals whom FBI agents subsequently arrested on charges of possessing or disclosing classified documents collapsed. Only three of the six were indicted, and two of the three received light sentences through a plea bargain. The third was never prosecuted.[15]

Bureaucratic rivalry and an unwillingness to subordinate agency independence to a broader national security purpose also influenced the handling of the single most significant intelligence accomplishment of the war—the breaking in 1940–1941 of the Japanese diplomatic code. U.S. policymakers should not have been caught completely off guard when the Japanese attacked Pearl Harbor in December 1941. They had the advantage of knowing the contents of Japan's confidential communications, one of which implied that Japanese government officials would resort to military action should diplomatic discussions in Washington not achieve a desired resolution. When U.S. officials did not budge during these negotiations, the Japanese launched a seemingly predictable attack resulting in the deaths of 3,435 naval and civilian personnel and the losses of 188 planes, eight battleships, three cruisers, and four other vessels. The Japanese suffered losses of only 29 planes, five submarines, and 100 personnel.

The intercepted communications should have forewarned senior U.S. officials of a planned Japanese attack. Why, then, were U.S. military personnel in Hawaii not warned? The failure was clearly not due to limitations in the collection capabilities of U.S. intelligence agencies. The story is more intriguing.

Secretary of State Stimson's May 1929 order had led to the dissolution of the jointly funded American Black Chamber. War Department officials had then created a special Signal Intelligence Service—late renamed the Army Security Agency and then, in 1952, the National Security Agency—with responsibility over codes and ciphers. SIS capabilities were at first quite limited, given the tight military budgets of the 1930s. Nonetheless this small agency developed a trained staff of code and cipher experts. Increased funding during World War II enabled Army Security Agency analysts in August 1940 to break the Japanese diplomatic code. MID and ONI officials then reached an agreement to handle the large number of intercepted communications. Under this agreement, MID officers would handle all even-numbered and ONI all odd-numbered dated messages. MID would deliver the deciphered messages to the secretaries of war and state, and ONI to the secretary of the navy and the White House. This arrangement enabled MID and ONI analysts to process a large volume of traffic and ensured that both agencies would receive credit.

But the operation of this code-named Magic project was a bureaucratic delight. Owing to their independence, ONI, MID, and State Department officials did not coordinate their differing analyses of the intercepted Japanese messages. In part their actions were determined by security considerations—an interest in ensuring that this intelligence breakthrough not become known to the Japanese. The deciphered messages, moreover, did not reveal specific Japanese plans and thus were subject to different assessments. In fact MID analysts concluded that the Japanese intended to attack China or French Indochina, while ONI analysts anticipated a Japanese attack against either the Philippines, Thailand, or Borneo, and State Department analysts an attack on Thailand.[16] These analytical differences underscored the value of a central agency, one without a specific departmental interest, which could offer a less parochial interpretation and reconcile these differing assessments of Japanese intentions. This lack of coordination before the Pearl Harbor attack would prove to be an important factor in the creation of the Central Intelligence Agency in 1947.

5 | BUREAUCRACY AND CENTRALIZATION, 1945-1952

■ THE MILITARY DEFEAT of the Axis powers in 1945 did not usher in an era of peace and international cooperation but a new crisis. With the defeat of Germany and Japan, a power vacuum was created in Eastern Europe, the Balkans, and the Far East. Given Soviet military advances and the USSR's position bordering Eastern Europe and China, the geopolitical situation seemed to benefit the Soviet Union. Furthermore the exploitive occupation policies of the Axis powers had devastated the economies of Western and Eastern Europe, the Balkans, and Asia, creating opportunities for movements advocating radical change. Finally, the devastating effects of World Wars I and II on the economies of the European colonial powers—Great Britain, France, and the Netherlands—and their displacement by Japan's military advance made it difficult for these colonial powers to reestablish their prewar control or to mount the costly military effort that would be required to counteract nationalist revolutionary movements that had emerged in China, Indochina, and Indonesia in opposition to Japanese occupation.

As one result, the wartime alliance of expediency between the United States and the Soviet Union shattered. Exploiting the military advantage accruing from their repulsion of the German army, Soviet officials after 1945 imposed Communist governments in

Eastern Europe and the Balkans and supported revolutionary movements in Indochina, Indonesia, and China. U.S.-Soviet differences over the composition of provisional governments in liberated Europe—in Germany, Eastern Europe, and the Balkans—and then over the role of national Communist movements in Greece, Western Europe, and Asia ultimately ended any hope for an enduring peace based on democratic principles. The result was a cold war, formally enunciated with the Truman Doctrine of March 1947. U.S. officials thereafter adopted a more activist strategy to contain Soviet and Communist expansion: economic and technical assistance flowed to Greece, Turkey, and Western Europe through the Truman Doctrine and the Marshall Plan while military alliances were solidified through the formation of the North Atlantic Treaty Organization (NATO) in 1949.

National Security Council memorandum No. 68 of April 14, 1950, articulated the containment strategy that would remain the cornerstone of U.S. foreign policy until the collapse of Communist governments in Eastern Europe and then in the Soviet Union in 1989–1991. Its basic premise was that Soviet leaders were committed to imposing their "absolute authority over the rest of the world" and would seek to achieve this goal not through military invasion but through internal subversion. The Soviet leaders' objective, the framers of NSC-68 contended, was "the complete subversion or forcible destruction of the machinery of government and structure of society in the countries of the non-Soviet world and their replacement by an apparatus and structure subservient to and controlled from the Kremlin." This worldwide threat, "so implacable in its purpose to destroy ours," and placing "our independence as a nation" at risk, could be countered by a "bold and massive program of rebuilding the West's defensive potential to surpass that of the Soviet Union" and by fomenting and supporting "unrest and revolt in selected strategic [Soviet] satellite countries." This would require substantial increases in U.S. defense spending, the development of nuclear weapons, and a powerful conventional army—but also a simultaneous counterinsurgency capability. By funding a more powerful military, the United States could deter Soviets without recourse to military conflict as in World Wars I and II.[1]

The assumptions underpinning NSC-68 also brought changes in U.S. intelligence policy. By 1952 a more centralized intelligence system would emerge. This development, however, was not inevitable or the legacy of the institutional changes adopted during the war. For with the end of the war there emerged two conflicting perceptions of how best to ensure the nation's security. American conservatives, whose opposition to executive powers had sharpened during the New Deal era and when President Roosevelt secured support for an interventionist foreign policy in 1939–1941, reaffirmed their stance in the early postwar years. They questioned the need to fund costly foreign aid and military assistance programs as inflationary and therefore as threatening to the American economy. At the same time they feared that an internationalist foreign policy would enhance presidential powers and undermine limited government. In contrast, many liberals, who had endorsed Roosevelt's consistently activist approach, welcomed the expansion of presidential powers. These political differences fueled the debate that erupted after 1945 over the role of U.S. intelligence agencies in the conduct of national security policy, and more specifically whether a more centralized intelligence system was desirable. They were captured in the congressional hearings that convened in the fall of 1945 to examine the circumstances behind Japan's devastating surprise attack on Pearl Harbor.

The Japanese attack had temporarily silenced a divisive debate over President Roosevelt's non-neutral foreign policy that had raged since the mid-1930s. The extensive damage to the U.S. fleet had raised a series of questions. Why had local commanders been caught by surprise? Given the difficult ongoing negotiations between the Roosevelt administration and Japanese diplomats between November 16 and December 6, why had administration officials not placed the military on war alert? Why had U.S. intelligence not anticipated a possible Japanese attack?

To allay popular and congressional concerns, President Roosevelt had appointed a special commission, headed by Supreme Court Justice Owen Roberts, to look into these questions. The commission's report in January 1942 primarily blamed army and navy commanders in Hawaii, who were reprimanded for dereliction of duty. Questions nonetheless remained, and with the end of the war any concern that an independent inquiry could affect morale and national security interests no longer applied. Thus Congress in the fall of 1945 established a special committee to investigate this apparent intelligence failure. This inquiry now scrutinized an issue that the Roberts Commission had not uncovered—that U.S. intelligence as early as 1940 had broken the Japanese diplomatic code. Apparently senior military and administration officials, the recipients of these deciphered intercepts, should have known of Japanese plans for military action in the event of the breakdown of talks in Washington. Publicity in 1945 about this intelligence coup reframed the issue not as a failure of intelligence but as a failure to *act* on critical intelligence.

Administration officials and many in Congress and the media attributed the failure to a lack of coordination among the U.S. intelligence agencies—first in the inefficient system of assigning to the navy and the army alternating responsibility for deciphering the intercepted messages; then in the failure of a joint army-navy board to coordinate their analyses of this intelligence; and finally in the total lack of coordination among the military agencies, the State Department, and the Office of Coordinator of Information. For these critics, the solution was to create a centralized, professional intelligence service to ensure that policymakers would receive expert analysis. This approach would ultimately shape Congress's enactment of legislation in 1947 creating the Central Intelligence Agency.

But another assessment of the Pearl Harbor failure, and one that contributed to the bitterly contentious politics of the late 1940s and 1950s, attributed it to secretive and duplicitous actions by the Roosevelt administration. Charles Tansill's *Back Door to War* and George Morgenstern's *Pearl Harbor* best capture this more sinister interpretation. According to these and other anti–New Deal critics, President Roosevelt had invited a Japanese attack in order to ensure U.S. involvement in World War II. The Roosevelt administration's policies leading the nation into war and its insistence on the unconditional surrender of the Axis powers, these critics further argued, made possible postwar Soviet expansion and the crisis of the cold war. These policies reflected not errors in judgment but disloyalty, "softness toward communism" as later expressed by supporters of Senator Joseph McCarthy's anti-Communist crusade. This skepticism about secretive executive power defined the political stance of many conservatives in the late 1940s and early 1950s.[2]

These conflicting views influenced how members of Congress, the informed public, and Truman administration officials evaluated the issue of intelligence reform in the critical years 1945–1947. Initial steps in the process, though, had been taken in the waning months of Franklin Roosevelt's presidency.

A sophisticated politician, Roosevelt had become convinced of the value of intelligence in advancing his foreign policy goals during the late 1930s and in World War II, yet he recognized that he must develop a constituency to support a more centralized intelligence system. This awareness explained his resort to a series of ad hoc, secret initiatives—his 1936 oral directive authorizing FBI intelligence investigations, his 1940 wiretapping directive, his 1940 directive creating the FBI's SIS, and the executive orders creating COI in 1941 and OSS in 1942. Roosevelt's sole public actions—creating COI and OSS—did command support at the time owing to the national-security climate. Lacking legislative authorization, their creation had been accepted as a strictly wartime measure. A consensus had not yet evolved to ensure their permanence. Roosevelt's interest in results had also informed these primarily secretive initiatives, stemming from his increasing frustration over the cautious and parochial approaches of the established intelligence bureaucracies. By 1944 the president, in evaluating the contributions of OSS and SIS in furthering his wartime objectives, saw that enhanced intelligence and covert operations would be essential after the war. On October 31, 1944, he therefore solicited OSS director William Donovan's counsel about a postwar intelligence system "which would be in over-all supervision of all agencies of the Gov't as to intelligence matters."

Donovan leaped at this opportunity. The OSS director and senior OSS staff had long been frustrated by the difficulties they encountered in seeking greater coordination among the various intelligence agencies, and more specifically by FBI officials' insistence on excluding OSS from foreign intelligence operations in the United States and the Western Hemisphere. Donovan also objected to the limitations inherent in OSS's role as a wartime agency subordinate to the Joint Chiefs of Staff. On November 18, 1944, he submitted a carefully formulated plan to President Roosevelt for a "Permanent World-Wide Intelligence Service."

In his cover memo summarizing the key features of the proposed plan, Donovan deferred to the president as to whether such a service should be implemented through legislation or by executive order. But he argued for immediate action, if only to ensure an orderly transition to peacetime without waste or duplication.

The new service, Donovan proposed, should report "directly" to the president and should be responsible "to frame intelligence objectives and to collect and coordinate the intelligence material requested by the Executive Branch in planning and carrying out national policy and strategy." "Operational intelligence" pertaining to the existing departments' (Army, Navy, State, Treasury, FBI) "necessary intelligence functions," however, should "remain within existing agencies." Donovan moreover qualified his recommendation to headquarter this "central intelligence service" within the Executive Office of the President by proposing as well an advisory body composed of the secretaries of state, war, and navy, and any others appointed by the president, to "advise and assist" this new agency.

This new service should collect "either directly or through existing" agencies all "pertinent" intelligence and be responsible for "final analysis" and dissemination of the acquired intelligence; it should promote, train, and supervise intelligence personnel; and it should conduct "subversive operations abroad" as well as "such other functions and duties relating to intelligence as the President from time to time may direct." The service should have an independent budget but "no police or law-enforcement functions." In a follow-up memo of November 22, Donovan emphasized that any legislative or executive proposal should be precisely drafted. Otherwise, he pointed out, the matter would be "tied up" and the other intelligence agencies would "worm out of generalities."[3]

Donovan's proposed central intelligence agency provoked immediate controversy in that it would intrude on the long-established prerogatives and independence of the established intelligence services. Formally presented to the Joint Intelligence Committee of the Joint Chiefs of Staff, it was in turn passed to the State Department, ONI, MID, and FBI. The heads of these agencies, both independently and in concert, opposed a centralized system. Instead they endorsed a "federal" system to coordinate and plan intelligence, "but with no administrative or operating function."

Having recently acquired a "foreign intelligence" responsibility in the Western Hemisphere, FBI officials were determined to retain it as well as preserve their independence. FBI director Hoover accordingly ordered his aides to draft both a detailed critique of the Donovan plan's "objectionable factors as well as errors of omission" and an alternative proposal to continue the overseas work of MID, ONI, and FBI. Hoover in fact proposed that the FBI's "legal attachés" in American embassies be expanded and a new evaluation and analysis unit created within the State Department. A Joint Chiefs of Staff analyst echoed Hoover's critique, characterizing Donovan's plan as "unsound and dangerous." The new agency, the Joint Chiefs argued, would have the "power of coordination and control over all intelligence agencies of the government, without responsibility to the heads of the departments concerned, as well as the unlimited authority to engage in intelligence operations of its own." General Clayton Bissell, head of MID, even warned that the proposed new agency would not be "in the best interests of a democratic government . . . [but] of a dictatorship. I think it would be excellent for Germany, but I don't think it fits in with the democratic set-up we have in this country, where we run things by checks and balances."[4]

Donovan's critics did not confine their efforts to rallying opposition within the executive branch. Having developed close relations with Walter Trohan, Washington bureau chief of the *Chicago Tribune*, FBI officials in February 1945 leaked a copy of Donovan's memo to this ardent critic of the Roosevelt New Deal. Predictably, in a sensational front-page story on February 9, 1945, Trohan described the plan in emotional language. Carried in the *Tribune* and its sister papers (the *Washington Times-Herald* and the *New York Daily News*), Trohan's article was headlined: in the *Times-Herald*, "Super Spy System for Postwar New Deal / World Police Over FBI, Secret Service, ONI and G-2" and in the *Tribune*, "New Deal Plan to Spy on World and Home Folks / Super Gestapo Organization Is Under Consideration." The administration's conservative critics in Congress echoed these themes.[5]

The resulting furor temporarily killed further consideration of Donovan's plan and the less centralized alternative proposed by the Joint Chiefs. An astute diagnostician of the political climate,

President Roosevelt immediately instructed Donovan, after publication of the Trohan article, to "shove the entire thing under the rug for as long as the shock waves reverberate." Military officials, though receptive to a central intelligence service, shared this assessment of the political situation. Pressing the matter, they feared, would provoke a congressional investigation framed around the "charges of Gestapo" and "super spy agency," which might lead to disclosure of "our best sources of intelligence." Further consideration of the matter, they argued, should "be deferred." Then, on April 5, Roosevelt ordered Donovan to convene a meeting of the heads of MID, ONI, FBI, and State's intelligence service "so that a consensus of opinion can be secured." The various representatives responded by proposing revised versions of a postwar intelligence system that would support their own special interests. Action on these conflicting recommendations was aborted with President Roosevelt's death on April 12, 1945.

Thrust into the presidency at this critical juncture, Harry Truman did not immediately consider the matter of intelligence reform. The new president was not fully informed about Roosevelt's various initiatives involving postwar foreign and domestic policies, and he lacked his predecessor's political stature—which would be essential in pressuring intelligence agency officials to resolve their differences. Truman's immediate priority was to instill public confidence in his succession and to quell the rivalries between Roosevelt holdovers (in the Cabinet and the White House) over postwar policy. His most pressing responsibilities were to bring World War II to a successful conclusion and to resolve U.S.-Soviet differences over occupation policy and the status of postwar governments in Eastern Europe, the Balkans, and China, left unresolved at the Yalta and Potsdam conferences. Truman also had to avoid an economic downturn similar to what the Wilson Administration had experienced after World War I when it failed to ensure a transition from a wartime to a peacetime economy.

Domestic and foreign policy questions were inevitably inter-
twined, particularly as they involved the continuance of wartime
rationing and production policies and the demobilization of a con-
script army. Decisions on these issues provoked bitter controversy
from conservatives in Congress opposed to New Deal spending
and regulatory policies and a public eager to abandon wartime
sacrifices. This opposition denied the new president the luxury of
challenging the established intelligence agencies and lobbying for
the creation of a peacetime central intelligence service.

Both MID and FBI officials ensured that Truman knew about
OSS's excesses and shortcomings under Donovan while the FBI
worked behind the scenes to ensure that the new president would
be fully informed about the merits "of the Bureau's participation
in World-Wide Intelligence." In the interim Truman had no
choice but to decide on the status of the wartime OSS. Truman's
response, Executive Order 9621 of September 20, 1945, dissolved the OSS as of October 1. OSS's intelligence assets were to
be transferred to the State Department's Research and Analysis
Branch and its operational assets to the War Department—on
condition that the secretary of war could "discontinue" any such
activity "whenever he deems it compatible with the national interest."[6]

FBI officials' role in helping submarine the Donovan plan
only encouraged them to redouble their efforts to convince Truman to sustain the FBI's foreign intelligence role. On October 22
Hoover briefed Attorney General Francis Biddle on his plan for
"U.S. Secret Worldwide Intelligence Coverage" that would post
FBI, ONI, and MID agents in every foreign country, thereby essentially expanding the FBI's SIS into a worldwide organization.
Under this proposal, FBI agents would collect and report information to the State Department, with an advisory body composed of the secretaries of State, War, and Navy and the attorney
general setting overall policy. The FBI director also sent a flurry
of reports to the White House extolling the importance of an ex-

panded FBI intelligence role. Most of these papers apparently documented the value of the intelligence developed by the FBI's SIS. One report, however, informed the president that an OSS officer stationed in Paris had attempted to arrange with French intelligence "for the establishment of French espionage organization within the United States." FBI officials also employed friends in Congress: Republican congressman Karl Stefan wrote the president to extol "the effective intelligence work of the Federal Bureau of Investigation in Canada, Central America and South America" and called for continuance of the SIS for national security reasons.[7] Stefan's and Hoover's lobbying efforts failed, however; instead Truman dissolved the SIS.

Despite having failed to maintain their own foreign intelligence role, FBI officials worked with MID and ONI officials and conservative members of Congress to overturn the State Department's control over postwar foreign intelligence—pursuant to Truman's order dissolving OSS and transferring its intelligence assets to State. For when Truman dissolved OSS he also instructed Secretary of State James Byrnes to "take the lead in developing a comprehensive and coordinated intelligence program." Byrnes was to chair an interdepartmental intelligence group to draft a plan to ensure "complete coverage of the foreign intelligence field." This group, however, was to take into account that "the needs of both the individual agencies and the Government as a whole will be met with maximum efficiency."

The secretary of state interpreted Truman's order as reaffirming the State Department's historic role as the nation's principal foreign intelligence agency. Accordingly he appointed Alfred McCormack, a prominent New York attorney who had served in MID during World War II, as special assistant for research and intelligence to "collect," "evaluate," and "disseminate" "all information regarding foreign nations." McCormack would coordinate the collection efforts of the various State Department regional branches as well as the other intelligence agencies.

Announcing this appointment on September 27, 1945, Byrnes characterized the State Department's recent absorption of OSS assets as the "first step in the reorganization of the Department to meet its expanding responsibilities."

Byrnes's attempt at centralization was immediately challenged. Working closely with MID and ONI, FBI officials acted to subvert State's initiative. They provided derogatory information about McCormack's former associates to their ideologically sympathetic allies on the House Armed Services Committee, and further let it be known that McCormack had sought to purge information from FBI files about these associates' subversive actions. This tactic succeeded. The Armed Services Committee immediately publicized these contentions, and in April 1946 the House Appropriations Committee voted to withhold funds from the proposed Office of Research and Intelligence. McCormack thereupon resigned in protest.[8]

The successes of FBI, MID, and ONI officials in submarining both the Donovan plan and the State Department's effort underlined Truman's central problem—the continued rivalry of the various intelligence agencies and their departmental supporters—and their reluctance to surrender their recently expanded authority. The president, already embattled by internal opposition from Roosevelt holdovers, his own Cabinet appointees, and emboldened conservatives in Congress, at first hesitated to seek legislation for a centralized intelligence system. Stefan's intercession and the congressional response to Trohan's article had confirmed that the entrenched bureaucracies could rely on congressional conservatives for support, thereby highlighting the political price Truman would pay should he attempt to institute centralized intelligence. But Truman could not avoid the matter altogether. The difficult international situation provoked by Soviet actions in Eastern Europe, Germany, and the Middle East, and the onset of civil wars in Greece and China, demanded action.

Truman's order dissolving the OSS did not suggest an indifference to covert operations and foreign intelligence. Bureaucratic realities alone had constrained this politically vulnerable president. They further demanded that he would have to work within the established institutional order to advance his administration's foreign policy goals. Because his request that Secretary of State Byrnes devise a coordinated "foreign intelligence program" had become bogged down by interdepartmental rivalry, on November 7, 1945, Truman directed White House aide Matthew Connelly to convene a conference among the secretaries of State, War, and Navy to prepare "a plan for the establishment of a Central Intelligence Service that is acceptable" to these three departments. The study was to be completed by December 31.

Navy and Army opposition to the State Department's proposal ensured that Truman's deadline would not be met. The participants did eventually reach a compromise that Truman adopted. On January 22, 1946, by executive order, he established a National Intelligence Authority. NIA would be composed of the secretaries of State, War, and Navy and presidential representative Admiral William Leahy, and would "plan, develop and coordinate . . . all intelligence activities" to ensure the "most effective accomplishment of the intelligence mission related to national security." The FBI, however, was excluded from the NIA, though it could participate in an advisory capacity. A Central Intelligence Group (CIG) was also established, staffed by intelligence officers loaned by the State, War, and Navy departments. Denied its own budget, CIG would have no "police, law enforcement, or internal security" function but could perform "services of common concern," subject to the direction of NIA, and "coordinate and evaluate" submitted information but not control or direct intelligence policy. In effect, Truman created a cumbersome system, one that sustained existing agency independence and bureaucratic rivalries with no agency or official having overall authority to determine collection policies or ensure a common intelligence product.[9]

Truman's concession that the secretaries of State, War, and Navy agree on a plan to coordinate intelligence operations ensured that the newly created CIG would not overcome bureaucratic independence and parochialism. Were the president to circumvent these problems, he would have no choice but to obtain legislative authorization for an independent central intelligence agency. Truman nonetheless hesitated to endorse the institutional changes that frustrated CIG staff advanced. White House aides Clark Clifford and George Elsey reflected Truman's caution. At a July 1946 meeting with CIG officials Lawrence Houston and James Lay, they at first objected to the proposed plan because it departed "from the President's intention by establishing a separate and sizeable government agency." Lay and Houston, however, succeeded in overcoming the hesitancy of these key White House aides. CIG suffered from "being a step-child of three separate departments," they observed, while recent "experience showed" that the president's interest in effective coordination required "enabling legislation" to create an "operating agency with a large staff of Intelligence experts."[10]

Within months the White House abandoned its indecision and endorsed legislation to create a central intelligence agency. The move was incorporated as part of a broader initiative to unify the armed services that eventuated in the National Security Act of July 26, 1947. Nonetheless, were the administration to achieve legislative support for a centralized intelligence system, it would inevitably have to overcome the opposition of both the established intelligence agencies and skeptical congressmen, some who identified with the established agencies and others who feared centralized government. During internal discussions over the proposed legislation, Major General Wilton Persons warned that "Congress and the American people have always looked upon any secret intelligence operation with suspicion." This "antipathy," Persons observed, was a formidable obstacle to creating a centralized intelligence system. Although the public might "at present" support such an institution, within ten to fifteen years such support would decline and thus affect needed funding. Administration proponents also realized that the existing intelligence agencies (notably the FBI, State, War, and Navy) could count on the support of powerful congressmen on the Appropriations, Armed Services, and Foreign Relations committees, congressmen who would have a major voice in determining final legislation.

Thus in drafting the bill that was introduced in Congress on February 28, 1947, White House and CIG officials considered both bureaucratic interests and the political realities that would influence legislative approval. They specifically sought the input of State, War, Navy, and Justice Department officials and consulted key congressmen. Their further attempts to allay congressional concern continued during executive sessions and informal deliberations on the bill. As finally enacted, the measure established an independent Central Intelligence Agency whose director would be appointed by the president, subject to Senate confirmation. The CIA would "plan, develop and coordinate the foreign intelligence activities of the United States," "correlate, evaluate and disseminate" intelligence, and perform "intelligence missions of common concern" and "such other functions and duties relating to intelligence affecting the national security" as the president and the National Security Council—another executive agency established by the legislation—"may from time to time direct." Denied any internal security or law-enforcement role, the new agency would, however, be responsible for protecting national security information. Just as important, the new agency would hire, train, and supervise its own personnel, have its own appropriations, and expend both documented and undocumented funds, the latter to be used for sensitive operations.[11]

Congress endorsed the proposed "comprehensive" and "integrated" intelligence system, but on the understanding that it would neither "merge" nor "replace" the existing intelligence services. Moreover the language of the bill that defined the parameters of the CIA's authority was vague, and this ambiguity raised questions whether the creation of a secret agency could threaten privacy rights and limited government. Some members of Congress demanded that the CIA's role be confined to evaluating and coordinating, that it not itself be permitted to collect intelligence; others questioned whether the section authorizing the CIA to conduct "such other functions and duties" would permit operations neither known nor authorized by Congress. These concerns were articulated during both executive sessions and floor debate. Nonetheless no member of Congress introduced an amendment to clarify this vague language, whether to limit the CIA's authority to analysis or to prohibit it from conducting covert paramilitary operations.

This ambiguity over the CIA's role was later clarified when in 1949 Congress enacted the Central Intelligence Agency Act. During the debate over this measure, which spelled out the duties of CIA officers and their remuneration, members of Congress described the CIA as an "espionage" agency and exempted its budget from routine accounting requirements. Indeed, the legislation was explicitly described as "an espionage bill," a description that implicitly recognized that CIA agents would secretly collect intelligence overseas and would not simply be analysts. Thus by 1949 the initial reservations articulated in 1947 about the scope of CIA operations had dissipated.[12]

A second concern, also articulated during executive sessions and floor debate in 1947, led Congress to adopt an amendment barring the CIA from any "internal security or police function." Conservative congressman Clarence Brown for one, in questioning Secretary of the Navy James Forrestal, had wondered whether this secret agency could become "an incipient Gestapo." Brown succeeded in securing the adoption of an amendment barring the

CIA from "police, subpoena, law-enforcement powers, or internal security functions."[13]

Whether or not the 1947 National Security Act authorized CIA officers to collect intelligence, the establishment of the agency led to the stationing of agents overseas who did indeed begin to collect intelligence. The scope of the CIA's role and status within the executive branch nonetheless remained unclear. Central questions remained: Would the CIA be anything more than a service agency? Would it merely respond to requests from the National Security Council, also established under the 1947 act? Would it merely "advise the President with respect to the integration of domestic, foreign, and military policies," or would it be an independent analyst reporting directly to the president? Would "subject to the direction of the President" mean that it would simply evaluate and recommend needed changes to current intelligence operations? The act's language furthermore left unresolved the CIA's relationship with other intelligence agencies. Would the CIA's responsibilities extend beyond coordinating the intelligence its agents collected with that acquired by other intelligence agencies? Had the National Security Act created an integrated and centrally directed intelligence system, one that would reduce bureaucratic independence and ensure full cooperation among formerly independent agencies having their own parochial priorities?

The 1947 act did not answer these questions. Instead the answers emerged from the Truman administration's various policy initiatives after July 1947 to counter the perceived Soviet threat. One consequence was the emergence of a more powerful and independent CIA, the product of a series of secret executive directives issued during the agency's formative years, 1947–1951. Political as much as international considerations determined this course of action. President Truman's unwillingness to seek congressional approval for his most sensitive initiatives also reflected his concern that the process would complicate efforts to win consent for the unprecedented and costly Truman Doctrine and Marshall Plan proposals.

The timing of the CIA's formal establishment in September 1947 coincided with Truman's official adoption of the containment policy. To arrest Soviet expansion, the Truman administration in March 1947 set forth an aggressive program that went beyond diplomatic negotiations to address the economic and political chaos of postwar Europe. Should the United States fail to promote economic recovery and political stability in postwar Europe, administration officials concluded, the vacuum would provide an opportunity for Soviet expansion. Success of the containment policy, moreover, depended on the acquisition of sound intelligence about Soviet plans and capabilities and the use of nondiplomatic measures to contain Soviet influence. Truman administration officials at the same time interpreted a series of developments in 1945—the *Amerasia* case and the defections of Soviet consular officer Igor Gouzenko and Communist courier Elizabeth Bentley—as confirming a serious internal security threat, one resulting from Soviet recruitment of American Communist party activists as spies. These international and domestic circumstances underlay deliberations within the administration in 1947–1948 about the CIA's relationship with State, MID, ONI, and FBI—in the case of the FBI, to coordinate counterespionage operations. While the administration's sense of crisis encouraged cooperation, the recent history of bureaucratic independence suggested that the established agencies would continue to attempt to operate independently.

The CIA's creation in 1947 did not affirm that a centralized intelligence system had won popular or institutional acceptance. To ensure passage various compromises had been adopted, and the resulting legislation did not explicitly recognize the CIA as the nation's primary intelligence agency. The CIA director might head an independent agency and command his own budget and personnel, but he had no supervisory or budgetary authority over the other intelligence agencies. The CIA director could coordinate intelligence and conduct "such special services" as requested by the NSC. But State and the Defense Department (which now replaced War and Navy), as members of the National Security Council, could ensure that the CIA would only supplement, neither replace nor direct, the activities traditionally performed by State, MID, ONI, and FBI. Earlier MID and ONI officials had resisted CIG Director Hoyt Vandenberg's efforts to act as their supervisor and not their servant; they continued to resist reporting to the CIA's first director, Roscoe Hillenkoetter. Similarly FBI officials only reluctantly provided the CIG and then the CIA with the records and assets their agents had developed as part of their wartime foreign intelligence service in the Western Hemisphere. Nor did FBI officials perceive the creation of the CIA as requiring changes in their conduct of counterespionage operations.[14]

Nonetheless the CIA differed from the CIG in that it operated under the direction of the NSC. Over time between 1947 and 1952, the NSC evolved into a key policymaking body, having its own staff and acting as the agent of the president. NSC staff and the council's members met regularly to discuss policy matters. The NSC subsequently issued secret directives drafted by the NSC's independent staff and an executive secretary (a presidential appointee). The NSC staff, moreover, was housed in the Executive Office Building and was independent of the intelligence services, who were supervised by the secretaries of state and defense and the attorney general. While it had not been planned, by 1950 the NSC evolved into a key policy deliberation and policymaking body. It became the president's agent, and its operation brought about a more efficient, centralized system that contrasted sharply with the cabinet system of independent departments. President Truman's administrative orientation and desire for efficiency, in addition, transformed the executive branch into an instrument of presidential power. NSC directives enhanced the CIA's independence and expanded its authority in the areas of intelligence analysis and covert operations.[15]

In enacting the legislation creating the CIA, Congress intended this new "central intelligence" agency to coordinate intelligence. How this was to be achieved remained unclear because the National Security Act failed to give the CIA director supervisory or budgetary authority over the other intelligence agencies. The act's legislative history also left unclear whether the CIA could conduct "covert operations." This possibility had been elliptically cited during executive sessions, but the act itself did not specifically authorize covert operations. The CIA could "perform such other functions and duties related to intelligence affecting the national security as the National Security Council may from time to time direct." Whatever Congress's intent, senior administration officials interpreted this language as authority for covert operations. This broader interpretation misrepresented the authorization language, which at best implied that such operations would be exceptional, not normative, and in response to unanticipated developments.

The assignment of covert operations to the CIA was at first a response by U.S. policymakers to their assessment of Soviet objectives and capabilities. By 1947 senior administration officials had concluded that U.S.-Soviet differences could not be resolved through diplomacy. Their conviction that Soviet leaders intended to exploit economic and political discontent worldwide led them to initiate programs of economic assistance to thwart Soviet expansionism. By late 1947 U.S. policymakers feared that the Communist threat was broader and more insidious than first recognized, and that a particularly worrisome aspect was the "vicious psychological efforts" of the Soviet Union and "its satellite Countries" to "discredit and defeat" the diplomatic and foreign intelligence efforts of the United States and its Western European allies. If this threat were to be repulsed, U.S. officials decided, the United States must resort to "covert psychological operations."

Such operations were temporarily assigned to the CIA subject to the "coordination of the Secretary of State" under a secret directive, NSC-4A, issued by the National Security Council on December 17, 1947. Neither State nor Defense wished to assume this role, fearing that the operations would entail intervention in the internal affairs of sovereign states and would thus chance compromising their diplomatic missions and military occupations. The NSC had thus turned to the CIA since its officers were already stationed in Europe and, in addition, the agency's access to undocumented funds would "ensure their secrecy and obviate costly duplication." State and Defense Department officials nonetheless intended that such operations would be undertaken only to advance U.S. foreign policy and military interests, and thus reserved to themselves the right to oversee and direct this onetime initiative. Programs implemented by the CIA included financial assistance to the Christian Democratic party to prevent a Communist victory in the April 1948 Italian parliamentary elections, and the funding of a non-Communist French trade-union movement to counter the Communist-led Confederation du Travail.

Eventually the CIA's conduct of covert operations became ongoing. By 1948 U.S. policymakers were convinced that Soviet officials intended to achieve world domination through subterfuge and would do so by capitalizing on the appeal of native radical movements. Thus they revisited this earlier December 1947 initiative and through another NSC directive, NSC-10/2 of June 1948, authorized ongoing CIA covert operations to meet this Soviet threat. Any such operations, they further decided, would have to be "so planned and executed that any U.S. Government responsibility for them is not evident . . . and that if uncovered the U.S. Government can plausibly" deny any responsibility. The operations were to be broader than those proposed under NSC-4A and would extend beyond psychological warfare to include "economic warfare, preventive direct action, including sabotage, anti-sabotage, demolition and evacuation measures; subversion against hostile states, including assistance to underground resistance movements, guerrillas and refugee liberation groups, and support of independent anti-communist elements in threatened countries of the free world."

Because the breadth and ambitious character of such operations made them not simply another task for CIA agents already stationed in Europe, a special Office of Policy Coordination (OPC) was created. It would be quartered in the CIA but subject to the direction of the secretaries of state and defense. To meet the expanded range of authorized covert activities, OPC's staff between the years 1949 and 1952 increased ninefold, from 302 to 2,812, and its budget twentyfold from $4.7 million to $82 million. The approved CIA programs included the funding of propaganda (Radio Free Europe and Radio Liberty) as well as of anti-Communist resistance movements in Eastern Europe, the Balkans, and Asia. Because such operations were no longer exceptional, NSA-10/2's requirement subjecting OPC operations to the direction of the secretaries of state and defense was reassessed. This cumbersome arrangement was abandoned under NSC-10/5 of October 23, 1951, with OPC now integrated within the CIA to ensure an "immediate expansion" and "intensification." OPC accordingly became the CIA's Directorate of Plans, ensuring a more efficient and effective conduct of covert operations because its functions were subject to a "single chain of command and a single set of administrative procedures." The head of the Directorate of Plans became the CIA director's "deputy for all CIA clandestine activities" and was charged to "coordinate" all such efforts and insure "prompt and effective compliance with operational directives." By 1952, then, the CIA had evolved into a more powerful institution, a development in response to the need for advancing the president's foreign policy initiatives without alerting the nation's adversaries to U.S. plans and capabilities, at the same time averting a potentially divisive domestic debate over the costs and consequences of operations that might precipitate armed conflict.[16]

The CIA's intelligence role underwent the same process of expansion and centralization. In authorizing this new agency to "coordinate" intelligence, Congress purposely refused to limit the role of the already established intelligence agencies. The decision simply to create another agency, however, was not sustainable. The confusion created by this policy of accretion inevitably forced Truman administration officials to resolve the central question: Was the CIA to be just another intelligence agency, or the first among equals? When it coordinated intelligence, were its analyses to be controlling as the final provider of intelligence to the president? Was the CIA director empowered to determine and allocate collection responsibilities? Were the other intelligence agencies obligated to forward all collected intelligence to the CIA? What would be the distinction between foreign intelligence and foreign counterintelligence? Between foreign intelligence and strategic intelligence? Between domestic intelligence and foreign intelligence?

Creation of the Intelligence Advisory Committee in December 1947 marked the first effort to resolve these questions. This committee was originally composed of representatives from MID, ONI, State, the Joint Chiefs, and the Atomic Energy Commission. (While the FBI was not an initial member, an FBI representative could be invited to attend specific meetings.) The committee would "advise" the CIA director about "surveys and inspections" of departmental intelligence and offer recommendations for cooperation. This process, it was hoped, would produce "intelligence relating to national security" without duplicating that of the other intelligence agencies. CIA officials' subsequent attempts to define the agency's role invariably provoked resistance and opposition from MID, ONI, FBI, and State Department officials. This resistance affected the CIA's ability to fulfill its coordinating function at a time of intensifying international crises—beginning with the

1948 Berlin blockade, the Soviet explosion of an atomic bomb in 1949, the Chinese Communist success in overthrowing the Chinese Nationalists in 1948–1949, and the North Korean invasion of South Korea in 1950. In all these instances, the president had not been forewarned about Soviet or Communist plans and capabilities. In their efforts to understand the objectives of a secretive adversary, CIA officials were hampered by a lack of full cooperation from MID, ONI, and State Department officials who clung to their authority to collect intelligence and shape administration foreign and military policy. This situation worsened in 1949 with the inclusion of an FBI representative on the Intelligence Advisory Committee to coordinate domestic and foreign intelligence. Efforts to curb inter-agency frictions ultimately changed the CIA's role to that of an independent provider of intelligence to the president, not an agent of the Intelligence Advisory Committee. Long-established intelligence agencies nonetheless sustained their independence and continued to resist attempts to subordinate their actions to the overall authority of the CIA director. Only in name, then, was the CIA *the* central intelligence agency.[17]

In effect, efforts to reform the intelligence system foundered on the shoals of inter-agency rivalries and independence. Decisions favored accommodation to the CIA's emergence as a new independent agency without a parochial departmental agenda. This process was exemplified in the FBI-CIA relationship, one that predated the inclusion of an FBI representative on the Intelligence Advisory Committee. Dating from 1947 when plans to define the CIA's foreign intelligence role were drafted, the NSC addressed how this invariably would also involve the agency in domestic activities—in the phrasing of NSCID-7, the CIA's "exploitation on a highly selective basis, within the United States of business concerns, other non-governmental organizations and individuals as sources of intelligence information."[18] Such actions did not violate the 1947 National Security Act's ban on a CIA "internal security" role. Nonetheless such CIA initiatives raised the question of how to ensure that the "domestic intelligence" operations of the FBI, MID, and ONI were not compromised.

The resolution of this matter, as in the case of the CIA's covert operations and intelligence functions, became a subject of NSC deliberations. In a departure, the NSC rejected the premise that such decisions were within the exclusive province of the interested department officials. Thus the delimitation agreements that FBI, MID, and ONI officials had independently concluded in 1940 became the subject of NSC review because "no one agency is solely or exclusively responsible" for the nation's internal security in light of the agencies' variety and distinctive responsibilities. The NSC staff eventually drafted a plan, adopted as NSC-17/4 in March 1949, to ensure "a thoroughly coordinated and integrated effort" to address the serious Communist internal security threat "at this time." Two committees were established and would be subject to NSC supervision. The first, an Interdepartmental Intelligence Conference (IIC), would be composed of representatives from the FBI, MID, ONI, and air force intelligence and would be chaired by the FBI. IIC would coordinate all investigations involving "domestic espionage, counter-espionage, sabotage, subversion, and other related matters affecting internal security." The second, an Interdepartmental Committee on Internal Security (ICIS), would be composed of representatives from the State, Defense, Treasury, and Justice departments. The ICIS would coordinate "all non-investigating internal security activities which are not within the purview of the Interdepartmental Intelligence Conference."[19]

The creation of the IIC, however, did not finally resolve the matter of how best to coordinate domestic intelligence investigations. As chair of the IIC, FBI director Hoover opposed State Department and CIA efforts to have a voice in coordinating and defining the priorities governing internal security policy. In fact Hoover had at first resisted the proposed inclusion of the FBI on the Intelligence Advisory Committee because he feared this would subject FBI domestic intelligence operations to the CIA's supervision and direction. Hoover's concerns were unwarranted; President Truman was unwilling, whether in domestic or foreign spheres, to challenge the bureaucratic independence of the established intelligence agencies. In addition, Hoover succeeded in containing any future CIA threat to the FBI's domestic responsibilities. Instead an informal liaison program was established under which CIA requests for FBI reports would be submitted in writing and required the FBI director's prior approval. Cooperation and assistance was volunteered, not mandated, through the appointment of special liaison officers who would forward to the CIA any FBI-obtained information having a "foreign intelligence" character.[20]

The crisis of the cold war, and the recognized importance of intercepting and decoding international communications, similarly fueled the centralizing of code-breaking and communication interception operations. The timing of this development stemmed from the failure of the military services to anticipate the North Korean invasion of South Korea on June 25, 1950. The internal debate provoked by this failure was finally resolved on October 24, 1952, when President Truman issued a secret directive creating the National Security Agency (NSA) to operate under the authority of the secretary of defense, not the Joint Chiefs of Staff. This new agency was assigned operational control over international communication intelligence—interception, code-breaking, and code security—that formerly had been separately conducted by the Army Security Agency, the Naval Security Command Group, and the Air Force Security Service. Creating the NSA implicitly recognized that earlier efforts, dating from 1948, had not integrated and coordinated the "foreign communications" activities of the State Department, the FBI, and the CIA. Each military and nonmilitary agency had jealously safeguarded its role, deeming this essential to its assigned responsibilities. Truman's secret directive thus did not effect a centralized communications intercept system so much as it resolved the conflicts among the three military services over targets, priorities, and the allocation of communication channels.[21] NSA's creation by secret directive, moreover, was by then consistent with what had become the Truman administration's overall approach to intelligence policy. For by 1950 Truman was unwilling to consult Congress, in part because he was concerned that the lawmakers would reject specific operations as contravening privacy rights or undermining limited government. His willingness to bypass Congress and avert public debate had also defined his administration's authorization of a particularly sensitive communications interception program, code-named Operation SHAMROCK.

Under a wartime censorship program that President Roosevelt had instituted in December 1941 and that Congress had authorized in 1942, military intelligence officials had reached agreement with the three international telegraph companies—Western Union, ITT, and RCA—for access to all international telegraph messages transiting through the United States involving the Axis and Axis-aligned powers and the Soviet Union. This program's legal authority expired with the end of World War II, and by executive order President Truman formally ended this censorship program. Before issuing this order in September 1945, Truman notified the director of the censorship program and the other participating intelligence officials of the planned termination.

Military officials nonetheless remained committed to continuing an arrangement they had found to be valuable. The executives of the international companies questioned the legality of continued assistance and suggested that it violated provisions of the 1934 Communications Act. Military officials overrode this reluctance in 1945, informing company executives of the attorney general's conclusion that the program was not illegal. On advice of legal counsel, company executives responded in 1947 with their doubts that the courts would affirm the attorney general's interpretations of the 1934 act and of Supreme Court rulings.

They also expressed their concern that labor union leaders might disclose such cooperation, thereby triggering adverse publicity and demands for prosecution. Again military officials obtained the executives' cooperation. In this case Secretary of Defense James Forrestal assured them that Attorney General Tom Clark, with President Truman's concurrence, had promised not to prosecute them. The administration, in addition, would draft and seek enactment of legislation amending the 1934 act to legalize this program.

Justice Department officials did draft such legislation in 1948 in consultation with the chairmen of the House and Senate Judiciary Committees. But the proposed amendment was never voted upon. After consulting with the chairman of the Senate Judiciary Committee, administration officials decided that opposition within the committee made such action unwise in a presidential election year. Still, the nonprosecution promise was reaffirmed to the company executives in 1949 by Forrestal's successor as secretary of defense, Louis Johnson. Johnson's assurance, however, was not accompanied by a renewed effort to have Congress legalize the program.

Truman administration officials instead pursued a different strategy, one reflecting their unwillingness to risk a public debate over efforts to amend the 1934 act. They introduced legislation with the narrow purpose of criminalizing the disclosure of code-breaking and communications interception activities. This measure would address company executives' concerns since it would make it illegal for union officials to disclose the companies' assistance. The provision was incorporated in an innocuous bill to amend the federal code and was approved by Congress in October 1951, in the waning days of the session, without public hearings, floor debate, or a recorded vote.[22]

Under the SHAMROCK program, FBI agents acted as intermediaries between the international telegraph companies and ASA (late NSA). They picked up the identified coded messages, delivered half to ASA/NSA, and kept the other half.²³ This cooperative arrangement characterized another relationship between the FBI and ASA/NSA involving an even more sensitive international communication interception program, code-named VENONA.

Soviet intelligence agents stationed in the United States during World War II, under cover as embassy or consular officials, had sent many of their reports to their superiors in Moscow through the commercial telegraph companies. The telegraph companies had then forwarded these—along with the communications of Axis and Axis-aligned powers and their suspected agents—to military intelligence. ASA agents, under a 1942 delimitation agreement with ONI and FBI, were granted exclusive responsibility to analyze and attempt to decipher foreign diplomatic and military ciphers.* Because the intercepted messages of Soviet consular and embassy officials had been transmitted in code, a special military intelligence unit was established in 1943 to attempt to break it. Until 1946 military analysts made only minimal progress. But that year an expanded and better-trained unit made a major breakthrough, discovering that, when transmitting the messages through a seemingly unbreakable "one-time pad," Soviet agents had used duplicate pages of the pad. Discovery of this duplication enabled military analysts, beginning in 1949, to decipher many of these coded messages that had been sent as early as 1940. Nonetheless, because the identities of the Soviet agents and their recruited spies were disguised through code names, ASA officials sought the FBI's assistance in 1948, and then in 1953 the assistance of the CIA, to identify these espionage agents. In many cases FBI agents were able to identify many of these disguised sources through a painstaking review of FBI surveillance files on American Communists and Soviet officials compiled during the 1930s and 1940s, and by reviewing the detailed testimony about their associates in Soviet espionage of Communist defectors, especially Elizabeth Bentley and

---

*The FBI maintained the messages of American citizens and alien residents.

Whittaker Chambers, and later the cooperative witnesses Harry Gold and David Greenglass. This liaison belatedly led in 1949–1950 to the uncovering and then the FBI's successful prosecution of some of the participants in Soviet espionage operations. The most notable were a low-level Justice Department employee, Judith Coplon, who was indicted for attempting to deliver classified FBI reports to a Soviet agent; and Julius Rosenberg, David Greenglass, and Harry Gold, who were indicted and convicted for participating in a conspiracy to steal atomic secrets.[24]

The FBI's cooperation with NSA and CIA in the VENONA project was not exceptional. FBI agents broke into various foreign embassies during World War II to photocopy codes, ciphers, and tables, then forwarded the information to military intelligence. FBI officials provided similar assistance to ASA/NSA and CIA throughout the cold war years until 1966–1970, with NSA officials periodically requesting break-ins to further their efforts to "break cryptographic codes." FBI assistance, moreover, extended beyond break-ins and included the installation of wiretaps and bugs, and the preparation of reports about the actions of foreign intelligence officers and their U.S. contacts. NSA officials, under a special program code-named MINARET, later forwarded to the FBI intercepted messages of Americans whose names the FBI had provided. CIA officials provided similar assistance to the FBI, forwarding copies of letters (sent between New York and the Soviet Union) they had intercepted. The CIA also investigated—at FBI request—and identified Americans who traveled abroad and who FBI officials suspected were involved in "subversive" activities. In 1966 FBI and CIA officials concluded an informal agreement to coordinate their investigations of anti–Vietnam War and civil rights activists who traveled overseas. Under this arrangement, CIA officials would "seek concurrence and coordination of the FBI" before monitoring activities within the United States to ensure that this "proposed action does not conflict with any [FBI] operation, current or planned, including active investigations [by] the FBI." Furthermore, whenever a source whom the CIA had recruited arrived in the United States, FBI officials would be advised, and the two agencies would "confer regarding the handling of the agent in the United States." The CIA would handle this source when in the United States for "foreign intelligence purposes" but would provide the FBI with any "information bearing on internal security matters."

The targets of this surveillance and the formal procedures governing this relationship cannot now be established because relevant records remain classified. Our understanding of this relationship and assistance is indirect, a by-product of congressional investigations of the 1970s, particularly those conducted by the so-called Church Committee, into the Huston Plan (described in detail in a later chapter). Records were then uncovered documenting NSA and CIA officials' protests in 1970 over the FBI's unwillingness to continue conducting break-ins, installing wiretaps and bugs, and pursuing mail coverage, all of which had been done for decades. NSA and CIA were protesting the effect of restrictive orders that FBI director Hoover had imposed in 1965–1966 prohibiting continued FBI break-ins and mail programs and imposing a cap on wiretaps and bugs.[25]

One known instance of FBI-CIA cooperation offers insights into the scope of this relationship. As part of his official duties to recruit private citizens who traveled abroad as foreign intelligence sources, CIA officer Joseph Bryan III in January 1951 arranged separate meetings with *New York Times* European bureau chief Cyrus Sulzberger and *New York Times* publisher Arthur Hays Sulzburger. Bryan at the time was employed in the CIA's psychological warfare division, and his specific purpose in meeting with the Sulzburgers remains in dispute. During an interview with former *New York Times* reporter Harrison Salisbury about this meeting, Cyrus Sulzberger recalled that Bryan had been traveling through Europe that year to "sign up people [reporters] for nondisclosure statements"—in other words, the reporter would agree not to disclose that the CIA was a source for leaked information. Bryan, in contrast, told Salisbury that Cyrus Sulzburger had been the only newspaper reporter he had met in Europe and that Bryan's purpose had been "to get information from him, not to give it to him." These tantalizing meetings, and the conflicting accounts of the *Times*-CIA relationship, nonetheless suggest that Bryan's 1951 initiative was part of a CIA program.

Whether or not Bryan's purpose in 1951 had been to recruit Sulzburger or *New York Times* reporters as CIA sources, his actions later that same year suggest that his request was part of a broader assignment consistent with his psychological warfare responsibilities. As recorded in FBI files, four months later, in May, Bryan, after first clearing this with the CIA's liaison to the FBI, secured access to the FBI's massive Obscene File. Why Bryan sought access to this file remains unclear—conceivably he was replicating OSS's 1944 counterpropaganda initiative. He might, then, have sought derogatory information on American Communists or Soviet officials who had been stationed in the United States.

The Bryan episode has another dimension: it offers insights into the tense nature of the FBI-CIA relationship. FBI director Hoover first learned that Bryan had been granted access to the FBI's Obscene File in early 1953. His discovery was the result of an investigation he had ordered about Bryan following a briefing that Bryan, at a dinner party on the eve of the 1952 presidential election, allegedly had claimed that Hoover was homosexual and that he could identify the FBI director's homosexual lover. Hoover had immediately demanded that his aides confirm this allegation and further that Bryan be forced to "put up or shut up." Hoover also ordered his aides to brief CIA officials about their former operative's comment—as a reflection of the character of CIA employees and an instance of CIA hostility.[26]

6 | SECRECY AND THE LOSS OF ACCOUNTABILITY, 1952–1965

■ SECRET EXECUTIVE ORDERS authorized the expansion of the intelligence agencies' powers and instituted rules to promote coordination. If the underlying purpose was to deny potential adversaries an awareness of U.S. plans and capabilities, secrecy at the same time foreclosed a public debate over the impact of proposed changes on privacy rights and governmental power. Just as important, the public could not know whether specific initiatives would violate the nation's democratic principles. In fact the process was inherently undemocratic: while the ability to act in secret might promote the objectives of presidents and bureaucrats, it exempted their decisions from congressional oversight.

President Truman's successors shared his preference for an executive-based government. Cold war presidents relied more heavily on secrecy to pursue an ambitious agenda of containing Soviet international influence and neutralizing potential internal security threats, but also to avoid the potentially destabilizing charges of "softness toward Communism." Leveled by McCarthyites, such accusations capitalized on a president's inability to achieve absolute security. At least until a shift in Congress's approach in the mid-1960s and 1970s, cold war presidents were for the most part able to act unilaterally, a tactic that was also a product of congressional deference to the executive. In the wake of McCarthy's irresponsible actions, principled members of Congress and the media, out of concern for national security, viewed secrecy as essential to countering the "subversive" character of communism. Congressional leaders willingly abandoned their potential checks—whether of public hearings or legislative proscription—on executive power and its secretive manner. This deference is best illustrated by Congress's response to one of the so-called Doolittle Committee's substantive recommendations.

Dwight Eisenhower's election to the presidency in 1952 ended twenty years of Democratic governance. Ike had won the Republican presidential nomination with the support of moderate Republicans who opposed the candidacy of conservative Ohio senator Robert Taft. For them, and the general public, Eisenhower was a more attractive candidate than Taft because he would not carry the senator's baggage as a strident opponent of New Deal domestic reforms and an isolationist in foreign policy. Eisenhower's nomination enabled Republicans to win the presidency and control of Congress in the 1952 elections. Republican candidates could campaign on the perceived failures of the Truman administration: a seemingly indecisive and ineffective foreign policy, a seeming indifference to the Communist internal security threat, and a seemingly inefficient and corrupt domestic policy. In contrast to the 1948 Republican presidential nominee, the moderate New York governor Thomas E. Dewey, Eisenhower successfully distanced himself from the militant anti–New Deal identity of the Republican congressional leadership. And, though Eisenhower did not propose to dismantle the New Deal, as a fiscal and philosophical conservative he did intend to scale back the role of the federal government and the level of federal spending. Achieving these objectives required a more nuanced and indirect approach, one that characterized the new president's early decisions in

1953, including the appointment of former Republican president Herbert Hoover to head a Commission on the Organization of the Executive Branch. This commission was to examine the operation of the expanded post–New Deal federal bureaucracy and recommend changes to increase efficiency, eliminate duplication, and reduce costs.

The Hoover Commission's investigation extended to the CIA. Yet, because of the sensitivity of CIA operations, two special committees were appointed to review its performance, one chaired by air force General James Doolittle to examine CIA covert operations, and the second by General Mark Clark to look at the CIA's other operations.

Because of their different responsibilities, the committees reported to different constituencies. The Doolittle Committee's classified report was submitted only to President Eisenhower while the Clark Task Force's declassified report was submitted to Congress along with the Hoover Commission's more extensive report on the federal government as a whole. Both the Doolittle and Clark reports criticized the quality of CIA personnel and recruitment efforts, administrative inefficiency, lax security procedures, and the quality of its intelligence on the Soviet Union.

In evaluating CIA covert operations, the Doolittle Committee endorsed "an aggressive covert psychological, political and paramilitary organization more effective, more unique and if necessary, more ruthless than that employed by" the Soviet Union. "It is now clear," the committee emphasized, "that we are facing an implacable enemy whose avowed objective is world domination by whatever means, and at whatever cost. There are no rules in such a game. Hitherto acceptable norms of human conduct do not apply. If the United States is to survive, long-standing American concepts of 'fair play' must be reconsidered. We must develop effective espionage and counterespionage services. We must learn to subvert, sabotage, and destroy our enemies by more clever, more sophisticated, and more effective methods than those used against us. It may become necessary that the American people will be made acquainted with, understand, and support this fundamentally repugnant philosophy."

Complementing this alarming recommendation, the Doolittle Committee, like the Clark Task Force, was concerned by the CIA's seemingly mindless growth and secret operations. Although the Doolittle Committee's critical report was not released, an abbreviated version of the Clark Task Force's report was. Significantly, the publicly released section of the Clark report criticized the inadequacy of congressional oversight of the CIA and recommended the creation of an oversight committee composed of respected lawmakers and "public spirited citizens" to limit the "possibility of the growth of license and abuses of power," given the need to conduct CIA operations in secret. Both these reports prompted administrative changes which President Eisenhower implemented secretly under NSC-5412 and then publicly in January 1956 in appointing the President's Board of Consultants on Foreign Intelligence Activities.[1]

Before the release of the Clark report, Democratic senator Mike Mansfield on July 20, 1953, had introduced a resolution to create a ten-member joint congressional committee to oversee the CIA. A freshman senator from the rural state of Montana, Mansfield at first commanded limited support for his initiative. It was referred to the Armed Services Committee in 1954, where it died. Release of the Clark report, however, changed the political landscape, and in February 1956 the Senate Rules Committee approved Mansfield's resolution for a floor vote. Acting quickly, the Eisenhower administration and CIA officials behind the scenes, as well as the leadership of the Armed Services Committee, notably Senators Richard Russell and Leverett Saltonstall, vigorously opposed passage. Russell and Saltonstall framed the issue as one of essential secrecy, at the same time extolling the current oversight role of the Armed Services Committee. Defending that oversight, Saltonstall argued, "It is not a question of reluctance on the part of CIA officials to speak to us. Instead, it is a question of our reluctance, if you will, to seek information and knowledge on subjects which I personally as a member of Congress and as a citizen would rather not have, unless I believed it to be my responsibility to have it because it might involve the lives of American citizens."

Russell echoed Saltonstall's stance on congressional oversight, emphasizing that "If there is one agency of government which we must take some matters of faith on, without a constant examination of its methods and sources, I believe that agency is the CIA." These arguments proved persuasive as the Senate voted 59–27 against Mansfield's resolution.[2] Given Saltonstall's description of current oversight and Russell's argument that CIA activities should be taken on faith, it is hard to understand how Congress could learn about CIA programs that affected the lives of American citizens. Saltonstall and Russell accurately described the informality and deference of congressional oversight at the time, a system that marked a sea change in congressional policy from that of 1945–1947. Without critical congressional oversight, CIA officials could initiate programs with profound domestic consequences and, in the process, intrude on FBI responsibilities. Only belatedly, in the 1970s, with the emergence of a more assertive Congress, would members assume this oversight role.[3]

Congressional deference also characterized its oversight of the FBI. Until the 1970s FBI operations were examined only by the House Appropriations Committee during annual appropriation hearings. These hearings resembled a lovefest—as Frank Donner has written in describing FBI director Hoover's testimony, "prepared and presented as a piece of theater with ritualistic concern for effect." FBI expenditures were never critically examined, nor did committee members challenge FBI officials' projected image of a professional, apolitical agency that respected First Amendment rights and the proscriptions of federal laws. In part, Hoover ensured this passivity through an arrangement he had forged with the chairman of the House Appropriations Committee in 1943. Three FBI agents were assigned as investigators to the committee's staff, to be replaced by a new group after three years. Hoover extolled the benefits of this arrangement during a 1970 conversation with White House aide Egil Krogh, commenting that it ensured "excellent relations with the committee" as the chairman of the committee "is very cordially inclined toward the Bureau and has been over the years."[4]

Congressional oversight of the National Security Agency was similarly nonexistent, though it differed in that Congress was for a time not even aware of the NSA's existence. As noted earlier, President Truman had created the agency in October 1952 through a secret directive authorizing it to conduct unspecified communication intelligence operations. Yet, despite the construction of NSA's expensive Fort Meade headquarters in 1957, its expensive technology, and sizable personnel (nine thousand by 1956), Congress first learned of NSA's existence in 1958 and only then because the Eisenhower administration introduced and lobbied for legislation to criminalize the disclosure of NSA operations. Despite its ignorance of the scope and objectives of the NSA's "functions or activities," and of how "foreign intelligence" was specifically defined, in May 1959 Congress approved a bill that criminalized the disclosure of information concerning the NSA's "organization or any function," "any information with respect to" its activities, and the "names, titles, salaries, or number" of NSA employees. As the nation's first official secrets act, Public Law 86-36 marked a significant departure in public policy. Congress's exemption of NSA operations from public scrutiny reflected its willingness to accept on faith that NSA's sophisticated technology would not be employed against American citizens or in violation of current laws, and further that NSA officials would fully cooperate with the other U.S. intelligence agencies.[5]

As a direct result of Congress's deference, in the 1950s and 1960s U.S. intelligence policy was at times set by presidents and at other times by the heads of the agencies. Neither presidents nor intelligence agency bureaucrats seriously considered the domestic ramifications of their actions or whether they were consistent with the initiatives of other intelligence agencies. Their actions instead were based on their personal conceptions of perceived national security threats, their assessment of the feasibility of specific measures, and the opportunity to act. As a consequence, each agency's bureaucratic independence was sustained while agency officials avoided any independent assessment of their programs as advancing legitimate security interests.

The philosophy governing both presidential and agency actions was the need to achieve absolute security for the United States. Agency officials were in effect accorded the latitude to consider and then adopt programs they believed could address the threat posed by a sinister and powerful adversary. NSC-5412, a secret National Security Council directive intended to ensure that CIA covert operations would advance the policy goals set by President Eisenhower, reflects this philosophy.

When he assumed the presidency in 1953, Dwight Eisenhower intended to pursue a more aggressive international course: to move beyond the containment of Soviet influence in Eastern Europe and China to the subversion of radical nationalist movements in the Middle East, Africa, Latin America, and South Asia. To achieve this objective, Eisenhower, beginning in 1953 and sustained throughout his presidency, turned to the CIA to orchestrate coups to overthrow nationalist leaders—in Iran in 1953 (Mohammad Mossadegh), Guatemala in 1954 (Jacobo Arbenz Guzman), and Indonesia in 1958 (Achmed Sukarno). For this reason Eisenhower sought to ensure that CIA operations would advance his policy goals and, just as important, that any action would remain secret. These concerns underlay his approval of an *internal* oversight system to monitor all proposed and approved CIA covert operations.

This system was instituted on March 12, 1955, through NSC-5412/1 with the creation of a special Planning Coordinated Group. It was to be the "normal channel for giving policy approval for such [covert operation plans] as well as for securing coordination of support thereof." Eisenhower further refined this system on December 28, 1955, under NSC-5412/2. A special oversight panel, known as the 5412 Group, was established to review proposed CIA covert operations. This panel would be composed of designees of the president, State, and Defense, with the president's designee his special assistant for national security affairs.

NSC-5412/1 and NSC-5412/2 were issued to ensure also that all CIA covert operations would be conducted in secret and yet, if exposed, permit presidential deniability. The planned scope of such operations had made internal oversight imperative—CIA officials were expected to "create and exploit troublesome problems for International Communism, impair relations between the USSR and Communist China and their satellites, . . . retard the growth of the military and economic potential of the Soviet bloc," "counter any threat of a party or individuals directly or indirectly responsive to Communist control," "strengthen the orientation toward the United States of the peoples and nations of the free world," and "develop underground resistance and facilitate covert and guerrilla operations and ensure availability of these forces in the event of war."[6]

President Eisenhower supplemented this system of internal oversight on February 6, 1956, by Executive Order 10656. It established the President's Board of Consultants on Intelligence Activities, to be composed of prominent citizens from the academic and business communities and retired military officers, and headed by retired General John Hull. A strictly advisory body, the board lacked supervisory or budgetary authority over the CIA or other U.S. intelligence agencies. It met monthly in Washington and submitted its findings to the president once or twice a year. The stature of its members ensured that its criticisms of the informality and relative independence of CIA operations could not be ignored. Nonetheless, because the members were presidential appointees and operated in total secrecy, the board had limited impact on presidential or intelligence agency policy. For Eisenhower's principal objective at the time had been to counter Senator Mansfield's pending resolution and to neutralize other demands for stricter congressional oversight. In this he succeeded.[7]

The creation of the board had one unanticipated consequence, however, stemming from President Eisenhower's appointment to the body of Joseph Kennedy: it enabled FBI officials to challenge the authority and reputation of the CIA. An FBI Special Service Contact,* Kennedy upon accepting this appointment immediately solicited Hoover's counsel. Kennedy expressed his frustration over the absence of staff assistance for board members and concern about the "duplication of coverage abroad by the military, CIA and the State Department." The FBI director eagerly exploited this opportunity to share with Kennedy "some of the weaknesses which we [FBI] have observed in the operations of CIA particularly as to the organizational set-up and the compartmentation that exists with that agency."[9]

The FBI director's comments capture the underlying distrust between FBI and CIA officials. They might have forged a formal

---

*FBI director Hoover had earlier required the heads of FBI field offices (SACs) to recruit prominent citizens in their area to serve as informers or to provide other services beneficial to the FBI. Joseph Kennedy was recruited by the Boston SAC in 1943 based on his extensive business interests in the United States and internationally, and particularly in the movie industry. Extolling Kennedy's anti-communism, the Boston SAC particularly cited Kennedy's contacts in Hollywood as potentially promoting the acquisition of information "pertaining to Communist infiltration" in that industry. In addition, he emphasized, Kennedy's contacts with foreign diplomats could be exploited "for any advantage the Bureau might desire in this field."[8]

relationship to share information and solicit specific assistance, but in fact CIA officials preferred to operate independently, even when their decisions to advance the agency's foreign intelligence responsibilities had troubling domestic ramifications.

One such initiative was intended to counter the closed nature of Soviet society. CIA officials had found it extremely difficult to obtain relevant information about Soviet plans and capabilities. Agents who were assigned under cover to U.S. embassies or as private citizens—businessmen, freelance reporters, tourists—could obtain only limited information about the economic, social, and political conditions in the Soviet Union and Soviet satellite countries. CIA officers also found it difficult to recruit Soviet officials as double agents. To offset these deficiencies, in late 1952 officers in the CIA's Soviet Division devised a creative solution—to secure information by intercepting letters sent to and from the Soviet Union that were handled at the U.S. Post Office's La Guardia Airport branch. (This mail program was expanded in 1957 to include mail to Latin America handled in New Orleans, and in 1969 to mail to China handled in San Francisco.) In theory such mail could provide insights into conditions in the Soviet Union through correspondence referring to prices, crop conditions, the weather, general living conditions, and unrest. It might also identify "subjects who if personally loyal to the United States, might be good agent material because of their contacts in the Soviet Union," or possibly "create a channel for sending communications to American agents inside the Soviet Union."

Post Office officials would have to cooperate in implementing such a program. Thus CIA officials originally sought permission from the Post Office only to survey how mail was handled, intending this to be a step toward a mail cover program—that is, one where only the names and addresses of the sender and recipient would be recorded without opening the letters. This plan worked. In 1953 Postmaster General Arthur Summerfield consented to a mail cover program, originally code-named SRPOINTER and then HTLINGUAL. The agency's Counterintelligence Division assumed operational control over this program by 1955, and its personnel began taking certain letters to the CIA's Manhattan office at night. These letters were then steamed open and their contents photographed, and they were replaced in the mail the next morning. At first agency personnel made random selections of the letters to be photographed. Over time, based on experience, the letters of certain correspondents were selected. The decision to open the mail was known only to participating CIA offices; extant records suggest that no postmaster general, president, or attorney general knew or approved this decision. Agency officials moreover acted to ensure that "the source [of the photographed letters] is concealed" whenever they circulated the photographed letters outside the New York office.[10]

HTLINGUAL, when first begun, had a defined foreign intelligence and counterintelligence purpose. But when they decided to expand the New York operation from a mail cover to a mail intercept program, should CIA officials have sought FBI assistance—as they had when asking the FBI to conduct wiretaps, bugs, and break-ins within the United States? They did not do so, preferring to retain exclusive control over the program. Thus they also denied to the FBI the potential fruits of their findings. This was a seemingly shortsighted and parochial judgment given the FBI's and CIA's shared counterintelligence responsibilities and CIA officials' belief in the program's counterintelligence value. CIA's belated decision of February 1958 to share the discoveries of this program with the FBI, moreover, was inadvertent, a consequence of FBI officials' independent decision of January 1958 to seek Post Office assistance for a proposed mail cover program involving letters sent to the Soviet Union.

FBI officials' request for Post Office assistance was the result of an internal reassessment of the bureau's counterintelligence operations. One ironic result of Elizabeth Bentley's defection in November 1945, and the institution of a Federal Employee Loyalty

Program in March 1947, had been that FBI agents found it more difficult to uncover planned Soviet espionage activities. For the Loyalty Program denied Soviet agents in the United States a principal source of recruitment for their espionage activities—Communists or Communist sympathizers who were employed in federal agencies and were willing to spy for ideological reasons. This loss eventually led Soviet agents to recruit individuals who would be willing to spy because they were handsomely paid. These efforts were somewhat successful, even though federal employees holding sensitive positions were subject to intensive FBI surveillance. In the years after 1947 the Soviets' most important recruits included FBI counterintelligence agent Robert Hanssen, former ONI officer John Walker, CIA officer Aldrich Ames, and former NSA employee Ronald Pelton.

After 1947, Soviet agents also relied on their own agents who entered the United States by using false passports. These "illegals"* were not readily identifiable, like members of Soviet consular, embassy, or United Nations staff, and were thus difficult to detect. FBI counterintelligence agents hit upon a method that might identify such spies when they apprehended Soviet espionage agent Rudolf Abel in June 1957.

Abel had entered the United States from Canada in 1948 under a false passport and had then established a base of operations in New York City. He was able to escape FBI scrutiny of his espionage activities until 1957. Even then, FBI agents discovered him only because of the defection of another Soviet illegal, Reino Hayhanen. Hayhanen had been ordered to meet his Soviet superior in East Germany. Suspecting that he might be fired or imprisoned, Hayhanen in May 1957 interrupted his travel on reaching Paris and approached the U.S. embassy there. In an interview

---

*The term "illegal" describes Soviet citizens who entered the country illegally, as opposed to consular, embassy, or U.S. employees who entered the country legally (even though they were not diplomats but spies).

with a CIA officer, Hayhanen described his own espionage activities that dated from his arrival in the United States in 1952 under a false passport, and identified his KGB handler in the United States, though not by name. Brought back to New York on the promise of resettlement, Hayhanen repeated this account to the FBI. Hayhanen was again unable to provide the name of his handler or the address where they had met. But he did provide sufficient background information to enable FBI agents to arrest Rudolf Abel on June 21.

Privately embarrassed by this discovery of Abel's and Hayhanen's evasion of their intensive counterintelligence operations, FBI officials sought to root out other such Soviet illegals. In this effort they hit upon the idea of identifying them through their possible communication by mail with their handlers in the Soviet Union—having learned that Soviet agents abroad allegedly contacted a particular address in the Soviet Union. The head of the FBI's New York field office was accordingly ordered to contact Post Office officials in New York "to determine the feasibility of covering outgoing correspondence from the U.S. to the U.S.S.R., looking toward picking up communications dispatched to the aforementioned address."[11]

In January 1958 the New York SAC requested the Post Office's assistance for such a mail cover program. The chief postal inspector demurred and then advised his CIA contact of this FBI request. In response, the head of the CIA's Counterintelligence Division, James Angleton, decided to brief Sam Papich, the FBI's liaison to the CIA, about the CIA's mail cover program, admitting, however, that CIA officers actually opened the mail. FBI officials were at first disturbed upon learning of Papich's discovery, since the CIA had clearly intruded on the FBI's jurisdiction. Nonetheless they decided to seek the CIA's assistance in view of the "complexity, size, and expense" and the "inherent dangers" involved in initiating their own program. CIA and FBI officials thereupon reached a formal arrangement in February 1958 whereby the CIA would provide copies of the intercepted correspondence to the FBI and in addition service specific FBI requests. They did so based on FBI officials' assurances that they would adopt safeguards to ensure that this interception program and assistance could not become known. The FBI's liaison to the CIA thereafter personally received this photographed correspondence, which was then maintained under a special FBI procedure, June Mail, which FBI director Hoover had instituted in June 1949.* FBI officials also established strict rules to govern the distribution of information from the intercepted letters, whether at FBI headquarters or to FBI field offices. Only supervisory staff could handle the letters, and they would paraphrase them to disguise the source, not process them through normal FBI channels, and destroy any copies.

In time this joint FBI-CIA program expanded in response to FBI requests that the CIA process the mail of identified individuals, eventually including women's, peace, and civil rights activists. But the program never realized its original promise. This was not surprising as CIA officials later conceded that it was unlikely that Russian correspondents would convey damaging information, suspecting that their mail would be read by Soviet censors. Furthermore, as trained professionals, Soviet agents would not risk compromising themselves by using the U.S. mails. CIA officials in fact later characterized the intelligence acquired from the HTLINGUAL program as of "no tangible operational benefit." FBI officials similarly admitted that the intercepted letters did not help them uncover a single espionage agent, and described 95 percent of the take as "junk." The interception program at best uncov-

---

*The June Mail classification was devised to safeguard "highly confidential" sources, "such as Governors, secretaries to high officials who may be discussing such officials and their attitudes," and "sources illegal in nature." June Mail was not filed in the FBI's central records system but was maintained "under lock and key" in a "special" file room with access on a "need to know" basis.

ered the travel plans of Communist party officials to the Soviet Union, the "pro-Soviet sympathies" of U.S. individuals, and the desire of U.S. exchange students to remain in the Soviet Union for "romantic" reasons.

In 1961 and then again in 1969, the CIA's Inspector General's office internally reviewed this program and recommended its discontinuance. They concluded that HTLINGUAL's "flap potential" should it be discovered—given the violation both of federal postal laws and of the 1947 National Security Act's prohibition of any internal security role for the CIA—outweighed any benefits. Senior CIA officials, however, did not discontinue the program because FBI officials sought its continuance, having by then received 57,000 letters. Furthermore, when in 1969 the Inspector General's office recommended handing the program over to the FBI, this offer was rejected. Pursuant to FBI director Hoover's 1966 order, the FBI had abandoned its own domestic mail programs. In this case, as they had in 1958, FBI officials welcomed the opportunity to acquire information without having to assume any political risk.[12]

HTLINGUAL was not the CIA's sole counterintelligence program with domestic ramifications. In 1953 CIA officials also instituted a second program that fell within the agency's jurisdiction to counter Soviet actions.

At the time CIA officials concluded that the Soviets were experimenting extensively with chemical and biological agents—specifically, mind-altering drugs such as LSD—and had used these drugs to extract confessions. They reached this conclusion based on the demeanor of U.S. soldiers whom the North Koreans had captured during the Korean War, and suspected that the Soviets and Chinese were using mind-altering drugs as a propaganda and intelligence weapon. In April 1953 CIA officials thus decided to fund a drug-testing program, code-named MKULTRA, for defensive reasons and to support "present or future clandestine operations." They nonetheless took great care to preclude discovery of this program. A 1957 CIA report stressed the need for "precautions" to protect MKULTRA "from exposure to enemy forces but also conceal these activities from the American public in general. The knowledge that the Agency is engaging in unethical and illicit activities would have serious repercussions in political and diplomatic circles and would be detrimental to the accomplishment of its mission." "No records" were to be maintained "of the planning and approval of [drug] testing programs." In 1973 CIA director Richard Helms ordered records relating to the program destroyed.

Two factors contributed to the decision not to preserve a full record of the MKULTRA program. First, in contrast to other sensitive CIA operations, CIA officials did not rely only on the agency's scientists but contracted with 44 colleges and universities, 15 private research foundations and pharmaceutical companies, and 12 hospitals and clinics employing a total of 185 research scientists. Such research, CIA officials recognized, "is considered by many authorities in medicine and related fields to be professionally unethical, therefore the reputations of professional participants in the MKULTRA program was on occasion in jeopardy." Their participation could be ensured only if they could be assured of secrecy—thus Helms's 1973 destruction order at a time when Congress demonstrated an interest in investigating the various activities of the intelligence agencies. Yet, despite Helms's order, all records relating to this drug program were not destroyed, specifically the project's financial records. These records permitted the reconstruction of the program's scope. In effect MKULTRA indirectly influenced scientific research that was unknowingly funded by Congress, without any evaluation of the allocation of limited scientific resources and personnel.

The second factor in the decision to destroy records is that in one experiment conducted under the program, LSD had been given to an unsuspecting Frank Olson. The effect of the drug led Olson to commit suicide. CIA officials thereupon immediately covered up their relationship with Olson and the reason for his death. Even afterward, CIA scientists continued to experiment with unwitting subjects at bars and safe houses. Such uses violated science ethics and laws—though no other cases of criminal negligence beyond Olson's suicide have been uncovered. The CIA scientists involved in the Olson case were lightly reprimanded; their subsequent careers were not affected.

MKULTRA did differ from HTLINGUAL in that it was not patently illegal. Other government agencies contracted with universities and private research institutes, and the 1949 CIA Act authorized agency officials to fund its programs secretly. Nonetheless CIA officials who knew about the program conceded that "some MKULTRA activities raise questions of legality implicit in the original charter," and further that the program's testing procedures "places the rights and interests of U.S. citizens in jeopardy." This realization only motivated CIA officials to adopt safeguards to avoid independent scrutiny of their practices. At no time were the program's scientific standards—in one case, for example, enticing heroin addicts to participate in LSD experiments by offering them heroin in payment—scrutinized to weigh its benefits against the continued expenditure of funds. MKULTRA research was conducted "without the establishment of formal contractual relations," since university and private research scientists would have been "reluctant to enter into signed agreements of any sort which connect them with this activity since such a connection would jeopardize their professional reputations."[13]

MKULTRA previewed what became a normative CIA procedure: recruiting or contracting with nongovernmental personnel for specific foreign intelligence and counterintelligence objectives, without coordinating such programs with the FBI or considering broader domestic ramifications. This approach recurred in the CIA's covert funding of the National Student Association, a nationwide student organization founded in 1947, headquartered in Washington, D.C., and ostensibly funded through dues paid by campus organizations and private foundations. The elected staff leaders organized the association's annual meeting, which was attended by delegations elected from participating colleges. These student delegates discussed and approved resolutions on domestic and international issues that commanded the interest of college students and selected delegates to attend international student conferences.

In the early 1950s CIA officials decided to forge a secret relationship with NSA leaders. Their purpose was to counter Soviet-supported international propaganda activities, which included the appointment of espionage agents in student delegations to international conferences and massive funding of such conferences. Through these efforts Soviet officials sought to secure the endorsement of Soviet policies and to exploit the revolutionary sentiments of Asian, African, and European students.

On a case-by-case basis beginning in 1950, CIA officials covertly funded the costs of sending NSA delegations to regional international conferences in Southeast Asia, and a team to study student groups in Europe and Asia. They successfully disguised their "penetration which we have made into the National Student Association."

In 1952 this initially informal, ad hoc arrangement was formalized. Committed to aggressively countering the Soviets, CIA officers decided to abandon their initial reluctance to exploit the NSA's image as a "private" organization. The timing of this decision was prompted by Congress's unwillingness to fund a State Department program for students, akin to the Fulbright program of sending faculty abroad. A secret agreement was concluded with the president of the National Student Association on the understanding that CIA financing would be known only to the president and the association's vice president for international affairs. Because association officers were elected at annual meetings, CIA officials reached similar agreements binding the new officers to secrecy and carefully vetted the association's officers.

Initially the NSA's funding source was disguised as private foundations, and funding was confined to defraying the costs of attending international conferences. But over the course of this covert relationship, which lasted from 1952 through 1967, the CIA funded 80 percent of the organization's expenditures—estimated at $3.3 million, including a rent-free national headquarters—and CIA officials interceded to ensure that the association's officers received draft deferments and tuition scholarships. While the original purpose had been simply to counteract Soviet propaganda activities, association delegates were encouraged to report on the attitudes of Soviet and Third World participants at international conferences, on the "political situation among student organizations abroad," and on Soviet counterintelligence methods, and to purchase Soviet-manufactured equipment. More disturbing, the operation of this program was not closely monitored even by senior CIA officials. When CIA director Richard Helms demanded a report in 1967 on past CIA funding of private organizations, including the National Student Association, his request could not be easily met because almost every agency component had its own set of programs and covert funding arrangements. A special inter-agency committee had to be established to compile the report.[14]

CIA officials forged a series of similar covert funding relationships with a variety of individuals and organizations. The CIA's assistance was again disguised through private foundations. Those recruited as CIA sources included hundreds of university administrators and faculty employed in more than a hundred universities and research institutions (such as the Asia Foundation, the African-American Institute, and American Friends of the Middle East), book publishers (notably Praeger), and approximately fifty American newspaper reporters and hundreds of foreign freelance reporters. The agency also secretly funded a foreign-based feature news service (Forum News); the filming of George Orwell's anti-Communist books *1984* and *Animal Farm* (films that circulated within the United States and around the world); Harvard's Russian

Research Center, Yale's Institute for International Studies, and MIT's Center for International Studies; foreign language and area studies (Eastern Europe, the Balkans, the Soviet Union); the research and publication of more than a thousand books (on the Soviet Union, Eastern Europe, and China); an exchange program run by a consortium of universities; and an international agricultural cooperative center. The decision to fund the agricultural center was to supplement the original funder, USAID, which was prohibited from addressing political goals since AID-funded programs "are part of official government-to-government programs and are designed for economic—not political—results." CIA officials also worked closely with CBS News president William Paley to obtain press credentials for their officers and to provide covert funding through the William S. Paley Foundation, and with Michigan State University's criminology department to train the South Vietnam police force. And it provided more than $1 million in subventions to the American Newspaper Guild for use in combating the Communist-dominated International Organization of Journalists.

If it was intended to promote the agency's foreign intelligence and counterintelligence objectives, the CIA's extensive funding inevitably influenced domestic politics. For example, some of the articles syndicated by Forum News were picked up by American newspapers while the scholarly publications of CIA-funded academics and researchers were adopted as texts in college courses and were read by the public. Because they were not directly attributed to the CIA, these publications had a greater impact on public understanding of the politics and history of Eastern Europe, the Soviet Union, and international communism. This indirect influence was especially true in a university system, where promotion and tenure would be based on the faculty member's research and publications. Recipients of CIA largesse not only benefitted personally but as tenured professors would influence subsequent promotion and tenure decisions. One overall effect was to sustain a militantly anti-Communist politics. This was not, however, a wholly unanticipated development. In 1961 the head of the CIA's propaganda unit extolled the "advantages of our direct contract with the author [of CIA-funded books] in that we can check the manuscript at every stage. Our control over the writer will have to be enforced . . . [and the agency] must make sure the actual manuscript will correspond with our operational and propagandistic intention." In evaluating the agency's recruitment of foreign-based reporters, CIA officials recognized that "fallout in the United States ostensibly from a foreign publication which we support is inevitable and consequently permissible."[15]

These concerns also underpinned CIA officials' efforts to counteract the appeal of communism to European intellectuals and Third World anti-colonial revolutionaries by enlisting European and Asian intellectuals. This was no easy task at the time, as the anti-Communist influence in the United States created two quite dissimilar problems. On the one hand, McCarthyite tactics had raised questions among foreign intellectuals about the status of civil liberties and the respect for unconventional political and social views within the United States. Then too, the influence of the McCarthyites made it unlikely that Congress would fund international cultural programs involving the very intellectuals who criticized McCarthyism or congressional restrictions on civil liberties.

The timing of the CIA decision to fund a cultural initiative stemmed from the State Department's decision in early 1950 to scale back appropriation requests for cultural programs. CIA officials acted to fill the vacuum. Through private foundations like the Kaplan and Fairfield Foundations, and by working closely with the Ford Foundation, they covertly funded the European-based Congress for Cultural Freedom in 1950 and the Congress's American branch, the American Committee for Cultural Freedom, in 1951. This funding enabled the Congress to organize international conferences, sponsor art exhibits and concert tours, and publish a variety of intellectual journals, including *Encounter*,

Preuves, Cuadenas, the *Chinese Quarterly, Hiwar,* and *Tempo Presente.*[16]

CIA officials intentionally sought to preclude FBI knowledge of their various programs, one of which (HTLINGUAL) violated federal laws and another (MKULTRA) involved criminal conduct by CIA personnel. In 1954 CIA director Allen Dulles concluded an agreement with FBI director Hoover whereby the CIA's Office of Security would handle all investigations of "irregularities" committed by CIA employees. CIA officials preferred this arrangement to avoid adverse publicity that might result from prosecution and to protect sources that might be disclosed during court proceedings.[17]

FBI officials as a result were kept in the dark about the actions of CIA personnel that intruded on the FBI's turf or augmented the FBI's domestic surveillance programs. For FBI officials had also instituted a series of programs—some of which violated the law—to influence university faculty and students, newspapers and films, and book publication.

FBI and CIA officials might have shared a common anti-Communist agenda, but they nonetheless differed in their approach. The impact of CIA programs on domestic politics was inadvertent and at the same time reflected the value that CIA officials placed on ideas. In striking contrast, the impact of various FBI initiatives was direct and purposeful, and reflected an underlying suspicion about ideas—namely, that for humanitarian or idealistic reasons a naive public might not support a militantly anti-Communist politics.

These differences may be seen in the two agencies' responses toward Harvard's Russian Research Center. While CIA officials valued the Center's faculty as a source of intelligence and as an aid in recruiting future officers or foreign assets, FBI officials worried about the loyalty and subversive influence of the Center's faculty and students. Indeed, FBI agents closely monitored the Center's faculty and students, recruited informers—notably

Charles Baroch, a graduate student on the Center's staff—and sought from Harvard administrators access to the records of these suspect individuals.[18]

This concern about the subversive views and associations of the Russian Research Center's faculty and staff was not exceptional and extended to university faculty and students as a whole.* FBI officials similarly developed secret collaborative arrangements with trusted faculty members and university administrators—notably Harvard political scientist Henry Kissinger and Yale liaison officer Harry Fisher—in an effort to purge "subversive" faculty and students. FBI agents were specifically instructed to take precautions to preclude discovery of their own monitoring activities. Advance approval from FBI headquarters was required before agents could seek information about a specific professor, and they would then have to provide assurances of the proposed informer's "discretion and reliability." A March 1953 FBI report illustrates the scope of FBI surveillance of university faculty. It recorded that "Communist subversion" was being investigated at fifty-six colleges and universities, including Harvard, Yale, the University of Washington, the University of Wisconsin, the University of Chicago, Swarthmore, the City College of New York, UCLA, Bennington, Sarah Lawrence, Cornell, Syracuse, Johns Hopkins, MIT, Smith, Duke, Northwestern, Tulane, Brooklyn College, Columbia, Howard, and Wesleyan. FBI agents also monitored the annual meetings of the American Sociological Association and the activities of Talcott Parsons, W. E. B. Du Bois, Ernest Burgess, Helen Lynd, Pitirim Sorokin, C. Wright Mills, and Edwin Sutherland,

---

*FBI officials' obsession with subversive influence also led to the monitoring of Supreme Court clerks in 1957 over a concern about the rumored influence of "a ring of left-wing law clerks" on recent Supreme Court rulings in the *Yates, Jencks*, and *Watkins* cases. FBI officials also worried about the political associations of Supreme Court Justices William O. Douglas and Felix Frankfurter.[19]

the nation's most prominent sociologists. Agents also kept tabs on the atomic scientists who helped establish the Federation of American Scientists for the purpose of lobbying Congress and influencing public policy related to the control of atomic weapons and access to classified information. These scientists concerned FBI officials owing to their "political orientation." Officials worried that their lobbying efforts "amount[ed] to Soviet espionage in this country directed toward the obtaining for the Soviet Union the knowledge possessed by the United States concerning atomic energy and specifically the atomic bomb."

Not content to compile reports on suspected faculty and students, FBI officials exploited secret arrangements with the House Committee on Un-American Activities and the Senate Internal Security Subcommittee to promote congressional investigations of "Communist subversion" at American universities. In October 1952, for example, FBI assistant director Louis Nichols recommended "furnishing" to the Senate Internal Security Subcommittee "any information as it occurs from time to time on college professors and teachers who are members of the Communist Party," to enable the subcommittee to prepare hearings. This practice extended FBI director Hoover's initiative when in 1951 he established a secret code-named Responsibilities Program. Under this program information about suspected Communist teachers was leaked to state governors on the strict condition they would agree not to identify the FBI as the source. Some governors used the information to purge the identified state college and elementary and secondary teachers; but, as ambitious politicians, they cited the FBI as the source of the information when their proposed dismissals were challenged. These snafus, which contradicted claims that FBI files were inviolate, led FBI officials in 1955 to terminated the Responsibilities Program.[20]

Anti-radical convictions also led FBI officials to question the public's understanding of the nature of the Communist threat. To rectify this perceived deficiency, FBI officials in February 1946 launched an "educational campaign" to undercut the "support" the Communist party received from its advocacy of "individual causes which are also sponsored by Liberal elements" and labor unions. This campaign was essential, FBI officials observed, to counter the anticipated "flood of propaganda from Leftist and so-called Liberal sources" should the FBI's proposed plan to detain Communist party leaders be implemented. FBI officials prepared "educational material which can be released through available channels so that in the event of an emergency we will have an informed public opinion" about the truth of the Communist threat.[21]

Two potential problems had to be addressed in implementing an educational campaign. First, the "educational material" could reach the public only if it was disseminated by newspaper reporters and members of Congress. But FBI cultivation of these sources carried a risk: should their leaking actions become known, FBI officials' presumed political neutrality and the confidentiality of FBI files would be exposed as fraudulent. Therefore FBI officials acted to ensure that the recipients of information would share their political ideas and honor their insistence on confidentiality.

In the case of newspaper reporters, columnists, and editors, FBI officials at first informally and later formally developed a system to identify those who both shared their politics and would not betray the FBI's covert assistance. FBI assistant director Louis Nichols had been appointed in the mid-1930s as the FBI's liaison to reporters and to members of Congress. As head of the FBI's Crime Records Division, Nichols had access to all FBI files which could be leaked, and to press clippings submitted by FBI agents of newspaper articles filed by reporters about the FBI or foreign policy and internal security developments. Thus Nichols was in a position to identify favored reporters to whom carefully selected information could be leaked to promote an image of the FBI as a highly professional, efficient, and apolitical crime- and spy-fighting organization, or to raise questions about the personal character and loyalty of radical activists. By the 1950s Nichols had refined this informal system. First, reporters were divided into two categories: "Do Not Contact" and "Special Correspondents." The former were denied assistance while the latter were leaked information. Second, FBI dissemination practices were refined and rationalized with the establishment in 1955 of a code-named Mass Media Program and then in 1956 of a code-named COINTELPRO program. The purpose of this new program was to "harass, disrupt and discredit" the leadership of and activists associated with the Communist party—by sowing dissension within the organization or by leaking derogatory personal and political information to the media. COINTELPRO was expanded during the 1960s to the Trotskyite Socialist Workers party, the Ku Klux Klan, the Black Panthers, and the Students for a Democratic Society.[22]

FBI officials also developed secret relationships with members of Congress, notably Senators Joseph McCarthy and Pat McCarran and Representatives (later Senators) Karl Mundt and Richard Nixon, and the chairmen and chief counsels of the House Committee on Un-American Activities and the Senate Internal Security Subcommittee. These members of Congress agreed not to disclose the FBI's covert assistance. When Senator McCarthy and the Senate and House committees failed to honor this condition, FBI officials terminated their informal assistance.

FBI officials also refined and expanded their informal system to identify "reliable" members of Congress. Under the terms of a more formal arrangement begun in the 1950s, FBI agents informally— that is, by not creating retrievable records—forwarded information to FBI headquarters about the "immoral conduct" and "subversive" activities of congressional candidates. This information was then regularly updated as long as they remained in Congress. To avoid discovery that the FBI was monitoring members of Congress, the information was incorporated in a "summary memorandum" on the member of Congress which would then be maintained in the FBI's Administrative Unit. This arrangement permitted FBI officials to compile and maintain information without risk. Officials could truthfully deny that the FBI's "central records system" contained a file on a member of Congress—"summary memoranda" were not files and were not maintained in the central records system.

The system had an additional deterrent advantage. Emanuel Celler, former chairman of the House Judiciary Committee, during a 1973 interview with Ovid Demaris attributed former FBI director Hoover's power to "the fact that he was the head of an agency that in turn had tremendous power, power of surveillance, power of control over the lives and destinies of every man in the nation. He had a dossier on every member of Congress and every member of the Senate." Were members of Congress aware of this? Demaris asked. Celler replied that they "certainly were," and that this influenced their willingness to challenge the FBI director.

A former FBI agent, testifying before the Pike Committee in 1975, described how this system worked. He recounted the response of FBI assistant director Cartha DeLoach* to his query about why the FBI collected personal information about members of Congress: "The other night we picked up a situation where this Senator was seen drunk, in a hit-and-run accident, and some good-looking broad was with him. . . . We got the information, reported it in a memorandum . . . by noon of the next day the good senator was aware we had the information and we never had any trouble with him on appropriations since."23

FBI officials' desire to counteract "subversive" ideas also led them to seek to influence the content of movies, radio, television, and books. On the one hand, they secretly assisted "reliable"

---

*DeLoach succeeded Nichols as head of the Crime Records Division and as the FBI's liaison to Congress and the media.

writers and television and movie producers to promote a positive image of the FBI and/or a militantly anti-Communist politics. On the other hand, they sought to discredit those writers and producers whom they suspected of disloyalty or Communist sympathies.

In one such effort, FBI officials in 1947 covertly leaked to the chairman and chief counsel of the House Committee on Un-American Activities information about the Communist party membership and affiliation of ten Hollywood producers, directors, or writers. These personalities became the subjects of the committee's highly publicized hearings that October, and their refusal to testify about their Communist associations led to their indictment for contempt of Congress and blacklisting by studio executives. Approached by the committee's chairman in May 1947 for assistance in the committee's intended inquiry into Communist influence in Hollywood, FBI director Hoover agreed to help, having concluded that "it is long overdue for the Communist infiltration in Hollywood to be exposed, and as there is no medium at present through which the Bureau can bring this about on its own motion, I think it entirely proper and desirable that we assist the Committee in Congress that is intent upon bringing to light the true facts in the situation."

FBI officials extended their purge initiative in 1951, prevailing upon their contacts with the Senate Internal Security Subcommittee to convene hearings "into the matter of Communist infiltration into the book publishing industry." Such hearings were needed, FBI officials emphasized, to "counteract the Leftwing element in the publishing business, which has been the source of the attacks on the Bureau . . . particularly the Max Lowenthal book, [Lowenthal's publisher] William Sloan[e] Associates, Merle Miller's *The Sure Thing*, and others." A special FBI index was created in 1960 to list those individuals who should be subject to detention because they posed "a greater threat [than identified Communists] in the event of an emergency than others." This index specifically listed "writers,* lecturers, newsmen, entertainers, and others in the mass media field."[25]

The scope of this secret containment campaign is hinted at in two quite dissimilar cases. The first involved Max Lowenthal, a former congressional counsel and informal adviser to President Truman. Over ten years Lowenthal researched and then in 1950 published a critical history of the FBI. Alerted to the book's pending publication, Hoover first solicited the assistance of prominent civil liberties attorney Morris Ernst to convince Lowenthal's publisher, William Sloane Associates, not to publish the book. When this failed, FBI agents pressured booksellers not to stock the book while FBI officials solicited critical book reviews and persuaded their contacts on the House Committee on Un-American Activities to subpoena Lowenthal to testify about his "subversive" activities and an NBC commentator to report the press reaction to the book as showing "how stooges do the Communists' work."[26]

The second case involved Hollywood actor Rock Hudson. Having learned of Hudson's homosexuality through a "confidential source," FBI officials alerted the Johnson White House to this discovery. Their briefing responded to President Johnson's demand for background information on prospective invitees to White House events. (The president had been embarrassed earlier that year when artists invited to a White House ceremony celebrating the arts had exploited the occasion to attack his foreign policy.) Reflecting their own quite different concerns, FBI officials feared that Hudson might play an FBI agent in a movie.[27]

---

*Natalie Robins and Herbert Mitgang filed a series of Freedom of Information requests for FBI files on prominent American writers. In every case the FBI had a file on the identified writer, which for some contained reports on their "loyalty and discretion." The FBI had files, for example, on syndicated columnists Drew Pearson, Jack Anderson, and Murray Kempton, and on authors Ernest Hemingway, Archibald MacLeish, Kay Boyle, Lillian Hellman, Dashiell Hammett, Sherwood Anderson, Pearl Buck, Truman Capote, Allen Ginsberg, Norman Mailer, Arthur Miller, E. B. White, Richard Wright, John Steinbeck, and Upton Sinclair.[24]

The contrast between the FBI's and the CIA's secret initiatives toward academics, reporters, writers, actors, and members of Congress highlights one positive advantage of their failure to co-operate closely, to coordinate their efforts to influence domestic policy, and to define the parameters of legitimate political debate. On this political front, the dangers of coordination are highlighted by the agencies' actions involving the syndicated columnist Joseph Alsop.

An ardent anti-Communist, Alsop had traveled to Moscow in February 1957 to interview Soviet premier Nikita Khrushchev. During his stay, Alsop became a victim of a KGB sting operation when KGB agents threatened to arrest him for his homosexual tryst with a young Russian the night before. Alsop was pressured to "help them if they were to help him" avoid a publicized arrest and ensure "absolute secrecy." The intervention of U.S. Ambassador Charles Bohlen enabled Alsop to leave the Soviet Union. On arriving in Paris before returning to the United States, Alsop confided to a CIA officer a detailed account of the Moscow incident and his own "incurable" homosexuality. At the time Alsop requested that the report on this interview be brought to the attention of CIA director Allen Dulles and FBI director Hoover and "kept out of the general file and kept in a special file."

Alsop's motivation for briefing the CIA and the FBI was to forestall any future Soviet advantage from this incident. He fully understood what was an unquestioned belief of the homophobic 1950s—that homosexuals were security risks owing to their vulnerability to blackmail. Alsop's request that this admission be closely held, however, was not honored. The CIA director immediately briefed Secretary of State John Foster Dulles, and the FBI director spoke with Attorney General Herbert Brownell and senior White House aide Sherman Adams. In addition, both the CIA and FBI directors were troubled by Alsop's refusal to make an "open" confession and by his intention to travel to the Soviet Union and Eastern Europe in the future. They agreed to continue to share any information about Alsop's future travel plans, with Hoover expressing his displeasure over Alsop's unwillingness to "furnish the identities of his homosexual contacts in the United States, particularly in Washington, D.C., and New York City."

By 1961 Alsop had second thoughts about his 1957 action, and he concluded that his request to keep this matter secret had not been honored. Accordingly he sought to exploit his close relationship with the recently elected president, John F. Kennedy, and his brother, the attorney general. In April 1961 he informed CIA director Dulles that he planned to ask "the President to take possession of the Central Intelligence Agency (CIA) file concerning this matter." CIA officials immediately briefed their FBI counterparts on this "highly irregular" request, adding that they "would be obligated" to comply should President Kennedy make such a request. When such a request was indeed made by Attorney General Kennedy in October 1961, FBI and CIA officials agreed that in the event that they received any future requests for background information about Alsop they "will be obliged to produce the facts" (from Hoover's secret office files).[28]

The commitment of FBI and CIA officials to smearing Alsop's reputation had little to do with legitimate security concerns. Alsop was not a government employee and could not be blackmailed into betraying government secrets. Furthermore he sustained his militant anti-Communist stance after the 1957 Moscow incident. In fact that militancy had brought him into conflict with the Eisenhower administration in 1959 during a controversial public debate precipitated by the so-called Sputnik incident of 1957. That year the Soviets' successful space launch led many analysts to contend that the United States had fallen behind the Soviets in missile technology. They attributed this "missile gap" to the Eisenhower administration's fiscal conservatism that had led to reduced defense appropriations. Alsop weighed in on this debate, claiming that, because of the reductions in defense spending, the administration was "playing Russian roulette with the whole course of human history at stake."[29]

Lacking any evidence that Alsop posed a security threat, senior FBI and CIA officials had nonetheless acted insubordinately to trump the president's intent. Their secret decision raises troubling questions in light of their other secret and unilateral actions: knowingly violating the law (HTLINGUAL and Do Not File) and initiating programs to influence public opinion. Their continuing ability to operate in secret was first challenged by a seemingly unrelated development: President John F. Kennedy's assassination on November 22, 1963.

Kennedy's assassination provoked a series of questions at the time, questions that expanded to include secret FBI and CIA operations as the result of revelations in the mid-1970s by the Church and Pike committees. In addition, the responses of FBI and CIA officials to Freedom of Information Act requests—the withholding in whole or in part of thousands of pages of records—intensified suspicions of the agencies' activities. Concerns about the actions of FBI and CIA officials dovetailed with a radical shift in public opinion about the assassination. Whereas an overwhelming majority of Americans had initially accepted the conclusion of the Warren Commission that Lee Harvey Oswald had been the lone assassin, by 1966 half of respondents to a Gallup poll no longer believed the commission's conclusion. In a 1976 Gallup poll, these doubts increased to 81 percent.

A veritable cottage industry of conspiracy theories soon emerged. Some doubted that Oswald possessed the markmanship to have killed the president. Others questioned whether Oswald had acted alone, with some suggesting that he might have been a scapegoat. Some cited as suspicious Oswald's ability to return to the United States in 1962 with his Russian wife following his defection in 1959; his open opposition to President Kennedy's Cuban policy; his visit to the Soviet embassy in Mexico City where he had met a KGB officer under cover as a consular official in the weeks before the assassination; and his presence in New Orleans in the company of anti-Castro Cuban exiles. Some suggested that Oswald might have acted on Soviet or Cuban orders, others that he might have acted in concert with anti-Castro Cuban exiles who bitterly opposed President Kennedy's Cuban policies. Still others found it suspicious that Dallas nightclub owner Jack Ruby could assassinate Oswald while in police custody, and before he could be fully interrogated. Ruby's questionable past and suspected associations with criminal elements led some to question whether his motivation was sincere grief over the president's death or whether he might have been recruited to prevent the uncovering of the role of organized crime in the assassination—given the Mafia's bitterness over the Kennedy administration's accelerated anti-organized-crime initiatives. Some even claimed that FBI officials, through the wiretapping of Mafia conversations, had not acted to forestall a Mafia plan to assassinate the president. Others, citing the bad blood between Kennedy loyalists and vice president Lyndon Johnson, were convinced that the vice president had either been involved or had had advance knowledge of a plot to assassinate Kennedy.

These theories received further support from the Church Committee's revelations of CIA plots to assassinate Cuban president Fidel Castro, which raised the question of payback. This possibility commanded further weight with the discovery that records relating to CIA plots to assassinate Castro had been withheld from the Warren Commission. The Church Committee's further revelations about the FBI's COINTELPROs, and then that FBI officials had also withheld relevant records from the Warren Commission, created similar doubts about a possible FBI cover-up.[30]

The unanticipated effect of President Kennedy's assassination was to shatter the wall of secrecy shrouding FBI and CIA operations. A heightened interest in learning the truth about the assassination eventually led many in Congress and the media to demand investigations of FBI and CIA operations and to reject their demands to preserve the secrecy of their records.

The first development that affected the FBI's stature was prompted by the Warren Commission's assessment of the FBI's handling of Oswald after his return to the United States and its failure to warn the Secret Service about Oswald as a potential threat to the president. For although the Secret Service was responsible for protecting the president, it lacked the resources to identify Oswald as a potential threat. By 1963, however, the FBI had compiled a massive security file on Oswald, dating from his defection to the Soviet Union in 1959 and including reports on his activities after his return to the United States. These reports recorded his criticisms of U.S. policy toward Cuba; his membership in the Fair Play for Cuba Committee and his arrest in New Orleans while demonstrating on behalf of this committee; his contacts with Cuban exile groups when residing in New Orleans and his offer to help train anti-Castro military forces; his subscription to the Communist *Daily Worker* after returning to the United States, contradicting his FBI interview that he "was disillusioned with the Soviet Union"; his radio interview in which he claimed to be a Marxist and praised the Castro government of Cuba; his visit to the FBI's Dallas field office, where he left a note threatening to blow up the office or the Dallas Police Department unless FBI agents ceased their efforts to interview his wife; and his visit to the Soviet embassy in Mexico City in September 1963.[31]

The Warren Commission, in its published report of September 1964, among other matters criticized the FBI for not cooperating fully with the Secret Service. FBI and Secret Service officials sought to address this problem and ensure better coordination through a delimitation agreement of February 1965. Under this agreement, the FBI would retain "general jurisdiction" over investigations of "subversive activities" and would report to the Secret Service all information about "subversives, ultrarightists, racists and fascists" who expressed "strong or violent anti-U.S. sentiments" or made "statements indicating a propensity for violence and antipathy toward good order and government."[32]

In contrast to its preassassination relationship with the Secret Service, the FBI's relationship with the CIA was both cooperative and contentious.

On the one hand, CIA officials provided the FBI with copies of Oswald's correspondence from the Soviet Union that had been intercepted under its HTLINGUAL mail program. They also informed FBI officials that Oswald had visited the Soviet embassy in Mexico City in September 1963 and had met a suspected KGB officer "functioning overtly as a consul." CIA officials moreover had earlier concerted with the FBI about their plan to plant "deceptive information" to embarrass the Fair Play for Cuba Committee "in foreign countries." They would take no action, they added, "without first consulting" the FBI to "make certain the CIA activity will not jeopardize any Bureau investigation." Having already employed disruptive techniques against this committee, FBI officials responded by giving the CIA the committee's "foreign mailing list."

At the same time CIA officers' interest in secrecy led them to withhold from the FBI—but also from senior CIA administrators and Presidents Eisenhower, Kennedy, and Johnson—their recruitment of Sam Giancana, John Roselli, and Santos Trafficante for a plot to assassinate Cuban president Fidel Castro. FBI officials learned of this plot only through a wiretap of Giancana and were appalled by such a harebrained scheme. It would have negated any future FBI prosecution of these crime bosses by giving them leverage to threaten to disclose this sensitive initiative. The FBI's wiretap in fact recorded Giancana and Roselli bragging about this CIA request, suggesting that this super-secret CIA operation had already been compromised.[33]

A quite different and bitterly contentious CIA-FBI relationship occurred following the defections of two Soviet intelligence officers, Yuri Nosenko and Anatoliy Golitsyn. Golitsyn was the first to defect, in 1961. At the time he told CIA officers that the Soviets had created a special disinformation unit to divert U.S. intelligence from Soviet espionage operations. This unit's activities, he claimed, included the use of false defectors. In addition, Golitsyn maintained, the Soviets had successfully infiltrated foreign intelligence services, including the CIA. Persuaded by Golitsyn's account and thereafter deeply suspicious of the veracity of future Soviet defectors, CIA counterintelligence chief James Angleton launched a decade-long inquiry that deeply divided CIA officials and eventually poisoned the agency's relations with the FBI.

CIA officials' handling of Golitsyn's defection was consistent with their reluctance to share sensitive foreign counterintelligence information with the FBI. As a result, FBI officials were not told about Golitsyn's defection until a year later, in 1962. This delay denied to the FBI information that could have been helpful in its counterespionage operations. FBI agents eventually interviewed the unstable and self-important Golitsyn and reached a quite different assessment of his veracity. These agency differences over Golitsyn's reliability became crucial in the aftermath of Nosenko's defection.

Nosenko had first approached the CIA in 1962 to offer information about Soviet activities in return for monthly payments. CIA officers found his information to be of limited value in that he essentially repeated Golitsyn's earlier accounts about Soviet disinformation and bugging of the U.S. embassy in Moscow. At the time Nosenko had expressed a desire to remain in the Soviet Union out of loyalty to his family and country. In February 1964, however, he suddenly defected, claiming to be concerned that Soviet intelligence might have discovered his espionage activities. At this time he said he had seen the Soviets' file on Oswald and affirmed that Oswald had not been recruited as a Soviet spy owing to his unreliability. Thus the Soviets, according to Nosenko, had played no role in Kennedy's assassination.

Angleton, however, doubted Nosenko's account and concluded that the defector was part of a Soviet disinformation campaign. FBI officials reached a different judgment, regarding Nosenko as legitimate. These differences over Nosenko and Golitsyn should not be seen as reflecting the agencies' differing cultures. They point up the difficulty of evaluating the accounts of defectors whose claims could neither be conclusively refuted nor confirmed. The resulting FBI-CIA conflict, moreover, was primarily shaped by the irrational suspicions, bordering on paranoia, of CIA counterintelligence chief Angleton. His obsessions over suspected Soviet "moles" also poisoned his relations with other CIA officers and were later an important factor in CIA director William Colby's 1974 decision to demand Angleton's resignation.[34]

The contretemps between the FBI and the CIA over the Nosenko-Golitsyn defections remained secret at the time. It nonetheless underscores a further consequence of CIA and FBI officials' obsession with secrecy: the promotion of a public belief that the agencies were involved in a sinister cover-up of their role in the Kennedy assassination. The agencies' withholding or heavy redacting of documents requested under the Freedom of Information Act furthered this belief.

Congress responded to these widespread suspicions in 1992 by passing the John F. Kennedy Assassination Records Collection Act, creating a special review board composed of historians, archivists, and political scientists. The board was authorized to order the release of classified records; assassination-related records could be withheld "only in the rarest case," and then only if there were a "legitimate need for continued protection." The act further authorized the board to override FBI and CIA objections to the release of records; its disclosure decisions could be countermanded only by the president.

The board eventually ordered the release of tens of thousands of formerly classified FBI and CIA records. These records revealed no government cover-up or conspiracy to assassinate

Kennedy, but they did confirm an insatiable obsession with secrecy. Thus, even though it was widely known that the CIA maintained station chiefs in the capitals of foreign countries, CIA officials had objected to the release of records acknowledging this. They reluctantly acceded to a compromise: to release records identifying station chiefs only for the years 1960–1964. FBI officials in contrast resisted the release of records that confirmed that organized-crime leaders had been wiretapped—hardly a secret and already suspected by the targets of these taps—and that documented FBI monitoring of critics of the Warren Commission report.[35]

The revelations produced by the review board offered insights into one effect of secrecy: immunizing CIA and FBI officials from public scrutiny and emboldening them to pursue programs that could not have commanded public support if known. Another such case involved a CIA covert operation to assassinate the charismatic Congolese leader Patrice Lumumba.

NSC staff member Robert Johnson recounted to the Church Committee in 1975 what had transpired in the aftermath of an August 18, 1960, National Security Council meeting. Johnson had attended this meeting at which the assassination of Lumumba was discussed, and was responsible for debriefing NSC staff on the important decisions taken at the meeting, and preparing the minutes. Consulting his superiors, Johnson testified, he had been told to omit the president's authorization of Lumumba's assassination from his debriefing and to use euphemism or omit the matter entirely from his minutes. The staff of the Church Committee then interviewed Johnson's superiors, Deputy Executive Secretary Marion Boggs and Executive Secretary James Lay. Both claimed not to remember having been consulted by Johnson. Boggs added, "I am not saying I was not consulted; merely that I do not remember such an incident. If I had been consulted I would almost certainly have directed Mr. Johnson to omit the matter from the memorandum of discussion." A matter as sensitive as an assassination order would not have been recorded in NSC minutes, Lay affirmed, and then described NSC record practices: "If extremely sensitive matters were discussed at an NSC meeting, it was sometimes the practice that the official NSC minutes would record only the general subject discussed without identifying the specially sensitive subject of the discussion. In highly sensitive cases, no reference to the subject would be made in the NSC minutes."[36]

By this and other tactics, allowing them to formulate plans and conduct operations in secret, FBI and CIA officials could pursue policies they believed would best advance the national interest. And because they would not have to account for their actions, they could be indifferent to public or congressional evaluation. Their principal concern was for results. Former FBI assistant director William Sullivan fully captured this mind-set in reflecting on his ten years' service as the FBI's representative to the U.S. Intelligence Board. "Never once did I hear anybody, including myself," Sullivan told the Church Committee, "raise the question: 'Is this course of action which we have agreed upon lawful, is it legal, is it ethical or moral?' We never gave any thought to this realm of reasoning, because we were just naturally pragmatists. The one thing we were concerned about was this: will this course of action work, will it get us what we want, will we reach the objective that we desire to reach."[37]

7 | THE BREAKDOWN OF THE COLD WAR CONSENSUS, 1965-1978

■ A HOST OF dissident movements emerged in America in the 1960s to challenge the cold war consensus. Women, civil rights, and youth activists organized to demand fundamental changes in national policy and to shift the focus from national security to economic and social injustice at home. They demanded an end to racial and sexual discrimination, rejected a politics of deference toward the presidency, and questioned national security claims as justifications for secrecy. These movements at first commanded the support of only a minority of Americans, but over time they reoriented the national political debate to individual liberty and the right to dissent. Their militancy, however, provoked two contradictory societal responses.

For one, the success of the activists in pointing up injustice or the economic and social costs of anti-Communist containment policies that led to the nation's involvement in the Vietnam War provoked a public debate over government priorities and the nation's failure to live up to long-acclaimed egalitarian principles. But activist militancy and the outbreak of urban race riots and violent anti-war demonstrations also provoked a conservative backlash. Many Americans were repelled by the disdain of militant, youthful activists for traditional morality and established authority, and denounced them as responsible for a national crisis of "law and order." The 1960s and 1970s, then, were decades of both change and reaction.

As they had in the 1950s, conservatives responded by questioning the loyalty of liberal and radical activists who demanded an end to racial and sexual discrimination and the nation's involvement in the Vietnam War. In one sense they reiterated what had been a long-term critique of New Deal programs, now decrying Kennedy's New Frontier and Johnson's Great Society programs as wasteful and counterproductive. By the end of the sixties, however, conservatives were articulating another theme that resonated with the broader public: liberal programs, by creating unrealistic expectations, had caused disrespect for authority. Criticisms of federally imposed solutions and a reaffirmation of limited government moreover had the indirect consequence of challenging an unquestioned tenet of cold war politics—the need for secrecy and for deference to experts. In their campaign for the presidency in 1968, both Richard Nixon and George Wallace championed these themes. Both emphasized not simply anticommunism but the liberal threat to "law and order," and they condemned liberal elites for seeking to impose their will on the people.

Despite their different policy objectives, liberals and radicals too began to challenge, if more directly, the tenets of cold war politics. This new liberalism ultimately led to a questioning of the secrecy and independence of the intelligence agencies and provoked a more critical examination of executive policy and secrecy. In the 1940s and 1950s these themes had been articulated from a Marxist perspective by isolated radical activists. Their criticisms had then been readily dismissed as "subversive," motivated by pro-Communist sympathies. By the late 1960s and early 1970s—as reflected in the presidential candidacies of Eugene McCarthy, Robert Kennedy, and George McGovern—such criticisms, if more nuanced, commanded broader support. Liberals more often questioned the wisdom of a presidentially based foreign policy and the effect of "national-security politics" in undermining dissent.

The rise of these dissident movements also influenced the actions of presidents and the heads of the intelligence agencies directly. At first their responses paralleled those of their predecessors in the 1940s and 1950s. FBI agents not only aggressively monitored liberal and radical activists involved in civil rights, student, anti–Vietnam War, women, and gay and lesbian movements but sought to counter the increased support and legitimacy of these movements. As a result, FBI surveillance and containment actions intensified, encompassing the scope of the new, more militant dissent.* Those targeted groups included the American Civil Liberties Union, the Congress of Racial Equality, the Southern Christian Leadership Conference, the NAACP, the Mississippi Freedom Democratic party, the Black Panthers, the Council of Federated Organizations, the Poor People's Campaign, the Student Non-Violent Coordinating Committee, Students for a Democratic Society, Black Student Unions, the American Friends Service Committee, the Women's Liberation Movement, Clergy and Laity Concerned About Vietnam, Vietnam Veterans Against the War (including future Democratic presidential nominee John Kerry), the Socialist Workers party, the National Lawyers Guild, the Nation of Islam, the Ku Klux Klan, and the American Christian Action Council. FBI investigations extended to monitoring the teach-in movement that swept across college campuses after 1965, Earth Day rallies, and the so-called underground press— weekly alternative urban newspapers that often appealed to disaffected youth.

Going beyond their earlier containment actions, FBI officials adopted even more aggressive—but covert—tactics with the ex-

---

*FBI agents conducted over 740,000 "subversive" investigations and 190,000 "extremist" investigations during the period 1955–1975.[1]

press purpose of influencing public opinion. The FBI's COINTEL-
PRO, which had been directed at the Communist party in the
1950s, was extended during the 1960s to non-Communist organizations such as the Black Panthers, Students for a Democratic Society, and even the Ku Klux Klan—with similar tactics
adopted to discredit Martin Luther King, Jr., and the Southern
Christian Leadership Conference. In these efforts FBI agents were
encouraged to devise means of sowing dissension within the
ranks of radical organizations or making derogatory personal
and political information available to influential reporters,
columnists, television producers, and members of Congress. Efforts were made to discourage private contributions to organizations such as the Southern Christian Leadership Conference and
to deter businesses from running advertisements in underground
newspapers or even printing them. In one case FBI officials wrote
a speech that Congressman Harold Smith delivered criticizing the
"subversive" character of anti–Vietnam War activists. Copies of
this speech were then sent to presidents of universities and corporations. FBI agents ratcheted up their investigations of student
groups' "subversive" activities but did so "in a most discreet and
circumspect manner. Good judgment and common sense must
prevail so that the Bureau is not compromised or placed in an embarrassing position." Copies of an article written by a San Francisco rabbi that supported the Vietnam War were mailed to members of the Vietnam Day Committee to "convince" them of the
"correctness of U.S. foreign policy in Vietnam." In yet another
case, derogatory information about Pentagon Papers discloser
Daniel Ellsberg's attorney, Leonard Boudin, was leaked to Copley News Service Washington bureau chief Ray McHugh, which
McHugh then ran on Copley's wire.[2]

FBI officials' most egregious covert political activism involved
the civil rights leader Martin Luther King, Jr. King first became
the subject of interest for FBI officials after his highly publicized
leadership of the Montgomery bus boycott movement in

1955–1956. FBI officials thereafter were troubled by King's charisma and his central role in forming a new civil rights organization, the Southern Christian Leadership Conference (SCLC) and its youth affiliate, the Student Non-Violent Coordinating Committee (SNCC), and in organizing nonviolent demonstrations throughout the South challenging racial segregation. To the FBI, King's support from Southern blacks and Northern liberals as a moral spokesman for nonviolent civil disobedience threatened the nation's security, as did his criticisms of racial segregation, legitimized in his award of the Nobel Peace Prize in 1964.

FBI officials accordingly devised a multi-pronged strategy "to discredit" King, owing to his "subversive" beliefs and the possibility that he might become a "messiah" who could "unify and electrify" the civil rights movement. FBI agents were ordered to recruit informers among black ministers, to check King's and SCLC's finances, to wiretap his office and home phones, and to bug his hotel rooms during his frequent trips around the country. The derogatory information obtained through this surveillance was then offered to friendly reporters on an anonymous basis, to promote critical news stories about King's immoral character and subversive associations; to the White House and to the pope to deter them from meeting with King; and to an FBI contact at a major magazine to "forestall" publication of an article written by King. Still, these were not FBI officials' most notorious actions.

FBI bugs of King's hotel rooms had intercepted the civil rights leader's illicit sexual affairs. Armed with this information, senior FBI officials in December 1964 transcribed the reels from this bugging operation and offered selected Washington-based reporters the opportunity to listen to these tapes—though no reporter subsequently filed a story based on this scurrilous information, or revealed that FBI officials had sought to peddle it. In an even more troubling action, FBI officials mailed an anonymous letter, postmarked from Florida, along with a copy of the tapes recording King's sexual activities, to King's residence. The letter threatened to "expose" King as a "complete fraud," adding that the public would "soon know you for what you are—an evil, abnormal beast." King was "done," the letter suggested, and had only one option before "your filthy, abnormal fraudulent self is bared to the nation"—he should commit suicide before accepting the Nobel Peace Prize thirty-four days later. King and his wife read the letter and listened to the enclosed tape but were not dissuaded from continuing their civil rights activities.[3]

While consistent with their covert actions of the 1940s and 1950s, the FBI's political activities in the 1960s changed in important ways as a result of Director Hoover's personal situation. On January 1, 1965, Hoover would reach the mandatory retirement age of seventy. In May 1964, however, President Johnson waived this requirement for an "indefinite period of time." Johnson's conditional waiver meant that Hoover's continuance as FBI director depended on the president's continued support. This new sense of vulnerability affected Hoover's relationship first with the Johnson and then the Nixon White House.

Since Franklin Roosevelt's presidency, the FBI director had regularly forwarded directly to the White House (in the process bypassing the attorney general) reports detailing information about the president's critics or other valuable political intelligence.* Some of these reports responded to specific White House requests, others Hoover had volunteered. Because presidents could not risk the possible discovery of their reliance on the FBI for essentially political intelligence, this had limited what they requested of Hoover. After 1965, however, Hoover's worries about his continued tenure as FBI director fundamentally changed the FBI–White House relationship to one in which Presidents Johnson

---

*This arrangement was temporarily severed during John Kennedy's presidency, owing to the fact that the attorney general was the brother of the president and had instituted rules requiring his clearance for all internal security matters.

and Nixon fully exploited the FBI's capabilities to advance their own political and policy interests.[4]

An emboldened Johnson did not hesitate to exploit this opportunity, having as senator and vice president taken advantage of Hoover's responsiveness and his ability to ensure that requested assistance would not become known.* The first such occasion occurred shortly after he assumed the presidency. Johnson had inherited a White House and a Department of Justice staffed by Kennedy loyalists, some of whom had opposed Kennedy's decision to offer him the vice presidency in 1960. To curry favor, Hoover in late 1963 and through early 1964 alerted Johnson to the plans and tactics of these Kennedy loyalists. They might be working behind the scenes to promote Robert Kennedy as a vice-presidential running mate in 1964, or Justice Department officials might be investigating former Johnson aide Bobby Baker "with the avowed purpose of trying to embarrass the President in every way possible" to force him "to pick" Kennedy as "his running mate in order to assure his re-election."[5]

Johnson did not hesitate to ask the FBI director for other helpful actions. In 1964 he asked the FBI to monitor the Mississippi Freedom Democratic party (MFDP) delegation to the 1964 Democratic National Convention. The president's concern then was to sustain an image of a strong supporter of civil rights and at the same time to minimize the political impact in the South of developments at the Democratic convention. Hoover dispatched a special thirty-four-man FBI squad to the convention, headed by FBI assistant director Cartha DeLoach, Hoover's liaison to the Johnson White House. This squad regularly reported to the White House—through a secure telephone line—the planned ac-

---

*Some of these requests were personal, including Johnson's solicitation of information about his daughter's boyfriend, his press critics who had reported on his questionable financial dealings, and radio personality John Henry Faulk, at a time when Johnson was considering hiring him to manage his radio stations in Texas.

tivities and contacts of the MFDP delegates and their liberal supporters, enabling the president to thwart a proposed resolution to seat the MFDP delegation and thus to avert a walkout by Southern delegations.[6]

President Johnson sought the FBI's assistance to address another potentially serious political problem: the arrest by a Washington, D.C., vice squad of White House aide Walter Jenkins on a morals charge in October 1964, in the closing weeks of the presidential campaign. Fearful that the Republican presidential candidate, Senator Barry Goldwater, might attempt to exploit this arrest, White House aide Bill Moyers requested FBI name checks* on all of Goldwater's Senate staff employees. Reports were submitted on fifteen Goldwater aides.[7]

FBI officials also helped Johnson counter the critics of his foreign and domestic policies. In June 1967, for example, FBI agents compiled derogatory information for "dissemination to the news media" about peace activists who were drafting a "Peace Party" ticket for the 1968 presidential elections. Their reports listed these activists' Communist associations and personal deficiencies, particularly their "scurrilous and depraved" character. Agents were informed that this "would be a real boon to Mr. Johnson." Every "possible embarrassment," the FBI director emphasized, "must be vigorously and enthusiastically explored." Hoover also honored a presidential request to "brief at least two Senators and two Congressmen, preferably one from each Party, on the [subversive character of anti-Vietnam] demonstrators so that they might in turn make speeches upon the floor of Congress but also publicly." Similar reports were prepared on the president's anti-war critics to "be used by prominent officials of the Administration whom the President intends to send in various parts of the country to speak on the Vietnam situation." FBI officials also honored Johnson's

---

*Name checks involved requests for a search of FBI files for all information on an identified person.

requests for name checks on prominent reporters—NBC anchor David Brinkley, *New York Times* reporter Harrison Salisbury, Associated Press reporter Peter Arnett, syndicated columnist Joseph Kraft, *Chicago Daily News* Washington bureau chief Peter Lisagor, *Life* magazine Washington bureau chief Richard Stolley, and *Washington Post* executive Ben Gilbert—whose critical reporting on the military situation in Vietnam had incensed the president. And name checks were conducted on individuals who had sent letters or telegrams (reprinted in the *Congressional Record*) commending Senator Wayne Morse's criticisms of the administration's Vietnam policies.

FBI officials serviced even more sensitive presidential requests. They prepared a report linking the critical comments made by senators during the Senate Foreign Relations Committee's hearings in 1966 on the Vietnam War "with the Communist Party line"; a memorandum on seven senators who in 1967 criticized the president's decision to resume bombing North Vietnam; and biweekly reports—based on information obtained through wiretaps on Soviet and Soviet-bloc embassies—on the contacts of members of Congress, congressional staff, and "any citizen of a prominent nature" with these embassies. Hoover also forwarded to Johnson a report listing derogatory information about Barbara Garson, the author of a satirical play about Johnson, *MacBird*.[8]

FBI officials continued to promote Johnson's political interests, even after he announced in 1968 his decision not to seek renomination as the Democratic presidential candidate. Johnson instead looked to ensure the nomination and then the election of his vice president, Hubert Humphrey, over anti-war challengers Eugene McCarthy and Robert Kennedy. First, Hoover agreed to Humphrey's request to send a special squad to the Democratic National Convention in Chicago to monitor and report on the activities of anti-war activists who had converged on Chicago. Then, responding to rumors that Republican vice-presidential nominee Spiro Agnew had concerted with a conservative activist, Anna Chennault, who had close ties with the South Vietnamese government, to undermine ongoing peace talks in Paris with North Vietnam, Johnson asked the FBI to determine if Agnew and Chennault were pressuring the South Vietnamese not to agree to peace terms before the election. FBI officials reluctantly complied, ruefully commenting that the request "put us in a most vulnerable and embarrassing position."[9]

During Richard Nixon's presidency the FBI–White House relationship fundamentally changed. One innovation involved the establishment in November 1969 of a code-named INLET program. Committed to enhancing presidential power and conducting policy in secret, President Nixon sought to rationalize what had, since 1940, been an informal arrangement whereby FBI officials either volunteered or responded to White House requests for reports on political developments of presidential interest. Under the INLET program, identified categories of information were to be automatically transmitted to the White House "on a continuing basis." The reported information was to have "the qualities of importance and timeliness to serve the President's interest and to provide him with meaningful intelligence for his guidance." It would include "security related" information; information about current or pending internal security cases; information about demonstrations, disorders, and other civil disturbances; and "items with an unusual twist or concerning prominent personalities which may be of special interest to the President or the Attorney General."[10]

Like Johnson, Nixon solicited FBI reports linking militant anti–Vietnam War and civil rights dissent with international communism. Over the first four years of his presidency, Nixon solicited reports on Americans for Democratic Action president Joseph Duffy, SCLC president Ralph Abernathy, producer of the anti-Nixon documentary Emil D'Antonio, opponents of a proposed anti-missile system and war production contracts, the women's liberation movement, church and civil liberties groups opposed to the Vietnam War, and organizers of Earth Day rallies. When they were told that famed Beatle John Lennon might lead demonstrations at the 1972 Republican National Convention and had urged youth to register and vote against the war, Nixon administration officials solicited derogatory information that could lead to Lennon's deportation. FBI officials also alerted the Nixon White House to the contacts of members of Congress and congressional staff with Soviet and Soviet-bloc embassies, provided information on the administration's right-wing critics (notably the American Christian Action Council), honored a name-check request on CBS correspondent Daniel Schorr, and monitored and wiretapped syndicated columnist Joseph Kraft.

The Nixon administration's most sensitive request, however, was that the FBI wiretap four Washington-based reporters and thirteen administration employees, including members of the president's White House and National Security Council staffs. This operation grew from a White House request to the FBI to identify the source of a leak to *New York Times* reporter William Beecher. It led to the wiretapping of prominent reporters and the president's own appointees. The operation soon acquired another dimension as the wiretaps continued after Morton Halperin and Anthony Lake left the NSC and joined Senator Edmund Muskie's staff. (Muskie was the leading aspirant for the 1972 Democratic presidential nomination.) The Halperin and Lake taps thereafter provided invaluable political intelligence and were welcomed by Nixon's key aides. Their sensitivity led FBI officials to maintain their copies of the wiretap intercept reports separate from other FBI wiretap records in the office of FBI assistant director William Sullivan, who personally delivered the originals to the White House. As FBI director Hoover's personal liaison to the Nixon White House, Sullivan also personally oversaw FBI monitoring and wiretapping of the syndicated columnist Joseph Kraft—and again maintained the FBI's copies of these reports in his office.

And, in a case that captures the paranoia and excessive secrecy of the Nixon White House, the FBI wiretapped a navy yeoman assigned to the staff of the Joint Chiefs in an effort to identify the source of a leak to syndicated columnist Jack Anderson and to determine how the Joint Chiefs had obtained access to certain NSC records.[11]

Presidents Johnson and Nixon also turned to the FBI to conduct certain foreign intelligence operations, reflecting their unwillingness to rely exclusively on the CIA.

The first such request involved an April 1965 coup led by junior Dominican Republic officers to restore the popularly elected Juan Bosch to the presidency of the country. Bosch had been elected president in 1962, following a 1961 coup that ousted dictator Rafael Trujillo. Bosch, however, himself became a victim of a military coup in 1963. Concerned about the political orientation of the leaders of the 1965 coup, President Johnson on April 24, 1965, sent U.S. troops to the Dominican Republic. His intervention was sharply criticized as undemocratic. To rebut his critics, Johnson released a report, prepared by the U.S. ambassador to the Dominican Republic, that justified this military operation as essential to avert another Cuba. It identified seventy-seven of the individuals aligned with the new Dominican government as being either Communists or Communist sympathizers. The evidence was almost immediately refuted, with press reports disclosing that many of those named either were out of the country at the time of the coup or were not Communists.

The questionable intelligence embarrassed Johnson, who confronted an additional problem of identifying Dominicans who could prove helpful in influencing the results of the forthcoming presidential election to be held in 1966. In this instance Johnson turned to the FBI to identify reliable candidates and to ensure that order could be maintained. Fourteen FBI agents were then dispatched to the Dominican Republic to conduct background checks on possible candidates for the provisional government.

The situation in the Republic, Hoover subsequently advised Johnson, was "touch and go," but FBI agents were "doing everything in their power" to further the president's desire to restore order. "Excellent results" were nonetheless being achieved in influencing the political situation, and preventive measures were being used to "prevent [Communist domination] when and if we had to." Working with NSC aide McGeorge Bundy, FBI agents screened prospective personnel to ensure that a "strong man who is anticommunist" would be elected. Former Trujillo associate Joaquin Balaguer, whom FBI agents found acceptable, won the 1966 presidential election. Johnson nonetheless asked Hoover to have the FBI's principal agent, Clark Anderson, remain in the Dominican Republic until the inauguration.[12]

President Nixon also turned to the FBI to supplement the CIA's foreign intelligence efforts, in this case seeking to exploit the FBI's long-term relationship with foreign police and intelligence agencies. This liaison dated from World War II, when President Roosevelt had the FBI conduct foreign intelligence and counterintelligence operations in Latin America. Agents in the FBI's Special Intelligence Service had then operated undercover, assigned to the staffs of U.S. embassies. When the SIS was disbanded with the end of the war, FBI agents continued to be stationed abroad under a new legal attaché program called Legat. By 1970 FBI agents under this program were assigned to embassies in fourteen European and Latin American capitals as well as Tokyo and Ottawa. While their principal purpose was to share information about international crime, including espionage, with foreign police and intelligence agencies, Legats also reported on political, military, and economic developments.

In November 1970 Secretary of State William Rogers relayed to FBI director Hoover President Nixon's request that he expand the Legat program to give the president "better intelligence." Aware that the CIA had not been notified about this request, Hoover assured Rogers that he "certainly" would not inform the

CIA, and he agreed to reopen offices in Manila, Rio de Janeiro, and Santo Domingo, and to open new offices in Canberra, Kuala Lumpur, and New Delhi. Welcoming this opportunity to expand the FBI's role, Hoover believed it would enhance the FBI's standing with the Nixon White House. Indeed, during 1971 the FBI sent the White House more than two hundred reports in the "political, economic, and social areas" and received "warm letters of appreciation" from National Security Adviser Henry Kissinger. Much of the FBI's reported information, Hoover privately conceded, had been "picked up in conversations, newspapers and various sources," but FBI personnel "are probably far more qualified than State Department personnel to put things in the proper perspective and to sense relative importance." An additional advantage of this expansion, Hoover observed, was that it enhanced the FBI's standing with foreign intelligence officials by enabling FBI personnel to "convey a true sense of the bureau's jurisdiction and efficiency."[13]

These isolated instances of FBI intrusion into the CIA's responsibility for foreign intelligence were not a product of bureaucratic rivalry. FBI officials had simply responded to presidential initiatives. Moreover in 1966 FBI and CIA officials reached an informal agreement to ensure better "coordination." Under this arrangement CIA officials would "seek concurrence and coordination of the FBI" before employing a clandestine action within the United States in order to avoid any "conflict with any operation, current or planned, including active intelligence [by] the FBI." CIA officials would continue to handle, for "foreign intelligence purposes," those agents entering the United States and whom they had developed. They nonetheless agreed to share any information bearing on "internal security matters" with the FBI.

This arrangement promoted both agencies' intensified efforts to monitor and contain radical civil rights and anti–Vietnam War activists during the 1960s and 1970s. Thus CIA agents relayed to the FBI information they developed about foreign nationals or U.S. citizens who were coming to the United States to attend conferences or to meet with prominent American dissidents. FBI officials, in addition, regularly requested CIA coverage of identified radical activists who traveled abroad—the number of such requests averaging over a thousand a month during the period 1967–1974. FBI officials, for example, were particularly interested in learning about the travel plans of black activist Stokely Carmichael to Cuba, North Vietnam, Czechoslovakia, Algeria, the United Arab Republic, and other foreign countries. In return, FBI officials relayed to their CIA counterparts information that FBI agents had developed about the associations of militant black nationalist leaders with the People's Republic of China and Cuba. CIA officials would then place the named individual on a special "watch list."[14]

This informal arrangement of divided responsibilities was nonetheless transgressed by particularly sensitive requests from Presidents Johnson and Nixon. As noted earlier, Johnson since 1965 had pressured the FBI to develop evidence linking militant civil rights and anti-war activists with international communism. FBI reports disappointed Johnson, though, for they cited only examples of shared ideology, not that radical activists were being financed or operated under the direction of the Soviet Union, Communist China, or Cuba. A frustrated president therefore turned to the CIA in 1967 to secure this desired intelligence. CIA director Richard Helms ordered CIA station chiefs overseas to keep tabs on radical students, African-American expatriates, and other U.S. citizens traveling abroad to determine the "extent to which Soviets, Chicoms [Chinese Communists] and Cubans are exploiting our domestic problems in terms of espionage and subversion." This limited initiative soon expanded as the CIA's counterintelligence division established a formal code-named program, Operation CHAOS. Rather than focus on sources developed abroad, CIA officers instead infiltrated radical civil rights and anti-war movements within the United States. This CIA domestic surveillance program was expanded and refined in 1969, in response to the Nixon administration's more intense pressure. Over the course of its operation from 1967 through 1974, more than 7,500 files were compiled by CIA operatives, containing information on more than 300,000 individuals and groups whose names were indexed by computer.

Yet Operation CHAOS too failed to produce the desired intelligence. CIA officials, in fact, regularly advised the White House that "no evidence" had been uncovered that "foreign governments, organizations or intelligence services now control the New Left movements and/or are capable at the present time of directing these movements for the purpose of instigating open insurrection or disorders; for initiating and supporting terrorist or sabotage activities; or for fomenting unrest and subversion in the United States." The source of unrest, CIA analysts continued, was indigenous, adding that the radical activists were responding to social, economic, and political concerns. CIA officials knew that this internal security program violated the ban of the 1947 National Security Act. CIA director Richard Helms called attention to this fact in a 1969 report to the White House. The section of this report on "American students," Helms emphasized, involved "an area not within the charter of the Agency, so I need not emphasize how extremely sensitive this makes the paper. Should anyone [outside the executive branch] learn of its existence, it would prove most embarrassing for all concerned."[15]

At the same time CIA officials had begun two additional programs, Projects RESISTANCE and MERRIMAC, ostensibly to counter anticipated threats to CIA personnel, facilities, and operations. While these programs fell within the CIA's counterintelligence responsibilities and focused on anticipated physical threats (a CIA recruiting office at the University of Michigan had been bombed in 1968, and CIA recruiters on college campuses were often harassed), CIA officials made no attempt to coordinate these domestic intelligence operations with the FBI. As they had done since the agency's creation in 1947, they relied on the agency's Office of Security. CIA officials preferred to retain exclusive jurisdiction over their personnel and projects, and contacted the FBI only in those instances when they learned of operations involving other than CIA personnel or facilities.[16]

Unable to develop the desired evidence that radical activists were subject to Communist control or direction, CIA and FBI officials solicited the NSA's assistance. Through its sophisticated technology the NSA could intercept virtually all international electronic communications. To be useful, such a capability required the identification of specific categories to be "sorted out from other information not of interest"—for example, the communications of Soviet military commanders about air defense or military exercises. (One indication of the NSA's capabilities involved its interception of Soviet Premier Brezhnev's unprotected communications from his limousine.) Beginning in 1967, FBI and CIA officials provided the NSA with the names of specific individuals and organizations—eventually totaling 1,200, of which the FBI provided 950—whose international communications were to be intercepted.* Those identified were suspected of participating in "civil disturbances [anti-war or civil rights demonstrations] or otherwise subvert the national security of the United States." This initially informal Watch List program was refined and expanded in 1969, and was then code-named Operation MINARET to ensure "more restricted control and security of sensitive information derived from communications as processed."

The intercepted communications—approximately two thousand between 1969 and 1973—were hand-delivered to FBI and CIA recipients. These communications were specifically not

---

*NSA officials also intercepted the international communications of identified drug traffickers at the request of the Bureau of Narcotics and Dangerous Drugs.

"identified with the National Security Agency," and the recipients were explicitly instructed to destroy them within two weeks or return the communications to the NSA. NSA officials moreover did "not serialize" or file these intercepts with other NSA records, and classified these records "TOP SECRET, stamped 'Background Use Only.'" These precautions were intended to preclude discovery that NSA officials were intercepting the communications of American citizens, including Jane Fonda, Benjamin Spock, and Martin Luther King, Jr. By doing so, NSA officials strayed from their military intelligence mission, indirectly assisted a domestic surveillance operation, and violated the 1934 Communications Act's wiretapping ban.[17]

This massive surveillance program, like earlier efforts, again failed to provide the Johnson and Nixon administrations with evidence that could discredit their domestic critics. In contrast to the McCarthy era, sweeping charges of Communist influence no longer commanded uncritical public acceptance. To the contrary, both administrations' attempts to question the loyalty of their critics won limited support and failed to intimidate dissenters. Instead such attacks only swelled the ranks of the dissidents and after the mid-1960s fueled a new skepticism about executive power and executive secrecy. A warier public, media, and Congress posed a new challenge to FBI and CIA officials who had long been accustomed to acting secretly and without accountability. Each agency responded differently to this challenge, mostly due to how their senior officials weighed the political costs of continuing questionable practices.

In contrast to their CIA counterparts, by the mid-1960s senior FBI officials began to reassess their long-standing practices. They encountered their first challenge to these methods in 1965–1966 in hearings initiated by the Subcommittee on Administrative Practice and Procedure, chaired by Senator Edward Long.

When he first convened public hearings in 1964, Senator Long was concerned primarily with the Internal Revenue Service's surveillance practices. Soon he was convinced by the subcommittee's staff to broaden the investigation in 1965 to all U.S. agencies. Before its public hearings, the subcommittee sent a detailed questionnaire to all federal agencies with a series of questions. These included: Had the agency installed or monitored telephone taps or requested another agency to do so on its behalf; if so, how many taps had been installed in the period 1959–1964? Had the agency purchased microphones and closed-circuit technology, and how many in the 1959–1964 period? Had the agency monitored mail and, if so, what was the extent of such actions and their purpose? Finally, the subcommittee demanded information about rules and procedures that agency officials had adopted to govern the installation and use of wiretaps, bugs, and mail covers.

The Long Subcommittee questionnaire and the prospect that they might be called to testify posed a serious dilemma for senior FBI officials. If they answered the subcommittee's questions truthfully, they would have to disclose the extent of FBI wiretapping, bugging, and mail-opening practices and, furthermore, the special—Do Not File and June Mail—records procedures that had been devised to preclude discovery of the FBI's illegal actions. The damning revelations would contradict FBI officials' public image of a principled law-enforcement agency that respected the law and the privacy rights of American citizens. Such disclosures might then trigger demands for a congressional investigation of FBI operations and possibly for Hoover's resignation as FBI director. Not surprisingly, senior FBI officials acted to contain this potential threat.

First, FBI director Hoover asked President Johnson to have Attorney General Nicholas Katzenbach pressure the subcommittee not to pursue an inquiry that could affect "sensitive security matters." The president agreed and in addition directed Vice President Hubert Humphrey to pressure Long to contain the subcommittee's zealous counsel, Bernard Fensterwald. At the same time Hoover contacted Senator James Eastland, chairman of the parent Senate Judiciary Committee, to "warn the Long Committee away from those areas which could be injurious to the national defense." These tactics apparently worked: Long agreed to limit the subcommittee's inquiry to the Internal Revenue Service and further to clear with senior FBI officials any proposed FBI witnesses to ensure that "any names involving national security [are] deleted."

But Long did "not keep his promise," and instead he demanded that Attorney General Katzenbach testify about FBI wiretapping and bugging practices. FBI officials soon learned that the subcommittee's staff had been "taking [executive session] testimony in connection with mail covers, wiretapping, and various snooping devices on the part of Federal agencies." They concluded that Long "cannot be trusted" and personally contacted the senator to exact his promise not to "call anyone from the department in connection with the hearings."

Assured now of Long's sympathy for the FBI's position, FBI officials nonetheless encountered a specific public relations problem: the senator would have to explain why no FBI official was called to testify during the subcommittee's public hearings. Acting as Hoover's liaison, FBI assistant director Cartha DeLoach urged Long to "issue a statement reflecting that he had held lengthy conferences with top FBI officials and was now completely satisfied after looking into FBI operations, that the FBI had never participated in uncontrolled usage of wiretaps or microphones and that FBI usage of such devices had been completely justified in all instances." When Long protested that he "did not know how to word such a release," DeLoach offered to provide him with the statement "on a strictly confidential basis." DeLoach did so. The subcommittee, his statement affirmed, had "not only conferred at length with top officials of the FBI, but . . . conducted exhaustive research into the activities, procedures, and techniques of this agency," concluding that FBI wiretapping and bugging operations were strictly controlled and limited to "serious crimes either affecting the internal security of our nation or involving heinous threats to human life." Long never issued this statement, knowing that had he done so the subcommittee's staff would have contradicted it. But the subcommittee called no FBI witnesses. Only the attorney general testified on behalf of the department.

Fearful of future leaks to the news media, FBI officials continued to monitor the subcommittee's proceedings. Hoover ordered his aides to prepare "summary memoranda" detailing whatever derogatory information the FBI had compiled on members of the subcommittee and on Fensterwald. The summaries contained derogatory information only on Senator Quentin Burdick and Fensterwald.[18]

Having squelched the Long Subcommittee threat, FBI officials immediately confronted a second challenge, prompted by a 1966 Supreme Court case involving Fred Black, a Washington-based lobbyist and influence peddler. Black had appealed his conviction on income tax charges, whereupon the solicitor general, arguing the government's case, advised the Supreme Court that the FBI had bugged Black. In response, the Court demanded answers to a series of questions, particularly when U.S. attorneys had learned that Black had been bugged and "the person or persons who authorized its installation; the statute or Executive Order relied on." These demands put FBI officials in a bind since FBI director Hoover alone had authorized the bug, without the knowledge or authorization of Attorney General Robert Kennedy. Admitting this would suggest that FBI officials had acted without proper supervision and had been willing to violate the Fourth Amendment's ban against unreasonable searches and seizures.

Unknown to the Court or to attorneys general, Hoover's unilateral action in the Black case had not been atypical. One internal FBI memo reported that FBI agents had installed 738 bugs during the period 1960–1966 but that FBI officials had "notified" Justice Department officials about only 158 of these installations. In private justifications for their unwillingness to brief the department about the scope of FBI bugging operations, FBI officials lamented that "to advise the Department at this time of our microphone coverage would result only in the Department running to the courts with resultant adverse publicity to the Bureau which could give rise in the present climate to a demand for a Congressional inquiry of the Bureau."

In preparing their response to the Court's questions, Justice Department officials first reviewed current policy, instituted by Attorney General Katzenbach in March 1965, and further consulted former attorneys general Robert Kennedy, William Rogers, and Herbert Brownell. Katzenbach's March 1965 order had altered his predecessors' policy of not requiring the FBI to obtain the attorney general's explicit authorization before installing bugs, and not requiring the bureau to seek reauthorization for ongoing wiretaps and bugs. Kennedy, Rogers, and Brownell, in addition, advised Katzenbach that they had never authorized FBI bugging installations during *criminal* investigations. Senior FBI officials were particularly alarmed on learning of Katzenbach's intention to so inform the Court, fearing that this admission would tarnish the FBI's reputation by implicitly confirming its independent streak and its willingness to violate the law. Press coverage, they concluded, could create demands for a congressional investigation. Accordingly they launched a campaign to pressure Katzenbach to submit a revised brief to the Court affirming that the FBI had acted under explicit departmental authority.

First, FBI assistant director James Gale advised Senator Long about the department's proposed brief to the Court. Department officials had learned of the FBI's bugging in August 1965, he claimed, at a time when the case was being reviewed by the appeals court. Expressing sympathy for the FBI, Long regretted this "most unfortunate development in that columnists like Drew Pearson, Fred Graham of the New York Times, and Dave

Kraslow of the Los Angeles Times together with liberals on his committee, and the anti-FBI group, would give rise to a hue and cry for the Long Committee to hold hearings on the FBI." The senator promised to contain the matter and to "figure out something with regard to handling his critics." Long subsequently warned Katzenbach in person that he intended to conduct hearings on the Justice Department's response to the Court in the Black matter, to which the attorney general responded, "Oh my God, not that! Let's keep this stuff out."

In their boldest initiative, FBI officials interceded with President Johnson, both directly and indirectly. They first contacted White House aide Marvin Watson to claim that Katzenbach's proposed brief was an attempt to protect Robert Kennedy. At the same time FBI assistant director Cartha DeLoach attempted to exploit Supreme Court Justice Abe Fortas's close relationship with the president, which had continued after Fortas's appointment to the Court. A receptive Fortas advised the FBI assistant director that Katzenbach's handling "boils down to a continuing fight for the Presidency. Kennedy was of course out to capture that segment of the voters which in the past had belonged to Vice President Humphrey," Fortas told DeLoach, but "if facts as possessed by the FBI concerning Kennedy's approval of wiretaps [sic] were made known to the general public that it would serve to completely destroy Kennedy." Agreeing to consult with President Johnson, Fortas in conjunction with DeLoach formulated a plan to ensure that Katzenbach would modify the department's brief to the Court and vindicate the FBI.

Katzenbach bowed to this intense pressure and slightly modified the brief. The final text, however, did not concede that the Justice Department had authorized the FBI's bugging of Black. In fact it affirmed that "no specific statute or executive order was relied on" by FBI officials in their bugging of Black, that attorneys general had "delegated" to FBI officials the duty to "gather intelligence"—not evidence—when investigating violations of federal statutes, and further that under "Departmental practice in effect for a period prior to 1963" (when the bug was installed) the FBI had been "given authority" to install bugs for "foreign intelligence"—but not evidentiary—purposes. Based on "the aforementioned Departmental authorization" the FBI director had "approved" the bugging of Black.[19]

The Long Subcommittee investigation and the Black case rang alarm bells for senior FBI officials. They concluded that they could no longer count on a deferential Congress and media. Just as important, they began to question whether attorneys general would automatically defend the FBI's resort to illegal or controversial practices. An astute political operator who was always wary of adverse publicity—thus his adoption of special procedures to preclude discovery of the FBI's abusive practices—the FBI director now hesitated to continue employing illegal investigative methods. The risks of their discovery were too great; one possible consequence would be a call for his resignation. In 1965–1966 Hoover thus privately issued a series of restrictive orders. These included limits on the number of wiretaps and bugs; the banning of break-ins, mail openings, and trash covers (rummaging through a suspect's trash); and the raising of the minimum age of informers from eighteen to twenty-one, because immature college students might have second thoughts and reveal that the FBI had recruited them to spy on their peers.[20]

Although it was not due to any purposeful reassessment of the FBI's relationship with the CIA and the National Security Agency, Hoover's restrictions directly affected these connections. After 1965 FBI officials hesitated to conduct break-ins and install wiretaps and microphones requested by the CIA on domestic activists and organizations. The FBI director in 1969 moreover advised his CIA counterpart of a new FBI policy: future CIA wiretap or bugging requests would immediately be relayed "directly to the Attorney General for approval." Hoover also advised NSA officials Louis Tordella and Marshall Carter in 1967 that he would no longer honor NSA wiretapping and bugging requests. Tordella's and Carter's protests led Hoover to relent, but on condition that he would honor such requests only if specifically ordered by the attorney general or the president. Hoover's conditions left CIA and NSA officials in a bind; neither were willing to seek the president's or the attorney general's authorization for such illegal practices. Tordella in fact admitted, "I couldn't go to the chief law enforcement figure in the country and ask him to approve something that was illegal."[21]

Clearly the FBI and the CIA had different views of the drastically changed political realities. Since 1936 FBI officials had abandoned a law-enforcement mission when conducting intelligence investigations, and since 1940 they had authorized "clearly illegal" techniques. These activities had exploded in the 1960s as FBI officials—both on their own and in response to White House demands—sought to contain increasingly militant dissident movements. FBI director Hoover had not become a "born again" constitutionalist in his old age. But he astutely understood that in a changed political climate, continued resort to illegal activities would be uncovered and might lead to demands for his dismissal as FBI director.*

In contrast to Hoover, CIA officials remained committed to the use of illegal and abusive practices. Their different assessment

---

*Hoover's concern was on the mark. His continuance as FBI director after January 1965 derived from President Johnson's May 1964 executive order waiving the mandatory age 70 retirement requirement. Johnson's action was in fact publicly challenged in November 1964, prompted by Hoover's disparaging comments about civil rights leader Martin Luther King, Jr., during a press conference when he described King as "the most notorious liar in the country." (Hoover was responding to King's criticisms of the FBI's failure to pursue violations of civil rights.) Hoover's thin-skinned response to criticism provoked a *New York Times* editorial, headlined "Time to Retire," which cited Hoover's inability to accept legitimate criticism as justification for letting "the mandatory provisions of the federal retirement laws take effect on Mr. Hoover's 70th birthday."[22]

reflected a confidence that they could escape scrutiny, and it was illustrated by their response to the Long Subcommittee inquiry.

The subcommittee questionnaire could easily have exposed the CIA's HTLINGUAL program—and, in the process, could have confirmed that CIA officials had knowingly violated federal postal statutes and the 1947 National Security Act's ban on CIA "internal security" investigations. Such revelations could have rekindled the alarmist concerns that had been articulated by members of Congress in 1947 about the inherent dangers of a secret, centralized intelligence service responsible to the White House.

CIA officials at first deliberated whether to study the "security" of the HTLINGUAL program in light of the "dangers inherent" in the Long Subcommittee hearings. They considered whether the program should be "partially or fully suspended until the Subcommittee's investigations are completed." Eventually they decided against any suspension, concluding that the subcommittee investigation "would soon cool off." No Post Office official, they determined, was aware of the "actual operation" of HTLINGUAL— CIA personnel had actually opened the mail. CIA officials furthermore decided not to brief Postmaster General John Gronouski that they were now opening the mail, as he had recently denied when testifying before the Long Subcommittee that any mail had been opened at all. Rather than abandoning the program, CIA officials contended that it should be *expanded* to open more letters, and that this could be safely done under current tight security procedures which limited knowledge on "a need-to-know basis." Anticipating the possibility that future allegations might lead Congress to initiate another investigation, CIA officials were confident that "any problems ensuing could be satisfactorily handled." Should a disgruntled CIA employee reveal the program, this "may be answered by complete denial of the activity." "No good purpose can be served by an admission of the violation" of the law, since the agency had "no good cover story" and thus had no choice but to "vigorously deny any association, direct or indirect, with any activity as charged." Just as important, CIA officials doubted that any allegation could be supported by "presentation of interior items from the Project." Should such allegations occur, "it might be necessary after the matter has cooled off during an extended period of investigation, to find a scapegoat to blame for the unauthorized tampering with the mails."[23]

This brazen strategy of denial worked. Nonetheless CIA officials soon faced other challenges. Public hearings in 1964 by the House Subcommittee on Foundations, chaired by the populist congressman Wright Patman, posed the possible compromise of other CIA domestic programs. The Patman Subcommittee had identified eight private foundations that had served as conduits for CIA covert funding operations.

CIA officials responded by reevaluating the agency's funding practices. In this case they concluded that the "real lesson" of the Patman hearings was "not that we need to get out of the business of using foundation cover for funding, but that we need to get at it more professionally and extensively." Another potential threat surfaced when Senator Eugene McCarthy on January 24, 1966, introduced a resolution calling for a Senate Foreign Relations Committee investigation of all U.S. intelligence agencies. McCarthy's resolution was later amended simply to add four members of the Foreign Relations Committee to the Senate Armed Services Committee, which had oversight over the CIA. On July 14, 1966, the Senate referred McCarthy's amended resolution to the Armed Services Committee, where it died.

McCarthy's demand for an inquiry into intelligence operations predated the publication in April 1966 of a five-part *New York Times* series on the CIA. In their research for this series, *Times* reporters in Washington and overseas had asked troubling questions in interviews with CIA officials. One official, Stanley Grogan, headed his report on this inquiry, "Subject: NEW YORK TIMES Threat to Safety of the Nation." The *Times* series, Grogan feared, might force the president and Congress to take action against the CIA. To counter this possibility, CIA officials protested to the White House, which unsuccessfully sought to pressure *Times* publisher Arthur Ochs Sulzburger to kill the series as potentially threatening to national security. The published series did indeed raise questions about the CIA's expansion and accountability, suggesting that the CIA might have evolved into "a sort of Frankenstein's monster."[24]

McCarthy's resolution and the *Times* series reflected a new skepticism about CIA operations. Yet the most pressing challenge to the CIA was prompted by a relatively obscure left-wing magazine, *Ramparts*. In early 1966 CIA officials learned that the editors of *Ramparts* were pursuing leads relating to the agency's covert relationships with private foundations. Because *Ramparts* lacked the *Times*'s stature, CIA officials were willing to use aggressive tactics to neutralize any planned exposé. They ordered an investigation, at the same time seeking the FBI's help in obtaining "any evidence of subversion" on the part of the magazine's editors and staff and "devising proposals for [CIA] counteraction."

This preemptive effort failed. In February 1967 *Ramparts* ran full-page ads in the *New York Times* and the *Washington Post* to publicize its forthcoming March issue. In this issue *Ramparts* disclosed the CIA's covert relationship with the leaders of the National Student Association, thereby raising questions about both the agency's domestic surveillance and its violation of academic freedom. To forestall a more far-ranging investigation demanded by Senate Majority Leader Mike Mansfield, President Johnson appointed a three-man committee—chaired by Attorney General Katzenbach and including CIA director Richard Helms and Secretary of Health, Education and Welfare John Gardner—to investigate only the relationship between the CIA and "U.S. educational and private voluntary organizations which operate abroad." This narrow mandate avoided an inquiry into those more problematic CIA programs with domestic consequences: HTLINGUAL, MKULTRA, Forum News, and the funding of selected academics and freelance reporters.

The Katzenbach Committee's principal recommendations did not fundamentally alter CIA operations. "No federal agency," the committee concluded, "shall provide any covert financial assistance or support, direct or indirect, to any of the nation's educational or private voluntary organizations." CIA officials recognized the "different ball game" posed by critical press scrutiny but nonetheless concluded that the agency's "covert" relations with "commercial U.S. organizations" and "covert" funding of "foreign-based international organizations" would still be permitted. CIA officials also acted to withhold the agency's high-priority intelligence operations from the Katzenbach Committee and devised more secure funding arrangements through so-called surge funding and by narrowly interpreting the committee's recommended prohibition. These practices allowed CIA officials to continue after 1967 to fund their foreign news service (Forum News), hire foreign-based freelance reporters (even though privately conceding that the publications were "read by U.S. students"), labor union organizations, and the research of American academics as well as soliciting their help in identifying "suitable United States students for CIA employment."[25]

Thus despite the changed political climate of the 1960s, the CIA concluded that it could continue to operate with impunity. National security claims would immunize CIA operations from public scrutiny. Illegal programs or methods need not be rescinded but could be continued or even expanded.

Senior Nixon administration officials shared this view of their own invulnerability. The willingness of the president and his senior aides to authorize illegal activities, based on the expectation their actions would remain secret, proved to be their downfall as a far more assertive media and Congress launched a series of highly publicized exposés. One indirect consequence was to shatter the reputations of the CIA and the FBI and to precipitate demands for limits on their authority and greater scrutiny of their operations.

This arrogance characterized the Nixon administration's 1969 demand that the FBI and CIA document "foreign Communist support of the revolutionary protest movements in the country." Dissatisfied with the subsequent reports, on June 20, 1969, White House aide Tom Charles Huston instructed FBI and CIA officials to "liberally" construe foreign Communist support "to include all activities by foreign Communists designed to encourage or assist revolutionary protest movements in the United States." The president, Huston added, intended to "use" this information to discredit these militant activists as subversive. Huston at the same time criticized the "inadequacy" of the agencies' collection methods and their "low priority and attention" to this internal security threat.[26]

Huston was acting as White House liaison to the intelligence agencies, and in this capacity he met frequently with FBI assistant director William Sullivan, the agency's liaison to the Nixon White House. The two men developed a close working relationship. Sullivan at one point confidentially advised Huston that the seeming low quality of FBI reports was due not to FBI unwillingness or indifference but to "the various restrictions" that FBI director Hoover had imposed on FBI investigative procedures in 1965–1966. Huston and Sullivan agreed that broader collection methods must be reinstated and in time developed a strategy to achieve this result.[27]

A strategy to circumvent Hoover's restrictive orders became more urgent after two crucial political developments in 1970. The first stemmed from President Nixon's decision in May to authorize the military invasion of Cambodia, a decision that ignited a firestorm of protest on college campuses. The intensity of this protest impelled many university officials to suspend the academic semester abruptly. Its virulence further alarmed an administration deeply frustrated because it had been unable to discredit its increasingly militant critics. The second event involved the so-called Thomas Riha affair.

An associate professor of Russian history at the University of Colorado, Riha had mysteriously disappeared in March 1969. Rumors about his disappearance prompted an investigation by the local district attorney and speculation within the local press that he might be involved with the FBI and the CIA. CIA officer Michael Todorovich in February 1970 sought to allay these suspicions and advised the district attorney that Riha was "alive and well," claiming to have learned this from an unidentified FBI agent. In disclosing this information, Todorovich had not gone through channels to secure FBI approval, as required under the so-called third agency rule. FBI director Hoover, briefed about Todorovich's action, was infuriated by the CIA officer's failure to consult the FBI and demanded that CIA officials identify the FBI agent who had been Todorovich's source. Although he was pressured by CIA director Helms to do so, Todorovich refused. Helms sought to mollify Hoover, assuring the FBI director that he had taken "administrative action" against Todorovich but could not force him to identify the FBI agent. Helms emphasized the value of "closest cooperation and teamwork" between the FBI and the CIA and their "mutual respect," and he hoped for closer coordination in the future "in order to prevent the airing in public of conflicts or differences between the two agencies, . . . [since] representatives of the news media . . . are eager to exploit alleged differences on a national scale." Not assuaged by Helms's abject apology, Hoover instead ordered the FBI's Denver office "to have absolutely no contact with CIA" and further terminated "direct liaison here [in Washington] with CIA" with "any contact with the CIA in future to be by letter only."

As it turned out, the CIA's relationship with the FBI was not completely severed and continued informally by telephone. The Riha incident nonetheless rekindled the simmering differences between CIA and FBI officials over Hoover's 1965–1966 restrictive orders. This tension was exacerbated by Hoover's March 31, 1970, response to CIA director Helms's complaints about the reduction in FBI wiretapping, bugging, and mail cover operations. The FBI director had then designated FBI assistant director Sullivan to discuss these differences with the CIA but had meanwhile outlined to Helms the conditions that would govern future wiretapping, bugging, and mail activities. Commenting on the CIA director's "belief" that the FBI should "have taken more aggressive action" in collecting intelligence, Hoover conceded: "There is no question as to the frequent value of such operations [wiretapping, bugging, mail opening] in developing needed intelligence. On the other hand, the use of these measures in domestic investigations poses a number of problems which might not be encountered in similar operations abroad. There is widespread concern by the American public regarding the possible misuse of this type of coverage. Moreover, various legal considerations must be borne in mind, including the impact such coverage may have on our numerous prosecutive responsibilities. The FBI's effectiveness has always depended in large measure on our capacity to retain the full confidence of the American people. The use of any investigative measure which infringes on traditional rights of privacy must therefore be scrutinized most carefully. Within this framework, however, I would be willing to consider any proposal your Agency may make."

At their meeting, Sullivan advised CIA counterintelligence chief James Angleton that the FBI "has not received the necessary support" for its wiretapping and mail interception activities from the attorney general. In the past the FBI had willingly provided "substantial amounts of coverage of this type in the interest of both of our counterintelligence responsibilities as well as in the national security interest," Sullivan confided, but "we had to retrench in recent years largely as a result of the lack of support for such operations." CIA officials had been urged by the FBI in

1966 to take up the matter with the attorney general, Angleton conceded, and though they had given this matter "considerable thought," that consultation would require a "whole new set of procedures and policy considerations" which were currently under study. Angleton promised to "be in touch with us [FBI] when they have firmed up various proposals." He would keep on top of this matter, Sullivan assured Hoover, and would make "no commitments" without the FBI director's "prior approval."[28]

The combination of a sharp increase in student unrest, the Riha affair, and its aftermath for FBI-CIA relations provided the background for Huston's ambitious plan to address the Hoover problem—to persuade the FBI director to rescind his restrictive orders of 1965–1966 so that FBI agents could resume illegal investigative practices. NSA and CIA officials also shared this concern. White House aide Huston, working closely with FBI assistant director Sullivan, thereupon devised a strategy: the appointment of a special inter-agency task force to evaluate current "intelligence collection procedures; identify restraints under which U.S. intelligence services operate; and list the advantages and disadvantages of such restraints." The task force, appointed by President Nixon in June 1970, was comprised officially of the heads of the FBI, CIA, NSA, and DIA (the Defense Intelligence Agency), though its actual working group included Huston, as the White House representative, and senior officers from these agencies. Sullivan was the FBI representative. The key problem, however, was that any report drafted by the working group for submission to the president would be subject to the review of the heads of the various intelligence agencies, notably Hoover. Huston and Sullivan finessed this problem by having the task force prepare a report that would simply list the pros and cons of various investigative techniques and reserve to the president the decision to endorse specific procedures. In addition, Sullivan allayed Hoover's possible suspicions by reporting daily to the FBI director on the progress of the working group's deliberations. His reports misrepresented his controlling role during these delibera-tions and instead implied that he and the other agency represen-tatives had simply been following the lead of the White House.

The task force's summaries of the pros and cons were aimed at rescinding Hoover's restrictive orders. The key "recommenda-tions," ostensibly for the president's consideration, involved lift-ing "current restraints which limit the [intelligence] community's ability to develop the necessary intelligence." These would in-clude intercepting international communications, conducting break-ins and mail openings, increasing wiretaps and bugs, and lowering the age of informers to eighteen. An additional recom-mendation, in this case reflecting President Nixon's principal ob-jective in appointing the task force, involved the creation of a per-manent inter-agency committee to operate under the direction of the White House, coordinating intelligence operations, preparing estimates on political violence, and developing new policies. Had this recommendation been permanently adopted, it would have established a coordinated intelligence system directly responsive to the White House.

Because the heads of the intelligence agencies had to sign off on the report before its submission to the president, FBI assistant director Sullivan faced a delicate problem. His cover memoran-dum sought to get around this by describing the "investigative re-straints and limitations" section as having been drafted "in ac-cordance with the President's request, with the pros and cons outlined and with no recommendation of any kind made by the committee." Hoover, however, was not deterred and instead de-manded that Sullivan draft a series of footnoted objections to the pros and cons section. These objections emphasized that while the FBI had employed such techniques in the past, their use was "becoming more and more dangerous and we are apt to get caught"; that the FBI director "would not oppose other agencies seeking authority of the Attorney General for coverage required by them and thereafter instituting such coverage themselves";

and that lowering the minimum age of informers "could result in charges that investigative agencies are interfering with academic freedom."

The heads of the other agencies were infuriated by Hoover's footnoted objections. Huston, however, dissuaded them from adding their own footnotes of explanation. In his cover memorandum to the president, Huston downplayed Hoover's objections as "inconsistent and frivolous," adding that even senior FBI officials opposed the FBI director's position. Hoover's action, Huston wrote, amounted to an attack on the president's authority. The "effective conduct" of intelligence operations "is possible only if there is direction from the White House." Hoover was a "loyal trooper," Huston added, and thus the president should invite the FBI director to the White House for a "stroking session" to seek his cooperation, convene another conference of the heads of the intelligence agencies to announce his decision, and then issue an "official memorandum setting forth the precise decisions of the President."

Nixon, however, rejected Huston's recommendation. No White House meeting was convened. Instead the president directed Huston to send the memorandum authorizing specific procedures (wiretaps, bugs, break-ins, mail openings, and interception of international communications) under his (Huston's) signature. Nixon was unwilling to issue even a highly classified directive, a decision that acknowledged his understanding of the risks involved should he personally authorize "clearly illegal" activities—the phrasing of the plan. Huston's signature would enable Nixon to retain presidential deniability should any of the activities become known.

The wily FBI director immediately understood the risks of this method of authorization for the FBI and advised Attorney General John Mitchell how he would act whenever the FBI conducted a specific operation (break-in, wiretap, bug, or mail opening): a memo would be prepared advising the attorney general that this action was undertaken "pursuant to the president's program." Hoover's intention to create a written record linking the specific action with the president in effect would undercut Nixon's strategy of deniability. Urging the FBI director to do nothing, Mitchell informed Nixon of Hoover's intentions. Such techniques "would likely generate media criticism if they were employed," Mitchell warned, adding that the "risk of disclosure of the possibly illegal actions . . . was greater than the possible benefits to be derived." Nixon concurred and rescinded the Huston Plan.[29]

The abortive history of the Huston Plan highlights what had been the core belief among intelligence agency officials—excepting Hoover after 1965: that they could and should safely conduct illegal or potentially controversial actions. Both CIA and NSA officials had welcomed the Huston Plan as an opportunity to rescind Hoover's restrictions on FBI domestic surveillance operations and, just as important, to win explicit presidential authorization for what they were already doing. NSA official Louis Tordella privately described the plan as "nothing less than a heaven-sent opportunity." And even though President Nixon reluctantly canceled the Huston Plan, he, the attorney general, and the heads of NSA and CIA remained committed to employing illegal investigative methods. They were willing to do so because they were still convinced that such operations could be safely conducted without risk of discovery.

In March 1971, accordingly, Attorney General Mitchell, CIA director Helms, and NSA director Noel Gayler made one last attempt to persuade Hoover to have the FBI resume these illegal practices. At a March 29 meeting with the FBI director, the three men urged a "broadening" of FBI "intelligence [operations] both domestic and foreign." Helms sought "further coverage of mail" while Gayler sought reinstatement of FBI foreign embassy break-ins. Responding, Hoover reiterated his willingness to assist the CIA and NSA officials, and further emphasized how intensively the FBI was currently monitoring radical activists and organizations. But the FBI director opposed the "proposed extension of operations insofar as the FBI was concerned in view of the hazards involved." Unwilling to pressure Hoover, Mitchell asked Helms and Gayler to conduct an "in-depth examination" of exactly what they wanted done and to report their results to himself and the FBI director. Helms promised to "take care of this promptly." Neither he nor Gayler, however, submitted any written recommendations; neither formally asked the FBI to break the law, or the attorney general to sanction this.[30]

President Nixon's unwillingness to abandon illegal investigative techniques ironically proved to be the undoing of his presidency. Subsequent revelations of Nixon's abuses of power also brought demands for an investigation of the FBI, CIA, and NSA. For since 1969 President Nixon had secretly authorized a series of illegal operations with far-reaching political consequences. These included wiretapping Washington-based reporters and members of his own White House and National Security Council staffs in 1969, authorizing the Huston Plan in 1970, requesting in November 1970 derogatory information about the homosexuality and "any other stuff" of members of the Washington press corps, and creating the so-called White House Plumbers in 1971. In all these cases the White House had purposely used the FBI and CIA for political purposes; and all the measures had been predicated on the belief they would never become known.

In the Plumbers operation of 1971, White House aides E. Howard Hunt and G. Gordon Liddy—formerly CIA and FBI employees, respectively—had recruited four Cuban Americans (who had earlier participated in the CIA's Bay of Pigs operation) to break into the office of Daniel Ellsberg's psychiatrist. The cost of this operation was defrayed through unexpended 1968 Nixon presidential campaign funds. In preparing for the break-in, Hunt also obtained the technical assistance of his former CIA colleagues. These same individuals and funding source were repeated in June 1972 when Hunt, Liddy, and the same four Cuban

Americans orchestrated a second break-in, this time of Democratic National Committee headquarters at the Watergate complex in Washington, with the costs defrayed through 1972 Nixon campaign funds. The arrest of the six and the grand jury proceedings that followed were key factors in the cover-up orchestrated by President Nixon and his chief aides in an effort to avoid the uncovering of the Plumbers operation during questioning of the six by the grand jury. Revelations in turn would have raised questions about the White House–FBI/CIA relationship. In a further unintended consequence, and as part of the cover-up initiative, after the arrest of the Watergate burglars President Nixon had urged the CIA to pressure the FBI to limit its investigation into the source of the funds that had been used in the break-in.

The White House–FBI/CIA connections were publicly disclosed in 1973 during hearings conducted by a special Senate committee, chaired by Sam Ervin, investigating the Watergate affair. The Ervin Committee's highly publicized hearings raised questions not only about Nixon's abuses of power but about White House relations with the CIA and the FBI. Questions about this relationship intensified after White House counsel John Dean's production of documents concerning the FBI's wiretapping of White House and National Security Council staff members and Washington-based reporters at the request of the White House in 1969; the formulation of the Huston Plan in 1970; and the creation and operations of the White House Plumbers in 1971. One result of these dramatic discoveries was that Congress in 1974 convened hearings to impeach President Nixon, culminating in his resignation that August. A second and unprecedented consequence was that Congress in 1975 launched a critical inquiry into the White House relationship with the intelligence agencies and the conduct of CIA and FBI officials.

FBI director Hoover's decisions of 1965–1966 to terminate the FBI's illegal activities, and his opposition in 1970 and 1971 to efforts to reinstate these practices, proved to be prescient. Hoover turned out to be a far more astute politician than Richard Nixon in recognizing the real possibility that such illegal practices could be discovered in the vastly changed political climate of the 1960s and 1970s. Hoover's actions might have put him at loggerheads with his counterparts in the CIA and NSA, who continued to press for the continued use of illegal practices. But these officials too came to recognize—belatedly—their own vulnerability. In the years 1973–1975 CIA and NSA officials either terminated ongoing intelligence programs or hurriedly destroyed some of the records documenting their illegal actions.

Following the events of Watergate, FBI officials were again the first to attempt, unsuccessfully, to cover up their past misdeeds and abuses of power. In the months after J. Edgar Hoover's death in May 1972, his administrative assistant, Helen Gandy, and pursuant to his earlier order, destroyed one of his two secret office files, his Personal and Confidential File. His second secret office file, his Official and Confidential File, however, was not destroyed, and its existence soon became known.[31]

Earlier, on March 28, 1971, radical activists had broken into the FBI's Media, Pennsylvania, resident agency and had photographed FBI records, which they distributed to the media and members of Congress. Some of these records were captioned COINTELPRO. In response, Hoover in August 1971 had terminated the COINTELPRO program "for security reasons because of these [COINTELPRO records] sensitivity." Hoover had to issue this order because COINTELPRO was a highly centralized program; its records would confirm that FBI agents had acted pursuant to the approval of senior FBI officials, in order to "harass, disrupt and discredit" targeted radical activists and organizations. Hoover's termination order did not, however, resolve a future public relations problem. Because one of the released Media break-in records was captioned COINTELPRO, NBC correspondent Carl Stern filed a Freedom of Information Act request for all COINTELPRO records. Stern's was a "blind" request in that he had no knowledge of this program, but his successful suit led in 1973 to the release of the massive COINTELPRO files.[32]

FBI officials' efforts to destroy or secrete potentially damaging records were not unique. In January 1973, shortly before leaving office to become U.S. ambassador to Iran, CIA director Richard Helms similarly authorized the destruction of the tapes and transcripts of his office telephone and room conversations* and of the records of the CIA's drug-testing program MKULTRA. Helms's orders were prompted by a query from his secretary how she should handle Senate Majority Leader Mike Mansfield's request that the CIA maintain "any records or documents which have a bearing on the Senate's forthcoming investigation into the Watergate break-in, political sabotage and espionage, and practices of agencies in investigating such activities."[33]

In February 1973, moreover, CIA officials, concerned about possible fallout from the Watergate break-in, terminated HTLINGUAL. They had earlier decided to continue this program despite its "known risks" because of its value to the FBI. But now Chief Postal Inspector William Cotter† advised his former CIA colleagues that he would have to admit the program's existence if he were called to testify before Congress about mail programs, unless he received "some indication that the program had been approved at an exceedingly high level in the United States Government." In light of this possibility, CIA officials concluded that continuing this program posed too great "a political risk."[34]

The Senate's Watergate investigation posed an equally serious problem for NSA officials. Their dilemma stemmed from an action

---

*In 1965 a taping system had been installed in the offices of the CIA director, the CIA assistant director, and an adjoining conference room to record all conversations. These recorded conversations were then routinely transcribed.

†Cotter had been appointed chief postal inspector in 1969, at which time he had not briefed the postmaster general that the CIA had opened the mail under the HTLINGUAL program. Cotter, however, was aware of this practice as a former CIA employee.

of defense attorneys for fifteen members of the Weather Underground faction of the Students for a Democratic Society, whose trial began at the moment of the Ervin Committee's disclosure of the Huston Plan. The presiding judge, Damon Keith, in an earlier case had struck down as unconstitutional the Nixon administration's authorization of warrantless wiretaps, a ruling upheld by the Supreme Court in 1972 in *U.S. v. U.S. District Court*. Defense attorneys effectively exploited the Huston Plan revelations and Judge Keith's constitutional concerns. Ordinarily they would have sought discovery only of whether the FBI had illegally wiretapped their clients, but now they broadened their discovery motion to include the NSA, the CIA, and the Defense Intelligence Agency, all identified by John Dean as participants in the formulation of the Huston Plan. Judge Keith honored this broad request. Nonetheless assistant U.S. attorney Will Ibershof initially confined the government's response to the FBI, affirming that the bureau had engaged in no illegal conduct. Judge Keith rejected this response as "perfunctory" and ordered the government to "fully comply" by "filing sworn statements from a person or persons with full knowledge of each specified agency."

After requesting additional time to respond because the identified agencies fell outside the Justice Department's jurisdiction, U.S. Attorney Ralph Guy advised Judge Keith that the government would submit an affidavit for his private inspection that involved "the interception of communications, none of whom are defendants presently before the court, by an agency of the government to obtain foreign intelligence information deemed essential to the security of the United States." Guy reserved the right to withdraw the affidavit should Keith rule against the *in camera* condition. Keith scheduled arguments on this request, but Guy subsequently moved to dismiss the case against the defendants.

Unknown to the defense attorneys or to Keith, the judge's order could have compromised MINARET and precipitated a governmental reassessment of this program. NSA director Lew Allen at first advised FBI director Clarence Kelley that NSA would continue to honor future FBI requests on the condition that its reports would be "proper[ly] handl[ed]" in light of the "ever-increasing pressure for disclosure of sources by Congress, the courts, and the press." In the interim, however, Attorney General Elliott Richardson, upon learning of MINARET, ordered the FBI to "cease and desist" submitting names to the NSA and further directed Allen to "immediately curtail the further dissemination" of intercepted communications to the FBI. This program, Richardson continued, "raises a number of serious legal questions," given the Supreme Court's ruling in *U.S. v. U.S. District Court*. The NSA, however, could continue to furnish to "appropriate" agencies "relevant information acquired by [the NSA] in the routine pursuit of the collection of foreign intelligence information," but not in "a matter that can only be considered one of domestic intelligence." Upon receipt of Richardson's ruling, Allen advised the attorney general that he had "directed no further information be disseminated to the FBI." Operation MINARET was formally terminated.[35]

The Ervin Committee's Watergate investigation not only provoked impeachment hearings but increased public and congressional skepticism about presidential "national security" and "executive privilege" claims—and specifically whether secrecy had permitted abuses of power by both presidents and the heads of the intelligence agencies. Two additional revelations of December 1974 and February 1975 offered further confirmation of a wider abuse of power. In December 1974 *New York Times* reporter Seymour Hersh, in a sensational page-one story, exposed the CIA's Operation CHAOS program whereby CIA officers had monitored domestic activists and organizations in violation of the agency's 1947 charter. Then, in February 1975, Attorney General Edward Levi informed a House subcommittee that former FBI director Hoover had maintained a secret file in his office—the Official and Confidential File—consisting of 164 folders of "derogatory" information on prominent Americans, including "presidents, Executive Branch officers and 17 individuals who were members of Congress."[36]

This crescendo of revelations* provoked Congress to launch the first intensive investigation of the operations, procedures, and claimed authority of the U.S. intelligence agencies. The Senate resolution of January 1975 creating the so-called Church Committee highlights this belated attempt to understand both the relationship between the White House and the intelligence agencies and the consequences of exclusive executive oversight. The resolution authorized a special committee to "do everything necessary or appropriate" to uncover "illegal, improper, or unethical activity" conducted by any U.S. intelligence agency. Its specific mandate was to determine (1) whether the CIA "had conducted" illegal domestic intelligence operations; (2) whether the FBI or "any other" federal agency had conducted "domestic intelligence or counterintelligence operations" against U.S. citizens; (3) the "origins and disposition" of the Huston Plan; (4) the "nature and extent of executive branch oversight of all United States intelligence activities"; (5) the executive orders, rules, or regulations, "either published or secret," that governed the U.S. intelligence agencies and whether these were expanded or "are in conflict with specific legislative authority"; and (6) whether any U.S. intelligence agency violated or was suspected of violating any state or federal statute, "including but not limited to surreptitious entries [break-ins], surveillance wiretaps, or eavesdropping, illegal opening of the United States mail, or the monitoring of United States mail."[37]

By 1975 the public climate of skepticism ensured that the Church Committee—and its House counterpart, the Pike Com-

---

*These included revelations of the FBI's COINTELPRO, FBI monitoring of Earth Day activities, and Acting FBI Director L. Patrick Gray's admission of having destroyed records that the Nixon White House had provided him at the time of the Watergate affair.

mittee—would have access to the classified records of the intelligence agencies. President Gerald Ford and the heads of the agencies were in no position to refuse to comply with requests for relevant records. This access, and the two committees' broad mandate, led to the uncovering of the wide scope of the agencies' abusive practices. These included plans to assassinate foreign leaders; extensive use of mail intercepts, break-ins, wiretaps, and bugs; actions to disrupt, harass, and discredit targeted organizations, including civil rights leader Martin Luther King, Jr.; CIA and NSA domestic surveillance programs; a lack of executive oversight, including the unwillingness of presidents and attorneys general to monitor the activities of the intelligence agencies to ensure compliance with the law; and the creation of secret record and record-destruction practices by presidents and intelligence agency officials with the explicit purpose of ensuring "presidential deniability" or precluding discovery of abusive practices. These included the willingness of FBI officials to act as the political agent of the White House.[38]

The Church Committee's intensive but necessarily incomplete investigation* concluded that "The Government's domestic intelligence policies and practices require fundamental reform." Needed reforms could not be instituted administratively, the committee declared, but required Congress to legislate "restraints upon [those] intelligence activities which may endanger the constitutional rights of Americans." Executive oversight had been inadequate when not purposely abusive. Conceding that finding the appropriate balance between legitimate security and civil lib-

---

*Given the tight one-year time frame, the limited prior knowledge of intelligence agency activities and programs, and the difficulty that congressional investigators confronted in obtaining all relevant information, the Church and Pike committees failed to uncover the full scope of intelligence agency and White House activities. Further revelations were subsequently uncovered through Freedom of Information Act requests filed by journalists, academics, and interested citizens and organizations.

erties would be difficult, the committee nonetheless found that the "potential for abuse is awesome and requires special attention to fashioning restraints which not only cure past problems but anticipate and prevent the future misuse of technology." The core of this problem, committee members affirmed, was the executive branch's exclusive control over intelligence policy and the resort by presidents and the heads of the intelligence agencies to secrecy in order to mask their abuses of power. "Abuse thrives on secrecy," the committee emphasized. And secrecy had subverted Congress's constitutional responsibility to oversee "basic programs and practices" and thereby check potentially abusive practices. "Knowledge is the key to control," the committee continued. "Secrecy should no longer be allowed to shield the existence of constitutional, legal and moral problems from the scrutiny of all three branches of government or from the American people themselves."[39]

The Church Committee's recommendations briefly defined the national debate on the proper role of the intelligence agencies. At minimum, the Senate in 1976 established a permanent oversight committee to examine the operations of the intelligence agencies and to conduct executive sessions or public hearings when appropriate.[40]

Congress meanwhile initiated hearings on proposed comprehensive charters that would define by statute the authority of the intelligence agencies. Deliberations over differing charter bills quickly bogged down as conservatives and liberals argued over their purpose: whether to specify in detail what the intelligence agencies could and could not do, or whether to delineate the broad parameters of the agencies' authority but reserve to the executive branch the responsibility to set specific standards. This debate centered on S.2525, a massive bill introduced in February 1978 by Senator Walter Huddleston, chairman of the Senate Select Committee on Intelligence Subcommittee on Charters and

Guidelines.* Proponents of S.2525 intended to ensure (1) that the executive branch would exercise effective control over intelligence agency activities, (2) that Congress would meet its oversight responsibilities, and (3) that intelligence activities conducted in the United States would be governed by legislatively defined standards.[42]

While Congress began difficult and lengthy deliberations over the proposed legislation, it moved more quickly to address FBI and NSA electronic surveillance practices.

In 1934 Congress had banned wiretapping when it passed laws regulating the communications industry. Justice Department officials at first privately concluded that this ban did not apply to federal agents, an interpretation that the Supreme Court rejected in 1937 and 1939 rulings. Nonetheless FBI wiretapping continued, authorized under President Roosevelt's secret directive of May 1940. Roosevelt's order had been based on the premise that the Supreme Court's rulings barred wiretapping during criminal but not "national defense" investigations, whose purpose was to anticipate, not prosecute, spying and sabotage. The directive governed only FBI wiretapping practices. FBI officials on their own authorized bugging until May 1954 when Attorney General Herbert Brownell, in a secret directive, authorized FBI bugging operations during "national security" investigations—again when the purpose was to anticipate, not prosecute. Neither Roosevelt's nor Brownell's directive legalized these practices. Recognizing this, dating from Roosevelt's presidency in 1941 through John Kennedy's presidency in 1962, presidents had unsuccessfully lobbied Congress to legalize FBI wiretapping. These efforts ultimately

---

*In April 1978 Senator Edward Kennedy, chairman of the Senate Judiciary Committee, convened hearings to "lay the foundation for the development" of FBI charter legislation to "clearly define the scope of the Bureau's responsibilities and the extent of its authority." The same divisions emerged as in the case of the deliberations over Huddleston's omnibus charter bill.[41]

succeeded when Congress in 1968 enacted the Omnibus Crime Control and Safe Streets Act.

This shift in congressional sentiment by 1968 was the result of "law and order" concerns that emerged in reaction to the sharp increase in violent crime and the upsurge of urban race riots and anti-war demonstrations that swept the nation in the 1960s. A new consensus emerged that recognized wiretapping as an essential law-enforcement tool. Nonetheless Congress remained leery of the possible abuses inherent in wiretapping and bugging. Thus the 1968 act required federal officials to obtain a court warrant before installing a bug or tap during a criminal investigation. Congress moreover would approve a broad loophole: "Nothing contained in this statute or in section 605 of the Communications Act of 1934 . . . shall limit the constitutional powers [*of the president*] to take such measures as he deems necessary to protect the Nation against actual or potential attack or other hostile acts of a foreign power, to obtain foreign intelligence information deemed essential to the security of the United States, or to protect national security information against foreign intelligence activities. Nor shall anything in this chapter be deemed to limit the constitutional power of the President to take such measures as he deems necessary to protect the United States against the overthrow of the Government by force or other unlawful means, or against any other clear and present danger to the structure or existence of the Government."

During Senate debate over the wiretapping section of the bill, Senator Philip Hart challenged this broad language, claiming that it failed to define the limits of executive power or the basis for a national security exception. In effect, he argued, this language would enable presidents to authorize wiretapping of radical groups "in areas that do not come within our traditional notion of national security." Senators John McClellan and Spessard Holland dismissed Hart's concerns as unwarranted. The section, they contended, did not "affirmatively" grant broad powers to the president but simply did not restrict a president's constitutional powers. "There is nothing affirmative in the statute," McClellan maintained.

The recently elected Nixon administration immediately exploited this loophole. But its decision not to seek court authorization in 1969 to wiretap radical activists was subsequently rejected by the Supreme Court. The president could not authorize warrantless wiretaps during "domestic security" investigations, the Court held, nonetheless implying that the president might have broader power in "foreign intelligence" investigations.

The FBI's wiretapping of radical activists became known at the time. Only later would the public and Congress learn of the scope of the Nixon administration's intelligence—that is, noncriminal—wiretapping practices.

Congress responded to the revelation of these practices by revisiting its earlier enactment of the 1968 Crime Control Act. Members now sought to plug the "foreign intelligence" loophole. After lengthy deliberations, Congress in October 1978 enacted the Foreign Intelligence Surveillance Act, which recognized a distinction between "domestic security" and "foreign intelligence" investigations. The latter would not have to be based on a "probable cause" standard that a federal crime had been or would be committed. Nonetheless, before a "foreign intelligence" interception of "U.S. persons who are in the United States" could be conducted, the president or a presidential designee would have to seek approval from a special court. The "certification" that the investigation involved "foreign intelligence" could be submitted in secret but would have to establish that the target was either a "foreign power"—a foreign government, a faction of a foreign government, a foreign-based terrorist group or political organization, or "an entity directed and controlled by a foreign government"—or "an agent of a foreign power." The special court was not authorized to determine the necessity or propriety of the proposed surveillance but simply to establish the "foreign" connection. In an emergency, interceptions of suspected conversations were permitted without advance court approval, but it would have to be secured within twenty-four hours.* Information obtained from an approved "foreign intelligence" interception, however, was explicitly barred for purposes of prosecution.[43]

Because Congress did not immediately enact charter legislation, the sole restrictions on intelligence agency operations were based on executive directives. Thus in March 1976, responding to congressional and public concerns, Attorney General Edward Levi announced new guidelines for FBI "domestic security" investigations. Levi addressed two major problems that had been identified during the Church and Pike Committees' highly publicized hearings, first, that such investigations had spilled over to monitor and at times to contain political activities, and, second, that attorneys general purposely or unwittingly had avoided their responsibility to ensure that such investigations were lawful and not used to violate privacy or First Amendment rights.

Under the Levi guidelines, FBI officials could authorize intelligence investigations based on "allegations or other information that an individual or a group may be engaged in activities which involve or will involve the use of force or violence and which involve or will involve the violation of federal law." Such "preliminary" investigations were to be limited to "verifying or refuting the allegations" and were to be confined to examining FBI files, public and government records, existing sources of information, or physical surveillance and interviews. In contrast, "full" investigations were to be based on "specific and articulable facts giving reason to believe that an individual or group is or may be engaged in activities which involve the use of force or violation of federal law." To address the oversight problem inherent in permitting noncriminal intelligence investigations, the Levi guidelines required

---

*In 2001 Congress extended this emergency exemption to seventy-two hours under provisions of the USA Patriot Act.

senior FBI officials to "periodically review the results of full investigations" and Justice Department officials "at least annually" to review the results of the FBI's "full" investigations and "determine in writing whether continued investigation is warranted."[44]

In a related action, far less restrictive guidelines were issued to govern FBI, CIA, and NSA counterintelligence investigations. President Ford's Executive Order 11905, issued on February 18, 1976, sought to "clarify the authority and responsibilities" of the intelligence agencies and to ensure that their "activities are conducted in a Constitutional and lawful manner and never aimed at our citizens." With the exception of an explicit prohibition of "political assassinations," Executive Order 11905 did not specifically ban intrusive or questionable tactics, such as those employed by the CIA and NSA under HTLINGUAL or MINARET. Furthermore Ford's order empowered the CIA to "conduct foreign counterintelligence activities . . . in the United States" but required the attorney general's approval if CIA officers were to wiretap or monitor American citizens traveling abroad. The order also permitted intelligence agency officials to use other investigative techniques directed at American citizens "reasonably believed to be acting on behalf of a foreign power." All intelligence activities authorized by the heads of the agencies had to be reviewed and approved by an Intelligence Oversight Board, whose members would be appointed by the president. Finally, executive branch officials and government contractors had to sign an agreement that they would not disclose information about "intelligence sources and methods."* (President Ford urged Congress to protect the secrecy of intelligence "sources and methods" by enacting legislation making it a "crime for a government employee who has access to certain highly classified information to reveal that information improperly.") In effect, Executive Order 11905 granted the intelligence agencies wide latitude

---

*This requirement would have prevented the future discovery of programs such as Operations SHAMROCK and MKULTRA.

to conduct operations approved by the White House and minimized the possibility of leaks to the media and Congress.[45]

Ford's order was issued before the public release of the Church Committee's final reports and the Senate's approval of a permanent Senate oversight committee. In the 1976 presidential campaign, Democratic nominee Jimmy Carter challenged Ford's relatively permissive standards. Following his election to the presidency, Carter issued his own Executive Order 12036 on January 24, 1978, in effect rescinding Ford's standards. His order, Carter said, would constitute "a basis for Congressional action on a charter to be written for the Intelligence Community."

Executive Order 12036 tightened administrative controls over the intelligence agencies and designated the CIA director as the "primary advisor to the president and the NSC on national foreign intelligence," with "full and exclusive authority" over the intelligence community's National Foreign Intelligence budget. Carter did not explicitly ban domestic surveillance activities but limited them to "agents of a foreign power." The CIA could "conduct counterintelligence activities within the United States," but only if coordinated with the FBI and approved by the attorney general. Carter reaffirmed Ford's ban on political assassinations, banned drug-testing programs, and empowered the NSA to collect and disseminate "signals intelligence information for counterintelligence purposes" and to investigate for "intelligence" purposes foreign residents, "foreign agents, and terrorists." The attorney general was empowered to ensure that any "intelligence activity within the United States directed against any United States person is conducted by the least intrusive means possible." Like President Ford, Carter also sought to curb unauthorized leaks to the media or Congress.[46] Although he intended it as a temporary measure, expecting that Congress would enact charter legislation, Carter's order proved to be a harbinger of a sharp reversal in the 1980s marked by a return to executive-defined policy.

8 | REAFFIRMATION OF THE NATIONAL SECURITY STATE, 1979–2005

■ THE CHURCH AND PIKE COMMITTEE investigations did not lead to fundamental changes in the status of the intelligence agencies. Congress never enacted their principal recommendation of charter legislation. This failure repeated Congress's inaction of 1924. Then, following a series of dramatic revelations of FBI abuses of power—the Palmer Raids of January 1920 and the investigation of senators who had demanded an inquiry into the Harding administration's handling of the Teapot Dome affair—Congress did nothing. Attorney General Harlan Fiske Stone imposed the sole restrictions designed to prevent future FBI abuses. His May 1924 executive order dissolved the GID, banned wiretapping, and confined FBI investigations to violations of federal law. Stone's restrictions, however, were later rescinded by President Roosevelt: first when in August 1936 he orally authorized FBI intelligence investigations, and then in May 1940 when he secretly authorized FBI "national defense" wiretapping.

In the immediate aftermath of the Church and Pike committee exposés, Congress appeared ready to enact a charter law. A consensus seemed to have emerged both within Congress and within the White House and the intelligence agencies that the agencies' authority should no longer be a matter of executive discretion but instead should be defined by statute. This apparent consensus, however, masked fundamental differences between liberals and conservatives over the nature of Congress's role and what presidents and intelligence agency officials would tolerate. Conservatives opposed strict legislative standards, preferring that presidents be granted wide latitude. Presidents Ford and Carter and senior CIA and FBI officials might have publicly endorsed the principle of charter legislation; but they did so while considering what was permissible and at the same time opposing well-defined restrictions. By 1980 FBI, CIA, and Carter administration officials had adopted a harder stance and would endorse very limited legislative changes: to reduce the burden of congressional oversight and curb leaks they claimed compromised the nation's security. Their specific legislative proposals included revising the Hughes-Ryan Act of 1974 to reduce from eight to two the number of congressional committees to whom presidents had to report authorized CIA covert operations; criminalizing the unauthorized disclosure of classified information (specifically identifying CIA agents' names); and exempting FBI and CIA records from the mandatory review and disclosure requirements of the Freedom of Information Act. This hardened position reflected a conviction that Congress had gone too far in its politics of exposure, thereby undermining legitimate security interests. Traditional conservatives and neoconservatives—notably Senators Barry Goldwater, Jake Garn, and Daniel Moynihan—forcefully endorsed this view.[1]

Differences over the content of appropriate charter law were never resolved. Instead Congress abandoned any effort to strike the balance that Senator Birch Bayh had articulated in opening hearings on charter legislation in 1980, "of giving our intelligence system what it needs to work with and also seeing that the temptation to direct this sophisticated intelligence-gathering operation against our own citizens is not there, that it is directed against our adversaries."[2] This attempt at balance fell victim to a political shift, reflected in Ronald Reagan's election to the presidency in 1980.

During his campaign in 1980, Reagan decried President Jimmy Carter's foreign and military policies as weak and as too accommodating toward the Soviet Union. Calling for a more militant anti-Soviet approach, the Republican nominee demanded substantial increases in defense spending to close a "window of vulnerability." He also wanted to "unleash" the intelligence agencies. The restrictions that had been imposed on the agencies in the wake of the Church and Pike committee hearings, Reagan charged, had damaged the nation's ability to anticipate, and thus be in a position to counter, potential threats to the nation's security. His complaints captured a new belief that these limits had emboldened Iranian militants to seize the U.S. embassy in Teheran and the Soviet Union to invade Afghanistan. After his election to the presidency, Reagan moved quickly to act on these criticisms.

In one of his first steps, on March 26, 1981, President Reagan pardoned former FBI assistant directors W. Mark Felt and Edward Miller, who had been convicted in November 1980 of having authorized illegal break-ins during an FBI investigation of radical activists. Reagan's action in pardoning these senior FBI officials symbolized his intent to pursue a more aggressive intelligence approach, one based on the expansion of agency powers with minimum safeguards against abuses of power. In December the president issued Executive Order 12333, rescinding President Carter's restrictive intelligence guidelines of January 1978. Under the new order, the CIA could conduct covert operations "unless the President determines that another agency is more likely to achieve a particular objective." It could also conduct "administrative and support activities," and "counterintelligence activities within the United States, in coordination with the Bureau, as required by procedures agreed upon by the Director of Central Intelligence and the Attorney General." The phrase "conduct of" that recurs throughout Reagan's 1981 order replaced what had been the key operative phrase of Carter's order: "restrictions on." The FBI, in addition, was empowered to "conduct" investigations "within the United States" to "collect foreign intelligence and to support foreign intelligence requirements." Reagan's order moreover did not require that proposed programs or procedures be reviewed by the attorney general to ensure that First Amendment rights or federal laws would not be violated.[3]

Meanwhile the Reagan administration successfully lobbied Congress to enact laws to minimize the possible disclosure of questionable CIA operations. It succeeded in part, first in June 1982 when Congress enacted the Intelligence Identities Protection Act, which criminalized the intentional, unauthorized disclosure of the names of undercover CIA officers; then in October 1984 when Congress enacted the CIA Information Act to exempt CIA "operational files" from the mandatory review and disclosure requirements of the Freedom of Information Act; and further in October 1986 when Congress amended the Freedom of Information Act to withhold information that might compromise ongoing FBI investigations. In addition, FBI agents processing an FOIA request could deny that any records existed pertaining to an ongoing investigation.[4]

The Reagan administration's efforts to promote greater secrecy, however, were not totally successful. Adverse reaction to Executive Order 12333 and to the president's proposal to exempt all FBI and CIA records from the Freedom of Information Act (leading to the more modest exemptions of the 1984 and 1986 acts) caused administration officials to proceed more cautiously before proposing further changes in the rules governing FBI intelligence investigations. Eventually, on March 7, 1983, Reagan's attorney general, William French Smith, announced new FBI "domestic security/terrorism" guidelines. The Levi guidelines' stringent "probable cause" requirement was rescinded. FBI officials could now "anticipate or prevent crime" and "initiate investigations in advance of criminal conduct." "Domestic security/terrorism" investigations could be started "when facts and circumstances reasonably indicate that two or more persons are engaged in an enterprise for the purpose of furthering political or social goals wholly or in part through activities that involve force or violence and a violation of the laws of the United States," with the "longer range objective of detection, prevention, and prosecution." Such investigations could be initiated simply on "statements advocating criminal activity or indicate an apparent intent to engage in crime." Of equal importance, "domestic security/terrorism" investigations would no longer be subject to the close supervision and written authorization of senior Justice Department officials. Instead senior FBI officials would have broad authority to initiate and continue such noncriminal investigations, their only obligation being to "notify the [Justice Department's] Office of Intelligence Policy and Review" at an unspecified time that they had begun a domestic security/terrorism investigation. The attorney general's supervisory responsibility was also watered down: he "may, as he deems necessary, request the FBI to provide a report on the status of the investigation."

The purpose of the new guidelines, Attorney General Smith announced, was to "clarify the scope" of the FBI's domestic security/terrorism investigations. Changes were needed, he emphasized, to "ensure protection of the public from the greater sophistication and changing nature of domestic groups that are prone to violence." Smith nonetheless claimed that the guidelines would "adequately protect lawful and peaceful political dissent." "Foreign intelligence, foreign counterintelligence and international terrorism matters," however, would be covered by separate classified guidelines.[5]

The vague language of both Executive Order 12333 and the Smith guidelines—including Smith's admission that rules for "international terrorism" investigations would be secret—left unresolved the scope of permissible FBI and CIA domestic operations and how the two agencies would coordinate their "foreign intelligence" and "terrorism" investigations. Because relevant records remain classified, it is impossible to evaluate the scope of such investigations and the FBI-CIA relationship, since by their nature intelligence investigations would not result in prosecution.

Nonetheless the instances when FBI intelligence investigations became known suggest that they had been ideologically based. Some of the records confirming this motive were released in response to Freedom of Information Act requests because the investigations had been closed and thus could not be withheld or their existence denied under the 1986 statute. The released records confirm that at minimum FBI intelligence investigations targeted the "nuclear freeze" movement; anti-nuclear groups such as Veterans Fast for Life and Silo Plowshares; the militant gay organization ACT-UP; and library patrons under the FBI's Library Awareness Program.* Further disclosures—in these cases because indictments had been obtained—confirmed that other FBI targets included militant white supremacist, survivalist, militia, anti–gun control, and anti-abortion movements, such as The Order, Freemen, and Operation Rescue. The most controversial of the known FBI "domestic security/terrorism" investigations involved the Committee in Solidarity with the People of El Salvador (CISPES).[6]

CISPES had been formed in 1981 to rally public opposition to the Reagan administration's Central American policies. Its principal support came from liberal religious activists (influenced by the tenets of Liberation Theology) and radical political, student, and labor union activists. In 1981 an FBI "terrorist" investigation of CISPES was launched, prompted by the unsupported alle-

---

*This program was established in the 1960s but was discontinued in the 1980s when its existence was revealed by librarians at research institutions who publicly protested FBI demands that they identify patrons of Eastern European descent seeking access to the library's nonclassified holdings of scientific literature.

gations of an informer who claimed that the organization was aligned with El Salvadoran rebels. This investigation expanded after 1983 and moved beyond CISPES chapters to include eighteen college student groups; branches of the United Automobile Workers and the National Education Association unions; nuns associated with two religious orders, the Maryknoll Sisters and the Sisters of Mercy; members of the Women's Rape Center in Norfolk, Virginia, and of the Southern Christian Leadership Conference; and religious and lay people active in the Sanctuary movement. This "terrorist" investigation, moreover, seemingly repeated the FBI's earlier investigations of "subversive" activities. Indeed, its reports confirmed that FBI agents had concentrated on political activists. One agent identified activists "actually involved in demonstrations, marches, etc., regarding US intervention in Central America"; another characterized the writing of a CISPES minister as evidence of a "mind totally sold on the Marxist Leninist ideology"; and yet another contended that it was "imperative at this time to formulate some plan of attack against CISPES and specifically against individuals . . . who defiantly display their contempt for the US government by making speeches and propagandizing their cause."[7]

The Smith guidelines' recaptioning of FBI intelligence investigations—from Levi's "domestic security" to "domestic security/terrorism"—captures the broader purpose of FBI investigations in the 1980s. This same expanded concern made counterterrorism a relatively more important CIA priority, though Soviet and Communist-directed espionage and expansionism remained the agency's major occupation. In contrast to the 1990s, however, CIA officials perceived this new international terrorist threat to be centered in the Middle East, involving attacks on U.S. personnel and facilities overseas and perpetrated by militant Egyptian Islamist movements, radical Palestinian activists, and the Libyan and Iranian governments' funding of organizations such as Hezbollah and Hamas. Attention to these groups corresponded to the location and character of the decade's terrorist incidents, rang-ing from the kidnapping by Hezbollah of U.S. citizens in Lebanon, including a CIA station chief; the bombings by Libyans of a Berlin discotheque—resulting in the deaths of five American soldiers and the wounding of another fifty—and of the Rome and Vienna air-ports; the hijacking by Palestinians of the cruise ship *Achille Lauro*; and the assassination by Egyptian Muslims of Egyptian president Anwar Sadat. To counter this increasingly serious threat, CIA officials in 1986 established a special Counterterrorist Center to coordinate operations within the CIA and among all U.S. intel-ligence agencies. In fact the new center did not lead to a more cen-tralized counterterrorist response, but it did improve FBI-CIA li-aison and in specific cases made coordinated operations possible.

Ironically, the most centralized and tightly coordinated of the Reagan administration's counterterrorist operations proved to be the most controversial: the so-called Iran-contra affair of 1985–1986. The principal objective of this covert operation was to secure the release of American citizens held hostage in Lebanon by Hezbollah through the sale of TOW missiles to Iran. An ancillary purpose was to improve U.S. relations with Iran by promoting the influence of Iranian moderates. The operation took a further turn as National Security Council officials diverted the surplus funds from the arms sales to Nicaraguan rebels—contras—seeking to overthrow the leftist Sandinista government of Nicaragua.

Normally the CIA would have conducted this covert opera-tion, but in this case members of the Reagan administration's NSC staff assumed control. The decision to rely on the NSC was due less to bureaucratic infighting than to the administration's in-terest in ensuring the secrecy of the operation given its potentially explosive domestic ramifications.* In further efforts to preclude

---

*This covert operation violated provisions of the 1984 Boland Amendment (the diversion of funds to the contras) and the Arms Export Control Act (by not reporting foreign arms sales exceeding $10,000).

discovery, the requirement of the Intelligence Oversight Act of 1980—that major covert operations advancing the nation's security must be reported to the House and Senate intelligence committees by the president—was purposely circumvented while NSC officials devised a special Do Not Log procedure.* Intended to ensure the undiscoverable destruction of sensitive communications, Do Not Log records were not indexed in the NSA's central records system.

This fail-safe system unexpectedly broke down with the publication of an article in an obscure Lebanese journal reporting that the Reagan administration had sold arms to Iran. The revelation brought an internal inquiry by the Justice Department and then the establishment of a joint congressional investigative committee. NSC officials quickly acted to neutralize this potential threat when NSC aide Colonel Oliver North destroyed the Do Not Log records. But North's ignorance that the NSC computer system maintained a backup memory to prevent the inadvertent destruction of records subsequently enabled congressional investigators to reconstruct many of the documents North had destroyed.[9]

The CIA's renewed counterintelligence emphasis was not affected by the collapse of Communist governments in Eastern Europe and the Balkans and then the dissolution of the Soviet Union itself in the years 1989–1991. But the end of the cold war did

---

*CIA officials also devised special records procedures to mask their involvement in the Iran-contra affair. For example, the communications of Duane Clarridge, who headed the agency's European Division, relating to the shipment of arms were sent through "privacy channels"—a special procedure to permit the temporary retention of records until the reported information was no longer needed and then destroyed. Clarridge's original copies of these communications, however, were maintained in a "shadow file" in his secretary's desk. Then, when the Iran-contra affair was publicly compromised in 1986, triggering investigations by a joint congressional committee and the independent counsel, Clarridge ordered the secretary to destroy this file. His action, however, was uncovered by the independent counsel staff during its investigation of the Iran-contra affair.[8]

usher in a more skeptical view of the CIA by many members of Congress—notably Senator Daniel Moynihan—and political elites who sharply criticized continuing secrecy policies.[10] CIA officials responded by releasing formerly classified records—especially the VENONA project—to confirm the contributions and continued importance of intelligence and counterintelligence operations. Furthermore, until the 1990s FBI and CIA counterintelligence efforts continued to focus on Soviet espionage initiatives. Nonetheless publicized disclosures of CIA counterintelligence operations prompted a critical examination of the agency's competence and its failure to cooperate fully with the FBI.

The CIA's counterintelligence deficiencies were first brought to light in the Edward Lee Howard case. A former Peace Corps volunteer and then an Agency for International Development employee, Howard in the fall of 1980 applied to become a CIA officer. His overseas and managerial experiences and academic training in international economics seemed to make him a valued recruit. He was accepted as a probationary officer in 1981 and underwent vigorous training in counterintelligence surveillance and interrogation techniques in preparation for an assignment to the CIA's sensitive Moscow station. Before this posting Howard had been briefed about the agency's Soviet assets—but only their code names—and communication methods. CIA officials, however, reconsidered the Moscow assignment in 1983 after again subjecting Howard to polygraph testing and psychological evaluation. He had admitted to abusing drugs and alcohol, even after his appointment in 1981, and had given deceptive responses to polygraph questions. Rather than assign him to other, less sensitive duties, CIA officials demanded his resignation.

Bitter over this rejection, Howard eventually obtained employment as an economic analyst for the New Mexico legislature. Then, in 1984, motivated by a desire for revenge, he flew to Austria where he met with Soviet intelligence officials. Capitalizing on his knowledge of CIA operations, Howard identified two Soviet intelligence agents whom the CIA had recruited as double agents, and described CIA "technical operations" in Moscow.

CIA officials first learned of Howard's espionage activities in August 1985 as the result of the defection of a high-level Soviet intelligence officer, Vitaly Yurchenko. In debriefing Yurchenko, CIA and FBI agents asked the defector if he could identify any American intelligence agent who had been recruited by the KGB. Yurchenko thereupon cited a "former CIA officer" whom the Russians had code-named "Mr. Robert," and described him as having been "pipelined for assignment to Moscow but fired for unsuitability issues and polygraph problems in 1983–1984."* Yurchenko then recounted "Robert's" specific assistance to the Soviets.

For CIA officials, Yurchenko's disclosure was potentially embarrassing, highlighting a major deficiency in CIA counterintelligence operations. As a disgruntled but knowledgeable CIA officer, Howard was in a position to provide critical intelligence to the Soviets that could undermine CIA operations. CIA officials nonetheless had failed to anticipate this possibility when they fired a trainee who possessed sensitive information about the agency's methods and assets. They compounded matters by not immediately alerting their FBI counterparts to the possibility that Howard might become a spy. At first they had no reason to suspect this would happen, but they never alerted the FBI even after learning of one of Howard's bizarre phone calls to the agency's Moscow station and his admission to a CIA officer that in 1983 he had contemplated approaching the Soviet embassy in Washington. Their withholding of information about Howard continued even after CIA officers recognized, during their joint debriefing of Yurchenko with the FBI, that "Robert" was Howard. They delayed for five days before advising their FBI counterparts about this conclusion—a delay that proved to be critical. In the interim,

---

*Yurchenko also identified an NSA employee, Ronald Pelton, as another Soviet recruit.

Howard flew to Vienna to contact Soviet officials. The Howard case turned into an even greater fiasco when Howard, upon his return to New Mexico, learned from another former CIA officer, William Bosch, about the FBI's interest in him; Howard then evaded FBI surveillance in September 1985, fleeing the United States to defect to the Soviet Union.[11]

The Howard case underlined CIA officials' reluctance to share with the FBI information about their employees. Since 1947, and reaffirmed in the 1954 Dulles-Hoover agreement, CIA officials had preferred to operate independently because they were confident they could keep matters under control. In this case, moreover, they did not immediately inform the FBI that Howard was "Robert" out of embarrassment over their failure to have earlier alerted the bureau that Howard might be a security risk.

This unwillingness to share information about the agency's personnel was repeated in the case of a second CIA defector, Aldrich Ames. In contrast to Howard, Ames was a twenty-five-year CIA officer who had held highly sensitive positions and had access to some of the agency's best-kept secrets. He had first obtained summer employment with the CIA while attending high school and college and then, after flunking out of the University of Chicago, was employed as a CIA clerk-typist while enrolled as a part-time student at George Washington University. He received a bachelor's degree in history in 1967 and two years later was appointed a CIA officer and assigned to Turkey. Recalled to CIA headquarters, he received training in Russian and in 1972 was assigned to the agency's New York office as a Soviet counterintelligence officer. Because of his expertise as a Soviet analyst, he was promoted in 1983 to head the counterintelligence branch in the agency's Soviet division and then, in 1986, was posted to the Rome station as a supervisor of intelligence operations against the Soviets. Returning to CIA headquarters in 1989, he held a variety of high-level counterintelligence appointments until being transferred in 1991 to the Counternarcotics Center.

Bored with his CIA career, a disillusioned Ames decided to sell CIA secrets to the Soviets. His principal motivation was to support his second wife's extravagant lifestyle. Paid $50,000 for his first delivery, he thereafter, during approximately nine years from April 1985 through February 1994, assiduously sought information about CIA counterintelligence operations and the identities of Soviet personnel whom the CIA had recruited as double agents. Eventually he sold thousands of records relating to CIA and FBI counterintelligence operations and identified at least ten double agents, for which he was richly rewarded—$2.5 million directly, with an additional $2 million deposited in foreign bank accounts. Ames recklessly spent this money on expensive cars and a luxurious house.

Ames's espionage activities began at a critical time for the CIA. Agency officials had already been embarrassed by Howard's defection in 1985. Over the next two years some twenty Soviet intelligence officers whom the agency had recruited "disappeared," suggesting that the Soviets had infiltrated the agency. CIA officials thereupon attempted to address deficiencies in the agency's counterintelligence operations. In 1988 a Counterintelligence Center was established to replace the more insular counterintelligence division. More important, on June 7, 1988, CIA director William Webster and FBI director William Sessions concluded a Memorandum of Understanding. Under its terms, the FBI would be notified in a "timely" manner whenever CIA officials had a "reasonable belief" that a current or former employee might consider "espionage, defection, or other compromise of classified information" or had an "unauthorized contact" with a foreign intelligence service. FBI officials would in turn notify their CIA counterparts "when the FBI independently develops information concerning a CIA officer or employee that may be of counterintelligence . . . significance to the agency."

These administrative changes did not prompt CIA officials to seek immediate FBI assistance regarding a possible spy in their ranks, despite having long suspected that the Soviets had turned a CIA officer. Ames in fact had escaped their attention despite his extravagant spending habits—exceeding his salary as a CIA officer—sloppy work routines, excessive drinking, and access to highly sensitive CIA records. Ames passed a lie detector test in 1986, before his posting to Rome. This success temporarily diverted attention that he might be the suspected mole. In addition, KGB officials acted to divert attention from Ames and toward two military employees stationed in the U.S. embassy in Moscow, Clayton Lonetree and Arnold Bracy. This Soviet diversionary tactic succeeded; for a time CIA officials concluded that the arrests of Lonetree and Bracy had resolved the security problem. By 1991, however, the suspicions of CIA counterintelligence officers led them to give Ames a second lie detector test, which he again passed. CIA officials in June 1991 now sought direct FBI assistance to identify the mole and delayed briefing the FBI until January 1993. An immediate FBI investigation was launched, which included wiretapping Ames and monitoring his computer, searching his trash, and tailing him and his wife. The FBI's investigation culminated with Ames's arrest on February 21, 1994, and his conviction on charges of Soviet espionage.[12]

CIA officials' handling of the Ames case and their delay in seeking FBI assistance provoked two administrative and legislative initiatives. First, in May 1994, President Clinton issued Presidential Decision Directive 24 to create a special inter-agency group to coordinate counterintelligence operations. Headquartered in the CIA's Counterterrorist Center, the group would be headed by an FBI agent. Congress supplemented this administrative change with the Intelligence Authorization Act of 1995. CIA officials were required under a section of this act to inform the FBI immediately whenever they suspected that any classified information had been compromised. FBI agents would have to be granted access to any CIA employee or file they deemed necessary.[13]

This simplistic assumption—that coordination could be mandated*—reflected a lack of appreciation for a more complex reality. CIA and FBI officials were never parochial bureaucrats committed to sustaining their own authority at the expense of the nation's security. Their actions in the Howard and Ames cases were based on a national security mind-set, one that had long defined their actions, dating from the creation of the CIA in 1947. Having for decades operated in secret, CIA officials were confident of their own abilities but, just as important, were committed to minimizing discovery of their controversial actions. The CIA's HTLINGUAL project provides insights into this mode of operation.

When CIA officials instituted the HTLINGUAL mail-opening project in the 1950s, they willingly broke the law and at the same time decided not to seek FBI assistance. Their purpose was to minimize the chance that their actions could be discovered. Their concern for secrecy led them to ensure that no one outside the agency—whether the Post Office, the FBI, or the White House—could learn of their actions. Then, when they decided in 1958 to share the intercepted letters with the FBI, CIA officials demanded that the FBI recipients adopt safeguards to prevent public discovery of their actions. This concern also influenced the CIA Inspector General's review of HTLINGUAL in 1961 and 1969 out of concern over its "flap potential." These officials decided to continue this program because they were confident that it could not be discovered; they ultimately reversed course in 1973 and only because they concluded that its secrecy could no longer be assured. CIA actions in the Howard and Ames cases reflected this same

*Both the Joint Committee and the Kean Commission repeated this response in 2002–2004 when recommending the creation of a national intelligence director who would report to the president. The purpose again was to ensure better cooperation between the FBI and the CIA. Congress adopted this recommendation in December 2004 in the Intelligence Reform and Terrorism Prevention Act.

conviction—that CIA officials could and should act alone. The sole difference in the Howard case was that when first confronted by their own failure in 1985, CIA officials (like other bureaucrats and politicians, including presidents) considered a cover-up.

In any event, the administrative reforms that were instituted to ensure better FBI-CIA cooperation after the Howard and Ames cases proved irrelevant in confronting an even more serious espionage threat—the activities of FBI counterintelligence agent Robert Hanssen. Hanssen had joined the FBI in 1976 and was assigned to investigate cases of white-collar crime. In 1979 he was transferred to the New York office's counterintelligence squad and, with the exception of brief stints in the inspection division and as FBI liaison to the State Department, thereafter held sensitive counterintelligence positions in the New York office and at FBI headquarters. Almost concurrent with his assignment to the New York office's counterintelligence squad in 1979, and off and on until his arrest in February 2001, Hanssen periodically delivered to the Soviet Union (and then to the Russian Federation) more than six thousand pages of records pertaining to FBI, CIA, and NSA counterintelligence operations. He also identified fifty Soviet agents whom the FBI and CIA had recruited as double agents. As in Ames's case, Hanssen's motivation was primarily mercenary. Over his twenty-two-year espionage career, he received $600,000 in cash and diamonds with an additional $800,000 deposited in a Moscow bank account.

Ironically, Hanssen's espionage activities had coincided with the start of a joint FBI-CIA counterintelligence operation to uncover a suspected "mole" within the ranks of the U.S. intelligence community. Agency officials had concluded, first following Howard's defection and then following Ames's arrest, that another mole had been recruited, given the continuing disappearance of some of their more productive double agents. Nonetheless, despite the intensity of the FBI's and CIA's joint operations, this suspected mole escaped discovery. Before Hanssen's arrest, in fact, the FBI's prime suspect was CIA officer Brian Kelly. Subjected to intrusive surveillance—including wiretapping and bugging of his office and home, monitoring of his movements, and searches of his computer—Kelly had been vigorously interrogated and, when he refused to admit his guilt, was suspended. The suspension was lifted only after Hanssen's arrest in February 2001.

The Hanssen case indirectly points up the inherent limitations of anticipating the operations of spies or terrorists. Hanssen himself was a highly trained counterintelligence officer who used that knowledge to avert discovery of his espionage activities. Thus he never revealed his name or employment status to his Soviet handlers, and thereby reduced the risk that he could be compromised by a Soviet defector. He wrote to Soviet officials at their home address and avoided personal meetings, knowing that FBI agents monitored the Soviet embassy. Hanssen moreover betrayed two U.S.-recruited double agents to the Soviets who might have called attention to himself had they defected. And although he was paid in cash and diamonds for his espionage activities, he sustained a frugal lifestyle. His reputation as a reclusive, hardworking technical expert and a conservative Catholic deflected attention while he cultivated the trust of his peers in FBI counterintelligence through his reputation as a helpful computer expert.

Hanssen was apprehended not because of the coordinated efforts of FBI and CIA counterintelligence agents but because of good luck. In 2000 a former KGB officer defected and gave to the CIA, in return for a $7 million payment and assistance in his relocation in the United States, the KGB's file on Hanssen, which he had somehow been able to steal from KGB archives. Hanssen was not identified by name in the file. Nonetheless it contained a tape of one of Hanssen's telephone conversations with his Soviet handler and a bag that he had used to deliver a batch of documents. These contents enabled FBI agents to identify Hanssen as the mole through fingerprints lifted from the bag and through his voice on the tape. Agents confirmed his disloyalty by closely monitoring his movements, wiretapping his office, and searching his computer. Hanssen was finally apprehended in February 2001 through an FBI sting operation.[14]

Hanssen's espionage activities had continued after the collapse of the Soviet Union in 1991 and the formal end of the cold war, confirming the importance of continued FBI and CIA counterintelligence operations. But by the late 1990s FBI and CIA counterintelligence operations also began to concentrate on an ultimately more serious domestic and international threat: terrorism.

Beginning in the 1980s FBI officials had become increasingly concerned about a new internal security threat posed by militant right-wing nationalists with strong anti-government views, whether because of their opposition to gun control, abortion, racial equality, or international organizations. A second concern was the militant anti-American sentiments of Islamic fundamentalists—recent immigrants or alien residents—who opposed corrupt authoritarian governments in the Middle East and Israel. These militant Islamists in time shifted their terrorist planning in the 1990s to target U.S. institutions.

FBI counterterrorist operations at first concentrated on the followers of Sheik Omar Abdel Rahman, a bitter critic of the Egyptian government of Hosni Mubarak and of that government's policy of accommodation with Israel. By the mid-1990s, however, FBI attentions also turned to a second leader, Saudi expatriate Osama bin Laden. Bin Laden and his jihadist supporters in Al Qaeda actively opposed the Soviet invasion of Afghanistan, then the Serbian persecution of Bosnian Muslims and the Russian persecution of Chechnyan Muslims. By the mid-1990s they began to target U.S. personnel and facilities.

The emergence of groups willing to resort to violence was confirmed by a series of unanticipated attacks launched in the 1990s. The first involved the truck bombing of the World Trade Center in New York in February 1993, resulting in six deaths and the wounding of one thousand. FBI agents were able to identify and secure the conviction of four Arab residents in New Jersey, who they learned had attended the Jersey City mosque of Sheik Rahman.* The four were apprehended through an FBI investigation that traced the vehicle identification number of the rental truck that had been used to convey the explosives, but also as a result of the ineptness of one of the participants who had attempted to collect his deposit fee from the rental agency, claiming that the truck had been stolen.

The World Trade Center truck bombing led FBI agents to focus on Sheik Rahman and Islamist militants influenced by his sermons. Alerted to the possibility of future terrorist attacks, FBI agents that year successfully recruited an informer, Emad Salam, who through his success in infiltrating another group of militants alerted FBI agents to a second planned terrorist operation: the bombing of the United Nations building, a federal office in New York, the George Washington Bridge, and the Lincoln and Holland tunnels. Eleven conspirators, including Sheik Rahman, were arrested in June 1993, before they could launch their planned terrorist operation.

FBI agents had not anticipated the 1993 World Trade Center truck bombing. Nor had they anticipated another terrorist attack in April 1995 when Timothy McVeigh, a former soldier attracted to the right-wing militia movement, detonated a rental truck containing a 4,800-pound bomb outside the Albert Murrah Federal Building in Oklahoma City, Oklahoma. FBI agents identified McVeigh as the bomber and his friend Terry Nichols as a co-conspirator in planning this terrorist operation. They did so through the identification VIN of the rental truck that had been used to convey the bomb, through an intensive investigation that traced McVeigh's and Nichols's purchase of bomb components,

---

*Two years later two other militants were arrested, one who had fled to Egypt and the second who had been in jail at the time.

and by pressuring McVeigh's and Nichols's friends to testify about the discussions leading to their attack.

These terrorist assaults within the United States were accompanied by a series of overseas incidents. The first involved a truck bombing in June 1996 at the Khobar Towers, a military barracks housing U.S. airmen stationed in Dhahran, Saudi Arabia. Other truck bombings occurred in August 1998 on U.S. embassies in Kenya and Tanzania; and the *USS Cole*, a navy destroyer, was bombed in October 2000 when it was moored in the harbor at Aden in Yemen. CIA and FBI officials later concluded that the 1998 and 2000 operations had been orchestrated and funded by Al Qaeda.

With the exception of the June 1993 arrests of Sheik Rahman and the other conspirators, none of these terrorist operations had been anticipated. They nonetheless refocused both CIA and FBI counterintelligence operations. As a direct result of the two New York terrorist plots (one executed, the second aborted), FBI officials in 1994 established a special Radical Fundamentalist Unit in the New York office. The discovery of the plans of militant Islamists in the United States and their contacts in the Middle East, illustrated by the Khobar Towers attack, led FBI officials in 1996 to establish a Counterterrorism Center at FBI headquarters and Joint Terrorism Task Forces in thirty-five field offices. Finally, the linking of bin Laden and Al Qaeda with the terrorist attacks on U.S. embassies in Kenya and Tanzania led to the 1999 establishment of a special Usama bin Ladin Unit in New York City to coordinate FBI counterterrorism investigations. This new priority was further reflected in the sharp increase in the FBI's counterintelligence budget, from $118 million in 1993 to $423 million in 2001. By that year the number of FBI agents assigned to counterterrorist investigations reached thirteen hundred. This new focus on terrorism moreover led FBI officials in 1999 to sever counterintelligence from counterterrorism operations with the creation of separate divisions.

Meanwhile CIA officials in 1996 established a special unit to analyze intelligence and plan objectives directed at containing bin Laden and his Al Qaeda network. This concern about the Al Qaeda threat intensified in response to a *fatwa* that bin Laden issued in 1996 and again in 1998, identifying the United States as the enemy of Islam and advocating the use of violence to evict U.S. troops from Saudi Arabia, where they were stationed in the aftermath of the 1991 Gulf War. To counter this international threat, President Clinton issued Presidential Decision Directives 39 (in 1995) and 62 (in 1998). The CIA was authorized to undertake "an aggressive program of foreign intelligence collection, analysis, counterintelligence, and covert action" while the National Security Council was assigned the responsibility to coordinate all domestic and international counterterrorism operations.

President Clinton's administrative changes fundamentally realigned FBI and CIA counterterrorist operations with an increased effort at coordination. CIA officials sought to limit Al Qaeda's funding and formulated plans to capture bin Laden and dismember the Al Qaeda network. These efforts included the attempted recruitment of Afghan tribal leaders to capture bin Laden and then to identify the specific locations of Al Qaeda training camps. Based on this intelligence, the United States launched cruise missile and drone attacks in Afghanistan. But these various plots to kill bin Laden and curb future Al Qaeda operations failed.[15]

These joint initiatives, however, did not lead FBI and CIA officials to anticipate the 9/11 terrorist attack. In their immediate post-9/11 responses, the Bush administration and congressional leaders attributed this intelligence failure to three factors, not all of them consistent: that FBI officials had been denied sufficient legal authority; that FBI personnel had been prisoners of a law-enforcement mind-set that deterred them from adopting more aggressive, proactive measures; or that FBI and CIA officials had not fully cooperated with each other.

The Bush administration quickly introduced legislation to expand federal surveillance powers. The implicit rationale was that such expansion could avert future terrorist attacks. Indeed, in lobbying Congress to authorize "roving" wiretaps, Attorney General John Ashcroft lamented that "It is easier to investigate someone in illegal gambling schemes than it is to investigate someone involved in terrorism."

Members of the House and Senate did resist some of the administration's sweeping demands, but Congress approved a complex and massive bill, the USA Patriot Act. The act authorized roving wiretaps—the monitoring of a suspect's telephone and computer communications, no matter where they occurred (this would permit the monitoring of an individual who switched cell phones); revised the standards governing "foreign intelligence" electronic interceptions—from a "direct" to a "significant" connection to a foreign power or movement; authorized federal agents when investigating individuals suspected of "harboring" or "supporting" terrorists to enter homes without first obtaining a search warrant, or to obtain secret access, again without a search warrant, to records of internet providers, credit card companies, libraries, bookstores, or indeed any business; authorized the detention for seven days and then the deportation of suspected terrorists without having to specify charges or present evidence justifying the detention; authorized the intelligence agencies to share information, including information obtained from grand juries; and authorized a suspension of banking ties to institutions that refused to assist U.S. law-enforcement agents. The Patriot Act, however, contained a series of so-called sunset provisions for some of these procedures, which would terminate unless Congress renewed them in five years. In 2006 Congress made them permanent.[16]

Although the Bush administration had asked Congress to permit the wiretapping of individuals having only a "significant" connection with foreign governments or movements, and to extend the emergency exemption from twenty-four to seventy-two hours, it did not seek changes in the requirement for prior court approval. Instead, in October 2001 President Bush secretly authorized the NSA to intercept international* internet and phone conversations of suspected terrorists without review and approval by a special court. The subsequent operation also involved the backdoor assistance of the major telephone companies, which agreed to provide millions of telephone records to be used in "pattern analysis." Presumably this would enable NSA analysts to identify individuals who might communicate with terrorist groups overseas. NSA was not authorized, however, to intercept purely domestic telephone and e-mail communications. President Bush had concluded that this would provoke intense public opposition should it become known. Nonetheless an allegedly small number of strictly domestic communications *were* intercepted. This was ostensibly accidental because of technical glitches that made it impossible for NSA to know that a communication was not international.[17]

While expanding surveillance, Bush administration officials also sought to foreclose any investigation into the FBI's failure to anticipate the 9/11 attack. They did so by announcing "a wartime reorganization and mobilization" of FBI operations to include a "comprehensive review" of the guidelines governing FBI counterterrorism operations.

Attorney General Ashcroft, at a joint press conference with FBI director Robert Mueller III, announced the results of this inquiry in releasing new FBI counterterrorist guidelines. The locus of FBI counterterrorist investigations, he explained, would be shifted from FBI headquarters to FBI field offices. In addition, "new priorities" and "new resources" were being instituted to put "prevention above all else" and change the FBI's "culture" from a "reactive to proactive orientation."

---

*That is, where at least one part of the communication involved a foreign terminal.

Ashcroft's guidelines, however, did not match these bold pronouncements. In essence, they reaffirmed the 1983 Smith guidelines—requiring agents to be "vigilant in detecting terrorist activities to the full extent permitted by law, with an eye toward early intervention and prosecution of acts of terrorism before they occur." Current wiretapping and undercover operations authority was not changed; indeed, the sole substantive changes permitted agents to "visit any place and attend any event open to the public" (demonstrations, meetings, religious services or meetings at mosques or churches) and to allow "online searches and accessing online sites." In response to these pressures to act more aggressively and to monitor public activities, FBI agents soon demanded records from car dealers, travel agents, pawnbrokers, and even the Social Security Administration and the Internal Revenue Service.[18]

The crisis atmosphere created by the 9/11 attack and the consequent attempt to change the FBI's culture and expand its surveillance authority misrepresented a far different reality. Since 1936 FBI agents had conducted proactive intelligence investigations with the objective of anticipating crime. Since the early 1940s, moreover, FBI agents had used illegal investigative techniques, though FBI officials had devised special records procedures to avert discovery of their actions. Nor had FBI investigations been circumvented by legal or constitutional prohibitions. In contrast to the 1940s, FBI agents in the 1990s had broad legal powers to wiretap or bug, through the Crime Control Act of 1968 and the Foreign Intelligence Surveillance Act of 1978. And in the aftermath of the Oklahoma City bombing of April 1995, Congress had given FBI agents broad powers in the 1996 Antiterrorism and Effective Death Penalty Act. That act criminalized "material support" of terrorism—vague language that would permit investigations of individuals who might only have given money to organizations that administration officials identified as terrorist or who simply attended terrorist training camps. It is revealing that the only terrorist cases the Bush administration brought after 9/11 involved indictments based on the 1996 act's "material support" section. Whether in the 1940s against espionage or in 2001 against terrorism, FBI agents had failed to anticipate crime.

Well before the 9/11 attack and the issuance of the Ashcroft guidelines, FBI agents had already been intensively monitoring individuals whom they suspected as would-be terrorists. None of these investigations led to the discovery of individuals who actually intended to engage in terrorism. Nonetheless these inquiries highlight the main reason for the FBI's failure to apprehend the 9/11 terrorists—not that FBI agents lacked sufficient authority but that they were unable to identify all individuals who *might* engage in terrorism.

The President's Daily Brief of August 6, 2001, indirectly confirms this. Captioned "Bin Ladin Determined to Strike in US," this brief's final paragraph reported that "The FBI is currently conducting approximately 70 full field investigations throughout the US that it considers Bin Ladin-related," and more specifically that "a group of Bin Ladin supporters was [in May] in the US planning attacks with explosives."[19] But not one of the 70 "full field investigations" involved any of the 9/11 terrorists. FBI agents, as it turns out, were monitoring the wrong individuals.

FBI agents' inability to identify real terrorists is further confirmed by the post-9/11 actions of the agents assigned to the FBI's counterterrorist squads. Before the 9/11 attack, FBI counterterrorist agents had hesitated to seek the court's approval to wiretap individuals who they suspected were Al Qaeda sympathizers. They had been unable to develop evidence of a "direct" connection with a foreign government or terrorist movement, as would be required for court approval. After 9/11, however, these agents exploited the crisis atmosphere to seek the court's approval to wiretap these suspects. But the wiretaps uncovered no information that the targeted individuals had advance knowledge or had assisted the 9/11 terrorists. Instead FBI agents simply learned that these militant Islamists were, in the words of *New York Times* reporters Neil Lewis and David Johnston, "overheard celebrating the attacks on the World Trade Center and the Pentagon" and that their conversations were "congratulatory, even gloating."[20]

FBI counterterrorist agents in New York were not alone in failing to identify prospective terrorists. Phoenix agent Kenneth Williams had apparently identified prospective terrorists when he recommended in July 2001 that FBI officials authorize a nationwide investigation of Middle Eastern men attending flight schools. As justification, Williams had singled out a militant political activist, Zakaria Soubra, who had helped organize public demonstrations against U.S. policy in the Middle East. Interviewed by Williams, Soubra had claimed that U.S. forces in the Middle East were "legitimate targets of Islam" and had displayed photographs in his apartment of Osama bin Laden and Chechnyan mujahedeen. In addition to Soubra, Williams had listed nine other Middle Eastern men in his July 2001 communication. His list, however, did not include Hani Hanjour. One of the nineteen 9/11 terrorists, Hanjour had attended flight school in the Phoenix area intermittently over the preceding five years and would go on to pilot the plane that crashed into the Pentagon. When FBI agents following the 9/11 attack investigated Soubra and the nine others whom Williams had named, they uncovered no evidence that any of these Middle Eastern militants had advance knowledge or provided any support to the nineteen hijackers.[21]

Future terrorist plots would not necessarily be revealed simply by expanding the intelligence agencies' surveillance powers. For example, under the NSA intercept program authorized in October 2001 by President Bush, NSA officials sent a steady stream of intercepted telephone and e-mail messages to the FBI. Based on interviews with FBI officials, *New York Times* reporters Lowell Bergman, Eric Lichtblau, Scott Shane, and Dan Van Natta, Jr., disclosed that "virtually all" of the NSA's submissions "led to dead ends or innocent" Americans. This "unfiltered information was swamping investigators." FBI officials said they had complained to their NSA counterparts, adding that the resulting FBI checks amounted to "pointless intrusions on Americans' privacy."[22]

Was the NSA intercept program of such limited value? After the *Times*'s disclosure, Bush administration officials claimed that this program was legal and had been of great value, but offered no evidence confirming either of these claims. They resisted release of internal memoranda that would document how Justice Department officials assessed the legality of the program or that led to the successful identification of terrorist plotters.[23]

The FBI investigation to identify the sender(s) of anthrax-laced letters offers a more striking example of the limited value of expanded surveillance authority. Letters containing anthrax powder had been sent through the mail in the month after the 9/11 attack to a variety of individuals, including a lowly hospital worker, an elderly woman, Senate Majority Leader Tom Daschle, Senate Judiciary Committee chairman Patrick Leahy, and NBC news anchor Tom Brokaw. Five individuals died as a result, including two postal workers who handled the mail. Because of their timing, shortly after the 9/11 attack, the anthrax letters were initially seen as part of a more general terrorist plot, perhaps by Al Qaeda or Iraq, in the latter case since that nation's scientists were known to have developed biological weapons. The variety of targets and the fact that the perpetrator(s) remained at large suggested an ongoing threat, which made the anthrax investigation a major FBI priority. FBI agents in this case apparently had two advantages: the increased surveillance powers of the Patriot Act and the knowledge that the sender(s) of the letters had both specialized knowledge and access to a laboratory.

But after an investigation lasting more than five years, FBI agents failed to identify the sender(s) of the anthrax letters. FBI officials eventually concluded that the perpetrator was a U.S. citizen, an unidentified loner with limited scientific expertise who could have obtained the needed laboratory equipment for as little as $2,500. FBI agents moreover were never able to develop evidence to secure indictments of their principal suspects: a former government scientist, Steven Hatfill, and a doctor and self-described bioterrorism expert, Kenneth Berry.[24]

The anthrax letters case illustrated the limited results of the FBI's post-9/11 counterterrorist initiatives. The claims of senior Justice Department officials of successfully meeting the terrorist threat also proved to be overblown. The relatively paltry results indirectly underscore the limited value of the expanded surveillance authority granted the FBI under the Ashcroft guidelines and the Patriot Act.

A critical examination of the Justice Department's terrorist prosecutions reveals that the vast majority resulted in sentences of only a few months, indirectly confirming their relative unimportance. Most, in fact, involved false documents or immigration violations. Of the 62 international terrorism indictments obtained by U.S. attorneys in New Jersey in 2002, all but two involved Middle Eastern students accused of paying imposters to take English proficiency exams for them. During the period between October 2005 and June 2006, of the 150 international terrorism referrals submitted by the FBI, U.S. attorneys declined to bring charges in 131. And Justice Department officials wrongly classified 46 percent of their claimed 288 terrorist convictions. The department's inspector general, after examining terrorist-related cases, concluded that almost all the cited statistics were either inflated or diminished by department officials' having included cases involving immigration violations, marriage fraud, and drug violations. These negligible results moreover occurred at the very time when Justice Department surveillance applications to the special court had sharply increased, from 50 applications in 2002 to 1,727 in 2003.[25]

How should this record be evaluated? Can the value of the FBI's enhanced surveillance authority be judged simply by the number of international terrorist prosecutions, the length of sentences, or the basis for convictions? A better standard might be to evaluate those specific cases cited by Justice Department officials as involving the apprehension of Al Qaeda "sleeper cells."

The first of these involved the FBI's arrest and detention in the week after the 9/11 attack of three Arab immigrants in Detroit—Karim Koubriti, Ahmed Hannan, and Youssef Hmimssa—as possible terrorist suspects who might have prior knowledge of the 9/11 attack. The three were found to have fraudulent immigration documents and badges granting them access to Detroit's Metropolitan Airport. Two of the three detainees and two other Arab immigrants—Farouk Ali-Haimoud and Abdel-Elah Elmardoudi—were indicted in August 2002 as members of a "sleeper operational combat cell" whose alleged mission was to obtain weapons and intelligence for terrorist operations. The specific charge was that these members of an Al Qaeda sleeper cell had provided "material support" of terrorism, had conspired to engage in fraud, and had misused visas.

Hmimssa emerged as a key government witness in the ensuing trial. He testified that the other four had planned a wide range of terrorist activities in the United States, North Africa, and Jordan, including the purchase of Stinger missiles to shoot down commercial airplanes. Hmimssa further acknowledged that he had provided false identification documents to the four defendants. During the trial, Attorney General John Ashcroft publicly praised Hmimssa's credibility, though his remarks were sharply condemned by the presiding judge as a violation of his ban on public comment about the case. Defense attorneys' efforts to impugn Hmimssa's credibility by suggesting that he was motivated by a desire for revenge failed, as did their efforts to portray a sketch that the government had submitted—allegedly of the U.S. air base in Incirlick, Turkey—as harmless doodling.

Elmardoudi and Koubriti were convicted in June 2003 on charges of providing material support for terrorism and conspiring to engage in fraud and misuse of documents. Hannan was found guilty of one count of document fraud, and Ali-Haimoud was acquitted of all charges. Attorney General Ashcroft immediately hailed the verdict as sending "a clear message" that the Justice Department "will work diligently to detect, disrupt and dismantle the activities of terrorist cells in the United States and abroad."

This success proved to be short lived, however. In January 2004 an internal Justice Department inquiry was launched into the case's handling. Ultimately, in September 2004, Justice Department officials petitioned presiding judge Gerald Rosen to drop the case and suspend the sentence, disclosing that the U.S. attorney prosecuting the case had withheld from the defense exculpatory evidence about the alleged sketch and Hmimssa's credibility. Agreeing to this motion, Judge Rosen blasted the department's handling of the case, commenting that the prosecution had early on developed a theory "and then simply ignored or avoided any evidence or information which contradicted or undermined" it. This fiasco culminated in March 2006 with the indictments of Richard Corventino, the U.S. attorney prosecuting the case, and a State Department official on charges that they had conspired to conceal evidence and obstruct justice.[26]

A second sleeper-cell case was far less problematic. In the spring of 2001 six Yemeni-American residents of Lackawanna, New York, traveled to Pakistan and from there to Kandahar, Afghanistan, where they attended an Al Qaeda training camp. The six returned to Lackawanna in late 2001 and resumed their normal family and occupational lives, though one traveled to Bahrain in September 2002 for an arranged marriage.

Before the six returned to Lackawanna, and in advance of the 9/11 attack, the FBI's Buffalo office received an anonymous letter in which the writer claimed that two terrorists had come to Lackawanna "for recruiting the Yemenite youth." FBI agents at first did not take seriously this uncorroborated charge. After 9/11, however, they launched an intensive investigation that included wiretapping and intercepting the e-mails of the six men and interviewing them. At first the six lied to FBI agents when questioned about their trip to Pakistan. They then admitted attending an Al Qaeda training camp but claimed to be disillusioned by that experience. Detained in September 2002, the six were indicted in October on the charge of providing material support for terrorism.

While claiming to have uncovered an Al Qaeda sleeper cell, Justice Department officials did not contend that the six men had conducted or recruited others for a terrorist operation. The six, they maintained, were awaiting an order to attack American targets. Evidence in support of this contention did not convince Magistrate Judge Kenneth Schroeder, Jr., who after a September bail hearing publicly stated, "I haven't heard of any act of violence or propensity of violence in the history of these men," adding that he could only speculate as to what threat they posed. Ultimately, rather than risk trial, the six agreed to a plea bargain whereby they admitted to having attended and received weapons training at an Al Qaeda training camp. They did not, however, admit that they had planned to conduct a terrorist operation. Because of their plea, the six received a reduced sentence of eight rather than ten years' imprisonment.

Significantly, the six were indicted only on the charge of providing "material support" for terrorism. They were not charged either with having planned, having attempted to recruit others, or having sought the materials needed to conduct a terrorist operation. The FBI's intensive year-long investigation uncovered no such evidence. The head of the FBI's Buffalo field office, Peter Ahearn, attempted to justify this failure, claiming, "If we don't know for sure they're going to do something or not, we need to make sure that we prevent anything they might be planning, whether or not we know or don't know about it." Dale Watson, head of the FBI's counterterrorism division, dissented from the CIA's characterization of the six Yemeni Americans as "the most dangerous group in the United States." "I have seen enough to know," Watson commented, "that they probably didn't have the means or the capabilities at this point to do something."[27]

This same scenario recurred in another of the Justice Department's well-publicized Al Qaeda sleeper-cell discoveries. In June 2005 two Pakistani-American residents of Lodi, California, Umar Hayat and his son Hamid, were indicted on charges of lying to FBI agents about Hamid's attendance at an Al Qaeda training camp during a visit to Pakistan. While not included in this charge, the U.S. attorney also claimed that the Hayats were members of a sleeper cell that intended to bomb malls and a food center in the Lodi area. But he never produced evidence during the trial that the two men had planned or conspired to effect a terrorist operation.

The U.S. attorney's principal evidence involved Hamid Hayat's taped conversations with a paid FBI informer, Naseen Khan, who had sought to persuade Hamid to travel to Pakistan and further had urged him to consider jihad. FBI agents had hired Khan as an informer, eventually paying him $250,000 even after he had told them an incredible story of seeing a key aide to Osama bin Laden, Ayman al-Zawahiri, at a Lodi mosque in 1998 or 1999. The perjury indictment was based on Hamid's and his father's admissions during lengthy interviews with FBI agents. The reports of these FBI interviews suggest that both father and son had sought to accommodate their FBI interrogators' questions (bordering on coaching) in the belief that agreement would enable them to avoid prosecution. Umar Hayat went so far as to admit that his son's training took place in the basement of a building and involved pole-vaulting exercises, further agreeing with a comment by the interviewing agent that it must have been a very deep basement.

Based principally on his FBI interview, Hamad was convicted while his father's case resulted in a mistrial. U.S. Attorney Scott McGregor thereupon cited Hamid Hayat's conviction as evidence of the government's ability to "prevent acts of terrorism by winning convictions against those who would plot to commit violence against our citizenry in the name of an extremist cause." President Bush, in a June 2005 press conference, then referred to the Hayat case as confirming the value of the Patriot Act in apprehending a Lodi sleeper cell. In April 2006 Attorney General Alberto Gonzalez claimed that the verdict made "the country . . . a safer place."[28]

The zealotry of FBI agents in the Lodi case, in recruiting an informer like Khan or in coaxing the Hayats to confirm Hamid's attendance at an Al Qaeda training camp, was repeated in the case of a Portland, Oregon, attorney, Brandon Mayfield. Mayfield was detained in May 2004 as a "material witness" who presumably could provide information about a terrorist bombing attack of March 2004 on commuter trains in Madrid, Spain. FBI agents claimed that Mayfield's fingerprints had been found on a bag containing explosives that Spanish authorities had recovered at the scene of the bombing. This identification, as it turns out, had been based on a faulty reading of the digital print circulated by the Spanish authorities in the course of their investigation. Spanish authorities immediately rejected Mayfield's identification as erroneous. But even after they were so advised, FBI agents investigated and wiretapped Mayfield and then detained him as a material witness. Forced to admit their error, they later apologized to the Portland attorney who successfully sued the government over the violation of his rights.[29]

The sleeper-cell and Mayfield investigations do not convey the full scope of FBI intelligence investigations. They became known only because Justice Department officials announced the arrests and sought indictments, thereby subjecting their actions and those of the FBI to public scrutiny. By their very nature, most FBI intelligence investigations would not result in indictments, leaving unresolved their scope and targets. Inadvertently, though, the underlying political character of FBI intelligence investigations of suspected "terrorists," like their earlier investigations of "subversives," has been disclosed.

One illustrative case came to light as the result of U.S. Attorney Stephen O'Meara's February 2004 decision to convene a grand jury and subpoena members of a student chapter of the National Lawyers Guild at Drake University as well as local peace activists who had organized a forum on the Iraq War on the Drake University campus in the fall of 2003. Those subpoenaed were specifically ordered to produce documents identifying the sponsors of this forum; the sponsoring organizations' leadership, annual reports, and office locations; and information about the event itself. Before their scheduled grand jury appearances, the witnesses publicized their subpoenas and the records they were asked to provide. Responding to this negative publicity, O'Meara at first denied that he intended to "prosecute persons peacefully and lawfully engaged in rallies which are conducted under the protection of the First Amendment." His sole purpose, he claimed, had been to determine whether "there were any violations of federal law, or prior agreement, to violate federal law, regarding unlawful entry onto military property"—nearby Camp Douglas. Owing to the adverse publicity, O'Meara canceled the subpoenas.[30]

In deciding to convene a grand jury, O'Meara unintentionally confirmed that FBI intelligence investigations extended to public anti-war activity.* Yet this example of FBI surveillance of political activities was not atypical. Other examples of political surveillance also became known after successful Freedom of Information Act requests or publicized interrogations of political activists. These disclosures confirmed that, at minimum, the subjects of post-9/11 FBI intelligence investigations included the Thomas

---

*The specified subpoenaed records involved "all requests for use of a room, all documents indicating the purpose and intended participants in the meeting, and all documents or recordings which would identify persons that actually attended the meeting."

Merton Center, an interfaith peace and social justice organization; student activists organizing demonstrations and rallies against the Iraq War; religious activists affiliated with the School of the Americas Watch, who participated in demonstrations at the U.S. Army's training school for Latin American military officers at Fort Benning, Georgia; Greenpeace, an environmental group involved in civil disobedience protest of the Bush administration's environmental policies; radical activists who planned to hold demonstrations at the 2004 Republican National Convention; the American Indian Movement—targeted for organizing demonstrations on Columbus Day in Denver, Colorado; Calyx Internet Access, an internet service provider widely used by radical activists; the Catholic Worker Movement, a peace and social justice organization; the People for the Ethical Treatment of Animals; Iraqi Americans and Iraqi students attending American universities (subject to surveillance dating from November 2002, based on the possibility the United States might go to war with Iraq, as occurred in March 2003); and people carrying almanacs—because FBI officials worried that such books could be used "to assist with target selection and pre-operational planning." Our awareness of the almanac episode comes from the disclosure that FBI agents had warned local police to watch such individuals, as "The practice of researching potential targets is consistent with the known methods of Al Qaeda and other terrorist organizations that seek to maximize the likelihood of organizational success through careful planning."[31]

The scope of the FBI's intelligence investigations is further confirmed by two highly critical reports of the Justice Department's inspector general. These findings assessed the FBI's extensive use, in one case, of wiretaps and, in the second case, of National Security Letters. In his March 2006 report on FBI wiretapping operations conducted under the Foreign Intelligence Surveillance Act during the years 2004–2005, Inspector General Glenn Fine uncovered more than 100 violations, with the number of such violations increasing from 47 percent in 2004 to 69 percent in 2005. Further, many of these interceptions had been "significantly" broader in scope than approved by the FISA court. Then, in a scathing report of March 2007, Fine found a "misleading and serious misuse" by FBI agents of National Security Letters (NSLs, relying on FBI officials' authorization without seeking court approval) to obtain credit card, bank, telephone, and internet records during the years 2003–2005—a total of 143,074.* He determined that FBI officials had "significantly understated" such uses in their reports to Congress;† that NSLs were improperly and at times illegally used to obtain records; and that many of the 739 "exigent letters" involving approximately 3,000 telephone numbers (used to obtain information in an emergency when a subpoena had already been obtained) were in nonemergency circumstances when a subpoena had not been sought.‡

---

*The USA Patriot Act reduced the standard for issuing NSLs from "pertaining to a foreign power or agent of a foreign power" to "an authorized" counterterrorist or counterespionage investigation. In addition, the total (143,074) involved only the number of NSL requests. In one case, for example, one FBI NSL request to a telephone company sought information on seven telephone numbers.

†In 2006, at a time when Congress was debating whether to renew sections of the USA Patriot Act pertaining to NSLs, FBI officials told House and Senate leaders that the FBI had issued 9,254 NSL requests in 2005 (a number comparable to the 8,500 NSL requests of 2000, the year before the enactment of the USA Patriot Act). This public report, however, did not include the FBI's semi-annual classified reports to Congress or Letters relating to consumer credit reports. The total NSLs for 2005 was in fact 47,221. The inspector general, however, discovered that this number understated the FBI's uses of NSLs owing to "inaccuracies" in the FBI's database. Reviewing a "judgmental sample" of 77 case files in four (of the FBI's 56) field offices, Fine concluded that FBI officials had underreported the use of NSLs by at least 6 percent.

‡The inspector general further discovered that of the sampled FBI case files examined by his office relating to NSL uses, 12 percent of FBI reports inaccurately identified the targets as non-U.S. persons "while the appropriate memoranda on the investigation indicated that the subject was a U.S. person or a presumed U.S. person." Furthermore, the inspector general con-

In addition, FBI agents visited at least 178 libraries; arrested a Saudi Arabian PhD candidate in computer science attending the University of Idaho on a charge he had provided "computer advice and assistance" to Islamic groups;* pressured internet companies to retain records on the web-surfing activities of their customers; and secured the major airline companies' passenger records for names, addresses, travel destinations, and credit card numbers. Proposed Justice Department rules (which were to go into effect in May 2007) authorizing FBI wiretapping of internet phone calls were pointedly criticized by a federal appeals court in May 2006 as "gobbledygook," "ridiculous," and "nonsense."[32]

Military intelligence agents, too, closely monitored political activities. They used National Security Letters to gain access to the bank and credit card records of hundreds of Americans who they suspected might be involved in espionage or terrorism within the United States. They also monitored a conference on Islamic law held at the University of Texas Law School, seeking the names of the participants and a videotape of the proceedings; student groups at the University of California–Santa Cruz and New Mexico State University protesting the presence of military recruiters on campus; a "Stop the War Now" rally in Akron, Ohio; anti-war activities of the Veterans for Peace and the American Friends Service Committee; and more generally the planning meetings of anti-war activists held at churches, in libraries, and on college campuses. Reports were then shared with the FBI on the premise that such activities constituted a "potential terrorist activity."[33]

cluded that NSLs were "most often" used for "intelligence purposes rather than for criminal prosecutions." Thus of the forty-six headquarters and field office units that responded to his inquiry, nineteen reported having made no criminal referral; the vast majority of the others reporting criminal referrals involved fraud, immigration, and money-laundering charges. Finally, the inspector general found that the number of NSL requests relating to U.S. individuals increased from 39 percent of all NSL requests in 2003 to 53 percent in 2005.

*Jurors voted not to convict.

In sum, the expansion of FBI investigative authority and the intelligence agencies' more aggressive conduct of investigations did not necessarily lead to the uncovering of terrorist plots but did lead to the resumption of FBI monitoring of political activities. The Kean Commission did not anticipate this possibility, or at least minimized it. Was the commission, then, on the mark in its criticisms of the lack of full cooperation between the FBI and CIA?

The Kean Commission specifically cited deficiencies in "information sharing" between the agencies before 9/11. These deficiencies, it concluded, were crucial to the failure to anticipate the terrorist attack. "No one was finally in charge of managing the case" of uniting foreign and domestic intelligence, commission members lamented, "and able to draw relevant information from anywhere in the government, assign responsibilities across the agencies [foreign or domestic], track progress, and quickly bring obstacles up to the level where they could be resolved." A more centralized system was needed, commission members continued, to "pool information gathered overseas with information gathered in the United States."

The commission then identified another reason for this intelligence failure: the principle of the "need to know" that governed the sharing of information among the intelligence agencies, notably the CIA and the FBI. The principal error of the "need to know" condition, the commission explained, was the assumption that officials could know in advance what information their counterparts might need, and further that "the risk of inadvertent disclosure outweighs the benefits of wider sharing. Those Cold War assumptions are no longer appropriate. The culture of agencies feeling they own the information they gathered at taxpayer expense must be replaced by a culture in which the agencies instead feel they have a duty to the information—to repay the taxpayers' investment by making the information available."[34]

To support this analysis, the commission cited two cases in which information about two of the nineteen hijackers, Khalid al

Mihdhar and Nawaf al Hazmi, was not shared—in one case between NSA and CIA, and in the other between CIA and FBI.

In 1999 the mastermind of the 9/11 plot, Khalid Sheikh Mohammed, had selected al Mihdhar and al Hazmi for the planned suicide operation. He had done so partly because, as Saudi nationals, they could more easily obtain visas to enter the United States. Both recruits first underwent intensive training at an Al Qaeda camp in Afghanistan, then traveled to an international conference among prospective terrorists held in Kuala Lumpur, Indonesia, in January 2000. From there they flew to the United States, arriving in Los Angeles on January 15. Al Mihdhar and al Hazmi settled for a time in San Diego, where they took English-language classes in preparation for pilot training. Because of their inability to master English, however, they never applied for training. Al Mihdhar returned to Saudi Arabia in June 2000 while al Hazmi simply bided his time in the San Diego area. Al Hazmi eventually met Hani Hanjour on his arrival in San Diego in December 2000, and moved with him first to Arizona that month, then to Falls Church, Virginia, in April 2001, and finally to Paterson, New Jersey, in May. Al Mihdhar returned to the United States in July and joined the other hijackers in Paterson in preparation for the 9/11 attack.

While the other seventeen participants in the 9/11 operation escaped scrutiny, NSA had intercepted messages that referred to men named Khalid, Nawaf, and Salem. NSA analysts concluded that these three were part of "an operation cadre" and that "something nefarious might be afoot," but they were unable to identify the three. Nonetheless NSA officials did not turn this incomplete information over to the CIA. Quite independently, CIA analysts had learned that al Mihdhar and al Hazmi had attended the Kuala Lumpur meeting, that al Mihdhar's passport recorded that he was to travel to the United States, and later that al Hazmi had departed from Bangkok, Thailand, on a United Airlines flight to Los Angeles. CIA officials did not, however, brief the FBI about these discoveries.[35]

As a result, FBI agents were denied information that could have led to their monitoring of al Hazmi and al Mihdhar, or to their alerting the State Department to al Mihdhar's return in July 2001. FBI monitoring of al Hazmi could also have led to the discovery of Hanjour and then of their meeting with other hijackers in Paterson.

The Kean Commission rightfully recognized that the CIA officials' decision not to share this intelligence with the FBI accorded with the "need to know" principle, not petty bureaucratic rivalry or parochialism. Yet commission members downplayed the underlying reason for this failure: that secrecy remained integral to CIA operations.

In hindsight this initial reluctance to inform the FBI about al Mihdhar and al Hazmi seems irresponsible. Yet this decision was based on what proved to be an erroneous assumption—that al Mihdhar and al Hazmi were involved in an *international* terrorist operation directed at U.S. personnel or facilities overseas. As the Pearl Harbor experience dramatically illustrated, the importance of murky intelligence is not always obvious at the time. CIA officials' actions in this case moreover differed little from those of FBI officials in 1944—in the Kravchenko case—or in the late 1990s—in the Hanssen case—when their obsession with security led to faulty decisions with serious security consequences. In the Kravchenko case, FBI officials had decided not to exploit his defection because of their belief that he might be a double agent; in the Hanssen case, FBI agents had focused on the wrong man, Brian Kelly.

Because their decision in the Kravchenko case remained secret, FBI officials not only evaded criticism during the early cold war years but could capitalize on the partisan tactics of conservatives who hammered the Roosevelt and Truman administrations during the 1950s for their alleged "softness toward communism" in hampering FBI investigations of Soviet espionage. Yet the real point is not that FBI officials escaped criticism but that incomplete intelligence and the political convictions of analysts can lead to erroneous conclusions. In the final analysis, it is unrealistic to expect that CIA officials, having a mandate to protect classified information and a proprietary interest in safeguarding acquired information, will abandon a commitment to secrecy and automatically share incomplete or incomprehensible information. Administrative reforms and centralization offer no solution to this intractable problem of intelligence analysis: the secrecy inherent in intelligence operations virtually ensures such errors in judgment and accountability.

9 | HOPES AND REALITIES

■ IN THEIR critical assessment of the U.S. intelligence agencies' failure to anticipate the 9/11 terrorist attack, the Kean Commission and the Joint House-Senate Intelligence Committee cited two causes: the FBI's failure to aggressively pursue crucial leads, and the lack of full cooperation between the FBI and the CIA.* Their assessment, however, ignored history and betrayed an ignorance of the complex character of the FBI-CIA relationship and the FBI's decades-long aggressive conduct of intelligence investigations.

Since World War I, FBI officials had moved beyond the bureau's assigned law-enforcement mission to initiate investigations in anticipation of internal security threats. In the process FBI agents willingly violated privacy and First Amendment rights and often relied on recognizably illegal investigative techniques—wiretaps, bugs, break-ins, and mail openings. The fruits of these investigations—which could not be used in trial prosecutions because they were illegally obtained or failed to reveal any violation of a federal statute—were regularly exploited by presidents or senior FBI officials to influence public opinion.

---

*Yet FBI agents had also not anticipated two other terrorist attacks: the February 1993 truck bombing of the World Trade Center and the April 1995 truck bombing of the Albert Murrah Building.

While these developments grew out of the FBI's more aggressive approach to domestic intelligence, for the most part FBI agents failed to uncover espionage or terrorism.

As for cooperation, since World War I the heads of the intelligence agencies had established first an informal liaison system to promote cooperation and then, after 1940, formally delineated their separate areas of responsibility and the sharing of information. Yet these executive and legislative measures* did not achieve full cooperation over time. Even in the known cases when the intelligence agencies cooperated fully, the question arises: Did interagency cooperation advance the nation's security interests?

Owing to stringent classification restrictions, the consequences of FBI-CIA cooperation cannot be comprehensively evaluated. But there is one notable exception: the CIA's HTLINGUAL program. When the CIA Inspector General decided in 1961 and 1969 to evaluate this program in view of its "flap potential," he concluded that it had provided "no tangible operational benefit" and had not provided "significant leads or information which have had positive operational results." Armed with this information, Church Committee investigators in 1975 pressed the chief of the FBI's counterintelligence section, William Branigan, about the program's value to the FBI. Branigan then conceded that not one Soviet espionage agent had been uncovered and that 95 percent of the 57,846 intercepted letters provided to the FBI were "junk."

Were the results of HTLINGUAL atypical? Did the NSA's Operation MINARET, for example, produce similarly meager results? And did the FBI's extensive resort to break-ins, wiretaps, bugs, and mail openings at the request of CIA and NSA officials pro-

---

*These included delimitation agreements of 1940–1941, legislation creating the CIA and NSC in 1947, an informal FBI-CIA agreement of 1966, President Carter's 1978 executive order, 1994 legislation and executive directives issued in the aftermath of the Aldrich Ames case, and President Clinton's executive directives of 1995 and 1998.

vide more tangible benefits? We do not know. But we do know that HTLINGUAL was continued even after CIA officials concluded that it produced no tangible results. They simply deferred uncritically to the FBI's interest in continuing the program, judging—until 1973—that they could do so without risk of discovery.

The Kean Commission and the Joint Committee never attempted to assess the benefits of earlier intelligence operations. Nor, for that matter, did they critically examine the reasons for the lack of full cooperation among the agencies or the FBI's earlier failures to anticipate security threats. The agencies failed not because of incompetence, indifference, or a narrowly bureaucratic mind-set, but because of the inherent difficulty of identifying individuals who *might* become spies or terrorists, before they acted. In those cases where counterintelligence and counterterrorism operations succeeded, FBI or CIA agents had acquired hard evidence in advance. The Kean Commission's rather parochial analysis was founded on the premise that absolute security is attainable, and that FBI and CIA officials should have been able to anticipate potential threats to the nation's security.

But the collection of credible evidence in advance has been the exception, and recognizing this reality is essential to a reasoned evaluation of the problems and opportunities confronting U.S. intelligence agencies. It is a reality that does not conform to one of the Kean Commission's main contentions: that the 9/11 crisis, because it is uniquely different from the cold war, requires a more centralized intelligence system. Comparing the problems posed by the 9/11 attacks with those posed by Soviet espionage operations during World War II and the cold war years challenges this assumption.

The 9/11 attack was a low-budget operation, costing between $400,000 and $500,000, financed through international fund transactions, and orchestrated by a relatively impotent organization, Al Qaeda. And because it was headquartered in a third-rate country, Afghanistan, Al Qaeda was vulnerable to a U.S. military operation. The participants in the 9/11 attack, moreover, were not trained professionals; they were alien residents who had entered the United States on visas as students or visitors, and were able to circumvent airport security when they boarded planes carrying knives and box cutters. Thus the 9/11 attack could have been averted without any input from the FBI and CIA, simply by tightening and enforcing visa standards, improving airport security, strengthening the cockpits of commercial planes, and restricting the international transfer of funds. Vastly superior U.S. military power led to the overthrow of the Taliban government in Afghanistan and the dismantling of Al Qaeda's base of operations.

In contrast the FBI and U.S. officials during World War II and the cold war years confronted a formidable adversary. The Soviet Union was a powerful state with a sizable industrial base and a well-equipped military that possessed nuclear, biological, and chemical weapons. Its power would make a military attack to curb espionage costly, and potentially suicidal. Soviet intelligence officers, moreover, were highly trained and disciplined, could enter the United States as members of the Soviet consular, embassy, or United Nations staffs, and could recruit U.S. citizens to conduct espionage.

Undeniably the Soviet and Al Qaeda threats were each unique. Nonetheless the Kean Commission's characterization of Al Qaeda as a threat requiring a centralization of intelligence that had never been achieved in the cold war era plays down the nature of the Soviet threat and the reality of the counterintelligence problem that FBI and the CIA officials faced.

FBI and CIA officials had aggressively initiated counterterrorist efforts during the critical years 1996–2001, when Al Qaeda's planning for the 9/11 terrorist attack reached fruition. Not only was counterterrorism a major CIA and FBI priority in the 1990s, but FBI agents commanded broad powers to uncover terrorist plots as a result of legislation that had legalized electronic surveillance, authorized the detention and deportation of alien residents suspected of terrorism, or criminalized "material support" for terrorism.

FBI agents failed to anticipate the 9/11 terrorist attack despite these broad powers; but this was not a unique failure. They had also failed to anticipate Soviet espionage operations during the 1930s and 1940s, even though under President Roosevelt's secret oral directive of 1936 they were authorized to conduct noncriminal intelligence investigations, and under other secret directives they were authorized to install wiretaps and bugs and conduct break-ins. The COMRAP investigation of 1943–1945 pointedly highlights that the source of this failure was not one of authority but of discovery.

Recapitulating that investigation: FBI officials in April 1943 had learned—from an illegal wiretap and then an illegal bug—of a Soviet plot to recruit American Communists to engage in industrial espionage.* The ensuing FBI investigation relied extensively on illegal techniques and yet failed to apprehend a single Soviet agent or American Communist engaging in espionage. Had Soviet agents recruited American Communists to conduct espionage? Yes, but FBI investigators had focused on the wrong Soviet officials and on the wrong American Communists. The experience indirectly confirms the limited value of simply expanding surveillance authority.

Two examples of FBI successes further highlight the inherent limitations of FBI counterintelligence operations: the indictments and convictions of Alger Hiss in 1948–1950 and of Robert Hanssen in 2001.

The FBI's intelligence investigations and reliance on intrusive investigative techniques had not led to Hiss's and Hanssen's apprehension. Hiss had been wiretapped and his mail opened in

---

*This advance, specific intelligence about an imminent security threat contrasts with the CIA's ambiguous discovery in 2000 of al Mihdhar's and al Hazmi's attendance at an international terrorist conference in Kuala Lumpur and their intent to enter the United States.

1945–1946 without discovery of his espionage activities. Hanssen had also been wiretapped and his computer searched in late 2000, but only because FBI agents already knew he was a Soviet spy. Further, despite having interviewed Whittaker Chambers in 1942 and again in 1945 and 1946, FBI agents first learned in December 1948 that he had served as a courier for the Soviets to obtain classified documents from individuals employed in the federal bureaucracy. Significantly, the source of the FBI's belated knowledge of Hiss's and Hanssen's espionage activities was extraordinary good luck: in Hiss's case, that Chambers had, despite having defected in 1938, maintained some of the classified documents that Hiss had given him; in Hanssen's case, that a former KGB agent had somehow pilfered the KGB's file on Hanssen and given it to the CIA in 2000.

Although the FBI and the CIA often failed to anticipate crime, the intelligence they acquired about "subversive" activities has often been used by White House and intelligence agency officials to shape the political culture. Aware that some of their actions were illegal, they devised safeguards to preclude discovery—and in the process came to interpret media and congressional oversight as harmful to the nation's security. Their commitment to secrecy made possible what might be called the Don Quixote syndrome: in their attempts to save damsels in distress, they tilted at windmills while all along thinking they were slaying dragons.

The principal recommendation of the Kean Commission and the Joint Committee—to centralize power in the executive branch—had been a prime objective of American presidents, from Roosevelt's initiatives of 1940–1945 through Nixon's creation of the inter-agency task force in 1970 that formulated the Huston Plan. Nonetheless presidents hesitated to seek legislative authorization because they recognized that the administrative proposals would meet opposition from libertarians or those who feared that a constitutional system of limited power and accountability would be undermined.

The history of these failed, or aborted, attempts at more effective intelligence suggests another, more reasonable solution: stricter congressional oversight. Relying on Congress would seem to fly in the face of the history recounted in this study. After all, Congress has been unwilling at crucial times to meet its oversight responsibilities; or, in periods of crisis, it has pressured presidents to pursue the very policies that have undermined individual rights without advancing security interests. But this history has also been marked by occasions when rigorous congressional oversight has breached the wall of secrecy erected by presidents and intelligence agencies to abuse power and cover up their failures. The range of such oversight activities began with the Post impeachment hearings of 1920 and continued with the Senate investigation of the Teapot Dome scandal of 1923–1924; the Long Subcommittee hearings of 1965–1966; the Senate Watergate Committee hearings of 1973; the Church and Pike committee hearings of 1975; the Joint House-Senate Intelligence Committee hearings of 1986 into the Iran-contra affair; the Senate Judiciary Committee pre-9/11 hearings of 2001 into FBI administrative practices; and the Joint House-Senate Intelligence Committee hearings of 2002–2003 into the 9/11 attack. Stricter congressional oversight would be consistent not only with the intent of the Founding Fathers to check the sway of the executive but with Lord Acton's axiom on the lessons of power, that power corrupts and absolute power corrupts absolutely.

NOTES

Introduction

1. U.S. Senate Select Committee on Intelligence and U.S. House Permanent Select Committee on Intelligence (hereafter Joint Committee), *Report on Joint Inquiry into Intelligence Community Activities Before and After the Terrorist Attacks of September 11, 2001*, S. Report No. 107-351, 107th Cong., 2d sess., 2003, Abridged Findings and Conclusions, pp. xi–xix; *The 9/11 Commission Report: Final Report of the National Commission on Terrorist Attacks upon the United States* (New York: Norton, 2004), pp. 268–278, 353–360.

2. Amy Zegart offers a thoughtful survey of the various proposals and why most of the various recommendations were not seriously considered. See "An Empirical Analysis of Failed Intelligence Reforms Before September 11," *Political Science Quarterly*, vol. 121, no. 1 (Spring 2006), pp. 33–60.

3. Joint Committee, *Report*, Recommendations, pp. 2–5, 6–9, 16; *9/11 Commission Report*, pp. 399–419, 423–427.

4. Athan Theoharis, "In-House Cover-up: Researching FBI Files," in Athan Theoharis, ed., *Beyond the Hiss Case: The FBI, Congress, and the Cold War* (Philadelphia: Temple University Press, 1982), pp. 21–37, 45–54; Athan Theoharis, "Secrecy and Power: Unanticipated Problems in Researching FBI Files," *Political Science Quarterly*, vol. 119, no. 2 (Summer 2004), pp. 272–288.

5. Memo, New York SAC to Files, May 10, 1955, FBI 62-117166-131 Bulky Enclosure.

6. Joint Committee, *Report*, pp. 20–22, 325–335, Appendix, The Phoenix Electronic Communication, pp. 1–8; *9/11 Commission Report*, pp. 2–4, 8–10, 225–227, 239, 242, 248, 261–262; *New York Times*, May 4, 2002, p. A10; May 9, 2002, p. A22; June 19, 2002, p. A18; September 25, 2002, p. A12.

7. *9/11 Commission Report*, pp. 269–276, 353–360, 399–415.

8. National Security Act of July 26, 1947, 61 Statute 495.

Chapter 1. The Origins of U.S. Intelligence

1. U.S. Senate Select Committee to Study Governmental Operations with Respect to Intelligence Activities, *Final Report, Supplementary Reports on Intelligence Activities* Book VI, 94th Cong., 2d sess., 1976, pp. 61–62; Jeffrey M. Dorwart, *The Office of Naval Intelligence: The Birth of America's First Intelligence Agency 1865–1918* (Annapolis: Naval Institute Press, 1979), pp. 3–29.

2. Senate Select Committee on Intelligence Activities, Book VI, pp. 63–64; Joan M. Jensen, *Army Surveillance in America, 1775–1980* (New Haven: Yale University Press, 1991), pp. 49–71; Bruce W. Bidwell, *History of the Military Intelligence Division, Department of the Army General Staff: 1775–1941* (Frederick, Md.: University Publications of America, 1986), pp. 12–66; Roy Talbert, Jr., *Negative Intelligence: The Army and the American Left, 1917–1941* (Jackson: University Press of Mississippi, 1991), pp. 3–6.

3. Senate Select Committee on Intelligence Activities, Book VI, pp. 73–74; Athan Theoharis, *The FBI and American Democracy: A Brief Critical History* (Lawrence: University Press of Kansas, 2004), pp. 14–17; Willard B. Gatewood, *Theodore Roosevelt and the Art of Controversy: Episodes of the White House Years* (Baton Rouge: Louisiana State University Press, 1970), pp. 236–247, 249–254, 257–287; Vern Countryman, "The History of the FBI: Democracy's Development of a Secret Police," in Pat Watters and Stephen Gillers, eds., *Investigating the FBI* (Garden City: Doubleday, 1973), pp. 33–38; Max Lowenthal, *The Federal Bureau of Investigation* (New York: William Sloane, 1950), pp. 3–17; Sanford Ungar, *FBI* (Boston: Atlantic/Little Brown, 1975), pp. 38–41.

4. Senate Select Committee on Intelligence Activities, Book VI, pp. 75–112; Jensen, *Army Surveillance*, pp. 141–177; Bidwell, *History of Military Intelligence Division*, pp. 109–243; Dorwart, *Office of Naval Intelligence*, pp. 96–142; Theoharis, *FBI and American Democracy*, pp. 21–23; William Preston, *Aliens and Dissenters: Federal Suppression of Radicals, 1903–1933* (New York: Harper, 1966), pp. 103–172; Joan Jensen, *The Price of Vigilance* (Chicago: Rand McNally, 1968), pp. 17–234; Melvyn Dubofsky, *We Shall Be All: A History of the Industrial Workers of the World* (Chicago: Quadrangle, 1969), pp. 398–456; Talbert, *Negative Intelligence*, pp. 8–134; John Fox, Jr., "Bureaucratic Wrangling over Counterintelligence, 1917–18," *Studies in Intelligence*, vol. 49, no. 1 (2005), pp. 9–17. The most comprehensive survey of World War I surveillance is William H. Thomas, Jr.'s forthcoming book *Policing the Nation: The U.S. Justice Department's Covert Campaign Against Dissent During the First World War.*

Chapter 2. A Period of Transition

1. Jensen, *Price of Vigilance*, pp. 236–291; Jensen, *Army Surveillance in America*, pp. 178–207; Talbert, *Negative Intelligence*, pp. 135–151; Bid-

well, *History of the Military Intelligence Division*, pp. 275–288; Senate Select Committee on Intelligence Activities, Book VI, pp. 124–126; Joseph Bendersky, *The "Jewish Threat": Anti-Semitic Politics of the U.S. Army* (New York: Basic Books, 2000), pp. 48–51, 120–136, 152–154, 160–204.

2. Senate Select Committee on Intelligence Activities, Book VI, p. 91; Jeffrey M. Dorwart, *Conflict of Duty: The U.S. Naval Intelligence Dilemma, 1919–1945* (Annapolis: Naval Institute Press, 1983), pp. 3–5, 11–18, 22–25, 38–46, 51–53, 65, 69, 81–83.

3. Theoharis, *The FBI and American Democracy*, pp. 24–36, 173; Unger, *FBI*, pp. 43–54; Preston, *Aliens and Dissenters*, pp. 208–229; Robert Murray, *Red Scare: A Study of National Hysteria, 1919–1920* (New York: McGraw-Hill, 1964), pp. 191–222, 253–257; Athan Theoharis and John Stuart Cox, *The Boss: J. Edgar Hoover and the Great American Inquisition* (Philadelphia: Temple University Press, 1988), pp. 53–57, 63–70, 80, 82–87, 92–96; Athan Theoharis, ed., *From the Secret Files of J. Edgar Hoover* (Chicago: Ivan R. Dee, 1991), pp. 295–300; Kenneth O'Reilly, *Hoover and the Un-Americans: The FBI, HUAC, and the Red Menace* (Philadelphia: Temple University Press, 1983), pp. 17–20; Kenneth O'Reilly, *"Racial Matters": The FBI's Secret File on Black America, 1960–1972* (New York: Free Press, 1989), pp. 12–18; Curt Gentry, *J. Edgar Hoover: The Man and the Secrets* (New York: Norton, 1991), pp. 75–80, 89–103, 118–142; Samuel Walker, *In Defense of American Liberties: A History of the ACLU* (New York: Oxford University Press, 1990), pp. 64–66.

4. Senate Select Committee on Intelligence Activities, Book VI, pp. 82–89, 115–119; Bidwell, *History of the Military Intelligence Division*, pp. 113, 124, 164–171, 253–254; David Kahn, *The Codebreakers: The Story of Secret Writing* (New York: Scribners, 1996), pp. 5–6, 326–360; Jeffrey Richelson, *A Century of Spies: Intelligence in the Twentieth Century* (New York: Oxford University Press, 1995), pp. 69–77.

Chapter 3. The Origins of the National Security State: Part I, Domestic Intelligence

1. Walter Trohan, "Chief of the G-Men—Record of His Career," *Chicago Tribune Magazine*, June 21, 1936.

2. U.S. Senate, Select Committee to Study Governmental Operations with Respect to Intelligence Activities, *Hearings on Intelligence Activities, Vol. 6, Federal Bureau of Investigation*, 94th Cong., 1st sess., 1975, pp. 558–559.

3. Theoharis, *The FBI and American Democracy*, pp. 50–51; Frances MacDonnell, *Insidious Foes: The Axis Fifth Column and the American Home Front* (New York: Oxford University Press, 1995), pp. 49–61.

4. Theoharis and Cox, *The Boss*, pp. 148–149; U.S. Senate, Select Committee to Study Governmental Operations with Respect to Intelligence

Activities, *Book III, Supplementary Detailed Staff Reports on Intelligence Activities and the Rights of Americans,* 94th Cong., 2d sess., 1976, p. 393.

5. Gentry, *J. Edgar Hoover,* pp. 202–204.

6. Confidential Memos, Hoover, August 24 and 25, 1936, Franklin D. Roosevelt folder, Official and Confidential File of FBI Director J. Edgar Hoover (hereafter Hoover O&C).

7. Strictly Confidential Memo, Hoover to Tamm, September 10, 1936, Franklin Roosevelt folder, Hoover O&C; Senate Select Committee on Intelligence Activities, vol. 6, pp. 562–563.

8. Senate Select Committee on Intelligence Activities, vol. 6, pp. 563–567.

9. Memo, Attorney General Jackson to All Department and Agency Heads, undated but ca. April 1941; Memo, Hoover to Jackson, April 1, 1941; Memo, Jackson to Hoover, April 4, 1941; Jackson, Robert H. folder, Hoover O&C.

10. Senate Select Committee on Intelligence Activities, vol. 6, pp. 567–570.

11. Confidential Memo on Division of Duties Between Military Intelligence Division, Office of Naval Intelligence, and the Federal Bureau of Investigation, May 29, 1940; Confidential Memo, Miles, Anderson, and Hoover, June 5, 1940; Proposal for Coordination of FBI, ONI, and MID, June 5, 1940; all in Duties of ONI, FBI, and G-2 folder, Official and Confidential Files of FBI Assistant Director Louis Nichols (hereafter Nichols O&C).

12. Athan Theoharis, "The FBI and the American Legion Contact Program," *Political Science Quarterly,* vol. 100, no. 2 (Summer 1985), pp. 274–278.

13. Memo, Jackson to Hoover, April 4, 1941, Jackson, Robert H. folder, Hoover O&C; Memo, Hoover to Watson, October 29, 1940, OF 10-B, Franklin Roosevelt presidential library; Theoharis, "The FBI and the American Legion Contact Program," pp. 273–275.

14. Confidential Memo, Roosevelt to Jackson, May 21, 1940, and Strictly Confidential Memo, Hoover to Tolson, Tamm, and Clegg, May 28, 1940, Wiretapping, Uses of folder, Hoover O&C. FBI officials authorized at least seventeen wiretaps without the attorney general's knowledge or approval. This is documented in seventeen wiretap cards captioned "Personal for LBN [FBI assistant director Louis Nichols] Only Cards from DML [FBI assistant director D. Milton Ladd] 2/1/54" plus nine note cards in Nichols's handwriting, Wiretapping folder, Nichols O&C.

15. Do Not File Memo, Sullivan to DeLoach, July 18, 1966, "Black Bag Jobs" folder, Hoover O&C; JUNE Memo, name redacted agent to SAC New York, April 26, 1954, FBI 62-117166-131.

16. Senate Select Committee on Intelligence Activities, Book III, pp. 636–640, 646–649, 652, 655–659; U.S. Senate, Select Committee to Study Governmental Operations with Respect to Intelligence Activities, *Hearings*

on Intelligence Activities, Vol. 4, Mail Opening, 94th Cong., 1st sess., 1975, pp. 147–149.

17. Memo, Hoover, October 1, 1941, reprinted in U.S. House, Subcommittee on Government Operations, *Hearings on Inquiry into the Destruction of Former FBI Director J. Edgar Hoover's Files and FBI Recordkeeping,* 94th Cong., 1st sess., 1975, pp. 154–155.

18. Letter, Matthew Aid to Athan Theoharis, August 17, 1996. Memo, Harris to AC of S, G-2, May 12, 1942; Letter, Hoover to Strong, November 24, 1942; Letter, Strong to Hoover, January 7, 1943; Letter, Hoover to Berle, January 28, 1942; Letter, Lee to Hoover, January 19, 1942; all in Record Group 319, File 311.5, Military Intelligence Division, National Archives. Letters, Hoover to Watson, October 31 and November 9, 1942, OF 10-B, Roosevelt Presidential Library. In addition to this FBI assistance, army codebreakers acquired similar information from the British that proved helpful in their attempts to decipher the coded messages of Argentina, Sweden, Turkey, Romania, Finland, Paraguay, Guatemala, and Brazil. See Memo and anonymous Annual Report to All Branches, Arlington Hall, April 21, 1943, Record Group 417, Box 832, National Archives.

19. Personal and Confidential Letter, Hoover to Watson, September 28, 1940, and attached Memo re: Washington Embassies, September 27, 1940, OF B, Roosevelt Presidential Library.

20. Memo, Wannall to Brennan, March 28, 1971, Intelligence Coverage Domestic and Foreign folder, Hoover O&C; Athan Theoharis, *Chasing Spies: How the FBI Failed in Counterintelligence but Promoted the Politics of McCarthyism in the Cold War Years* (Chicago: Ivan R. Dee, 2002), pp. 68–69.

21. See the FBI's National Security Electronic Surveillance index card file which lists the targets and dates of installation of specially sensitive FBI wiretaps and bugs. In processing my request for this file, the FBI withheld on personal privacy grounds all such cards recording FBI taps and bugs of individuals, releasing only cards on organizations.

22. Theoharis, *Chasing Spies,* p. 69; Theoharis, *The FBI and American Democracy,* pp. 143–144; Theoharis and Cox, *The Boss,* pp. 13–15; David Alvarez, *Secret Messages: Codebreaking and American Diplomacy, 1930–1945* (Lawrence: University Press of Kansas, 2000), p. 214; Alexander Stephan, *"Communazis": FBI Surveillance of German Emigre Writers* (New Haven: Yale University Press, 2000), pp. 117, 119, 122, 128–129, 192, 253–254, 257, 259–266, 275–276.

23. McDonnell, *Insidious Foes,* pp. 127–128; Raymond Batvinis, *The Origins of FBI Counterintelligence* (Lawrence: University Press of Kansas, 2007), pp. 226–256.

24. McDonnell, *Insidious Foes,* pp. 131–132; Louis Fisher, *Nazi Saboteurs on Trial: A Military Tribunal and American Law* (Lawrence: University Press of Kansas, 2003), pp. 1–36.

25. Personal and Confidential Letter, Hoover to Hopkins, May 7, 1943, OF 10-B, Roosevelt Presidential Library; Robert Benson and Michael Warner, eds., *Venona: Soviet Espionage and the American Response, 1939–1957* (Washington: National Security Agency/Central Intelligence Agency, 1996), pp. 51–54, 105–112; Kai Bird and Martin Sherwin, *American Prometheus: The Triumph and Tragedy of J. Robert Oppenheimer* (New York: Knopf, 2005), pp. 188–190; Report, San Francisco, April 22, 1947, FBI 100-203581-5421; Letter, Hoover to SAC New York, May 15, 1943, FBI 100-203581-5.

26. Letter, Hoover to SAC New York, May 15, 1943, FBI 100-203581-5; Teletype, Hoover to San Francisco, undated but May 1943, FBI 100-203581-47; Memo, Ladd to Welch, April 24, 1943, FBI 100-203581-64; Letter, Conroy to Hoover, May 24, 1943, FBI 100-2-3581-102; Letter, Hoover to Conroy, May 24, 1943, FBI 100-203581-102; Personal and Confidential Letter, Hoover to SAC San Francisco, June 22, 1943, FBI 100-203581-270; Personal and Confidential Letter, Pieper to Hoover, June 18, 1943, FBI 100-203581-407; Letter, Pieper to Hoover, April 7, 1943, FBI 100-203581-689.

27. Bird and Sherwin, *American Prometheus*, pp. 176, 184–193, 231–235; Letter, Pieper to FBI Director, April 7, 1943, FBI 100-203581-X; Letter, Hoover to Pieper, April 24, 1943, FBI 100-203581-X17; Letter, Hoover to Strong, April 22, 1943, FBI 100-203581-X25; Letter, Hoover to SAC New York, May 15, 1943, FBI 100-203581-5; Memo, Ladd to Welch, April 24, 1943, FBI 100-203581-64; Letter, Hoover to Strong, June 22, 1943, FBI 100-203581-87. Personal and Confidential Letters, Hoover to Strong, June 22, 1943, FBI 100-203581-176; June 25, 1943, FBI 100-203581-267; September 24, 1943, FBI 100-203581-487; September 18, 1943, FBI 100-203581-547. Confidential Letter, Hoover to Lansdale, September 8, 1943, FBI 100-203581-587; Report, San Francisco, April 22, 1947, FBI 100-203581-5421; Narrative, New York, January 30, 1945, FBI 100-203581-3914.

28. Theoharis, *Chasing Spies*, pp. 46–47, 81–82; Benson and Warner, *Venona*, pp. xii–xiii, xv, xix, xxv–xxvi, 201–202, 255–256, 299–300, 327–328, 335, 341–342, 363–364, 365, 381, 387–389, 425–426, 441–442.

29. Memo, Ladd to FBI Director, April 25, 1950, FBI 65-59122-15; Report, New York, May 10, 1950, FBI 65-59122-37; Report, Albuquerque, May 4, 1950, FBI 65-59122-38.

30. Bird and Sherwin, *American Prometheus*, pp. 285–287. Soviet consular officials record Hall's and Sax's self-appointed roles as volunteer espionage agents. See the relevant intercepted consular reports reprinted in Benson and Warner, *Venona*, pp. xxvi, 363–364, 441–442.

31. Theoharis, *Chasing Spies*, pp. 64–78.

32. Personal and Confidential Letters, Hoover to Hopkins, October 24, 1942, May 7, 1943, August 7, 1944, December 22, 1944 (and accompanying Quarterly Report on Espionage and Counterespionage Activities), December 24, 1944; Personal and Confidential Letters, Hoover to Watson,

September 30, 1943, August 3, 1943, October 27, 1943, March 21, 1944; General Intelligence Survey in the United States, January 1945; all in OF 10-B, Roosevelt Presidential Library.

33. Theoharis, *Chasing Spies*, pp. 47–49.

34. Athan Theoharis, "A Creative and Aggressive FBI: The Victor Kravchenko Case," *Intelligence and National Security*, vol. 20, no. 2 (June 2005), pp. 324–329.

35. Theoharis, *Chasing Spies*, pp. 41–43, 55.

36. Report, San Francisco, December 15, 1944, FBI 100-203581-3702.

37. Athan Theoharis, "The FBI, the Roosevelt Administration, and the 'Subversive' Press," *Journalism History*, vol. 19, no. 1 (Spring 1993), pp. 3–9.

38. Theoharis, *Chasing Spies*, pp. 58, 151–155.

39. Stephan, *"Communazis,"* pp. 2, 20, 35, 36, 43–45, 50, 67, 76, 77, 85, 89, 117, 119–123, 125–129, 138, 190, 192, 195–196, 253–254, 257, 259–266, 271, 275–276.

40. The full text of this massive report is reprinted, accompanied by a useful historical survey of the period, in Robert Hill, ed., *The FBI's RACON: Racial Conditions in the United States During World War II* (Boston: Northeastern University Press, 1995).

41. Memos, Ladd to Hoover, September 11 and October 21, 1942, FBI 62-116758; Hill, *RACON*, pp. 12–13, 56n55.

42. Memo, hab [Helen Boehm] to FBI Director, January 29, 1942 and Memo, Ladd to FBI Director, February 4, 1942, American Youth Congress folder, Nichols O&C.

43. Memo, Ladd to FBI Director, December 1, 1942, Miscellaneous A–Z folder, Nichols O&C.

44. Bidwell, *History of the Military Intelligence Division*, p. 288. Do Not File Memo, Burton to Ladd, December 31, 1943, and Memo, Nichols to FBI Director, January 18, 1950, Joseph Lash folder, Hoover O&C. Memos, Nichols to FBI Director, January 8, 1953, and February 2, 1954, Dwight Eisenhower folder, Nichols O&C. Memos re Bissell, Boyer, Waterhouse, Kraus, Kibler, Forney, and Ark (MID officials involved in the surveillance of Lash), Jones to Nichols, February 5, 1954, Eleanor Roosevelt folder, Nichols O&C. Athan Theoharis, "Military Intelligence, the FBI, and Mrs. Roosevelt," *Our Right to Know* (Winter 1984), pp. 5–7.

45. Memos, Hoover to Personal Files, April 14 and 23, 1959, Joseph Alsop folder, Hoover O&C. David Barrett, *The CIA and Congress: The Untold Story from Truman to Kennedy* (Lawrence: University Press of Kansas, 2005), pp. 368–369.

Chapter 4. The Origins of the National Security State: Part II, Foreign Intelligence

1. Athan Theoharis, "FBI Wiretapping: A Case Study of Bureaucratic Autonomy," *Political Science Quarterly*, vol. 107, no. 1 (Spring 1992), pp.

107–109. Letter, Vanderbilt to Tully, July 22, 1941 and Letter, Vanderbilt to Mrs. Roosevelt and Report, November 29, 1942, PSF Cornelius Vanderbilt, Roosevelt Presidential Library. Letters, Hoover to Watson, August 9, 1941, September 16, 1941, November 22, 1941, December 16, 1941, February 19, 1942, and November 12, 1942; Memo, ld to Watson, September 16, 1941; Letter, Vanderbilt to Roosevelt, January 15, 1942; all in OF 10-B, Roosevelt Presidential Library. Memo, Roosevelt to Hoover, March 18, 1943, PSF Justice Department J. Edgar Hoover, Roosevelt Presidential Library.

2. Dorwart, *Conflict of Duty*, pp. 162–163, 168–169; MacDonnell, *Insidious Foes*, pp. 141–142; Roger Daniels, *Prisoners Without Trial: Japanese Americans in World War II* (New York: Hill & Wang, 1993), pp. 24–25. Letter, Carter to Berle, February 20, 1941; Memos, Berle to Welles, February 20 and July 28, 1941; Memo, Berle to Director, Bureau of the Budget, June 9, 1941; Memo, Berle, September 16, 1941; Memo to Berle, October 17, 1941; Memo, Lawton to Berle, October 17, 1941; Memo, Smith to Roosevelt, October 16, 1941; all in Adolf Berle Papers, Carter, John Franklin, Roosevelt Presidential Library.

3. MacDonnell, *Insidious Foes*, p. 169; Dorwart, *Conflict of Duty*, pp. 114, 164–168; Thomas Troy, *Wild Bill and Intrepid: Donovan, Stephenson, and the Origins of CIA* (New Haven: Yale University Press, 1996), pp. 105–109. Memo, Kirk to Tully, March 20, 1941; Memo, Roosevelt to Tully, March 19, 1941; Letters, Astor to Roosevelt, February 5, 1940, June 7, 1940, and April 20, 1940; Memo, Roosevelt to Morgenthau, February 8, 1940; Letter, Astor to Lelfand, undated; all in PSF Vincent Astor, Roosevelt Presidential Library. Letter, Berle to Kirk, undated but March 1941; Memo, Chief of Naval Operations to Commander, Third Naval District, March 28, 1941; all in PPF 40, Roosevelt Presidential Library.

4. MacDonnell, *Insidious Foes*, pp. 167–169; Batvinis, *Origins of FBI Counterintelligence*, pp. 177–182, 207–225; Dorwart, *Conflict of Duty*, pp. 166–168; Douglas Charles, "'Before the Colonel Arrived': Hoover, Donovan, Roosevelt, and the Origins of American Central Intelligence, 1940–1941," *Intelligence and National Security*, vol. 20, no. 2 (June 2005), pp. 226–234; Beatrice Berle and Travis Jacobs, eds., *Navigating the Rapids 1918–1971: From the Papers of Adolf A. Berle* (New York: Harcourt Brace Jovanovich, 1973), pp. 320, 321, 337, 341, 373; William Stephenson, *A Man Called Intrepid: The Secret War* (New York: Harcourt Brace Jovanovich, 1976), pp. 76–80, 90, 105–106, 160–162, 171–172; Donald McLachan, *Room 39: A Study in Naval Intelligence* (New York: Atheneum, 1968), pp. 219–223, 227; H. Montgomery Hyde, *Room 3603: The Story of British Intelligence Center in New York During World War II* (New York: Farrar, Straus, 1962), pp. 24–28, 32–33, 52, 56, 60 63, 73, 134–144; Bidwell, *History of the Military Intelligence Division*, pp. 397–401; Jensen, *Army Surveillance in America*, pp. 213–217; David Rudgers, *Creating the*

Secret State: The Origins of the Central Intelligence Agency, 1943–1947 (Lawrence: University Press of Kansas, 2000), p. 7. Personal and Confidential Letters, Hoover to Watson, December 9, 1941 (and Report In Re: Censorship, December 8, 1941), and March 7, 1944 (and Report on Special Intelligence Service); Memo, Biddle to Roosevelt, December 22, 1941; Memo Prepared by Assistant Secretary of State Berle, June 24, 1940 and Approved by President; Memo Re: Foreign Funds, March 13, 1941; all in OF 10-B, Roosevelt Presidential Library. Censorship folder, Nichols O&C.

    5. Memos, Tamm to FBI Director, July 3, 4, 5, 7, 8, 9, 10, and 30, and August 1, 1941; Personal and Confidential Letter, Donegan to Hoover, July 4, 1941; Memos, Foxworth to FBI Director, July 4, 9, and 10, 1941; Personal and Confidential Letter, Hoover to Watson, July 5, 1941; Transcript, Telephone Conversation Hoover and Astor, July 5, 1941; all in Kermit Roosevelt folder, Nichols O&C. Memo, ld for Record, March 14, 1941; Letter, Belle Roosevelt to LeHand, undated but March 1941; Telegram, Watson to Belle Roosevelt, March 14, 1941, and reply, March 14, 1941; Memo, Eleanor Roosevelt to Watson, undated but July 1941; Letter, Belle Roosevelt to Watson, July 10, 1941; Letter, Miles to Watson, July 17, 1941; Letter, Watson to Davison, July 21, 1941; Message to Early, September 30, 1941; all in PPF 1224, Roosevelt Presidential Library. Message to White House, October 18, 1941, OF 10 B, Roosevelt Presidential Library. Telegram, Astor to Tully, July 7, 1941; Memo, Miles to Watson, July 29, 1941; Memo, Watson to President, September 15, 1941; Letter, Astor to Watson, September 3, 1941; Medical Report on Kermit Roosevelt, Ryan and Martin to Astor, August 27, 1941; all in PSF Kermit Roosevelt, Roosevelt Presidential Library. Memo, Biddle re luncheon with President, February 7, 1942, Francis Biddle Papers, Roosevelt, Franklin D., Roosevelt Presidential Library.

    6. Personal and Confidential Letter, Hoover to Watson, June 2, 1941, and accompanying Report on the Coordination of the Three Intelligence Services, OF 10-B, Roosevelt Presidential Library; Transcript, Telephone Conversation Hoover and Astor, July 5, 1941, Kermit Roosevelt folder, Nichols O&C; Correlation Summary, William Donovan, November 15, 1955, FBI 77-58706-50; Anthony Cave Brown, *The Last Hero: Wild Bill Donovan* (New York: Times Books, 1982), pp. 159–160.

    7. Memo, Tamm to Hoover, June 27, 1941, FBI 94-4-4672-5X. Correlation Summary, William Donovan, November 15, 1955, FBI 77-58706-5X. Personal and Confidential Letter, Foxworth to Hoover, October 22, 1941, and Memos, Tamm to Hoover, November 22 and 26, 1941, FBI 62-116758. Blind Memo, January 5, 1942, FBI 94-4-4672-10. Bidwell, *History of the Military Intelligence Division*, pp. 401–402; Troy, *Wild Bill and Intrepid*, pp. 108–133; Senate Select Committee on Intelligence Activities, Book VI, pp. 138–141; Arthur Darling, *The Central Intelligence Agency: An Instrument of Government to 1950* (University Park: Pennsylvania State University Press, 1990), pp. 7–10.

8. Memo, Roosevelt to Attorney General, Under Secretary of State, Donovan, MID, and ONI, December 30, 1941; Memo, Biddle to President, December 22, 1941; Confidential Directive, December 23, 1941; OF 10-B, Roosevelt Presidential Library; Gentry, *J. Edgar Hoover*, pp. 294–295.

9. Senate Select Committee on Intelligence Activities, Book VI, pp. 141–147, 155–156; Darling, *The Central Intelligence Agency*, pp. 10–14.

10. Memo, Roosevelt to Secretaries of State, Treasury, War and Navy, Postmaster General, and Chairman of the Federal Communications Commission, December 8, 1941; Memo, Biddle to Watson, December 8, 1941, and attached Report In Re: Censorship, December 8, 1941; OF 10-B, Roosevelt Presidential Library. Memo, Postmaster General to President, December 12, 1941, OF 1773, Roosevelt Presidential Library. Memo, Price to President, January 23, 1942; Letter, Price to President, February 19, 1942; Letter, Biddle to President, May 18, 1942; OF 4695, Roosevelt Presidential Library. Censorship folder, Nichols O&C.

11. Leslie Rout and John Bratzel, *The Shadow War: German Espionage and United States Counterespionage in Latin America During World War II* (Frederick, Md.: University Publications of America, 1986), pp. 29–40, 454–456; G. Greg Webb, "Intelligence Liaison Between the FBI and State, 1940–44," *Studies in Intelligence*, vol. 49, no. 3 (2005), pp. 25, 29–38.

12. Senate Select Committee on Intelligence Activities, Book VI, pp. 142–150; Darling, *The Central Intelligence Agency*, pp. 11–20.

13. Confidential Memo, Ladd to FBI Director, June 26, 1944, FBI 62-116758.

14. Mark Riebling, *Wedge: The Secret War Between the FBI and CIA* (New York: Knopf, 1994), pp. 37–42; Donald Downes, *The Scarlet Thread: Adventures in Wartime Espionage* (New York: British Book Center, 1953), pp. 87–88, 93–95, 97.

15. Theoharis, *Chasing Spies*, pp. 97–109.

16. Bidwell, *History of the Military Intelligence Division*, pp. 330–335, 443–500; Richelson, *Century of Spies*, pp. 115–123; *Report of the Joint Committee on the Investigation of the Pearl Harbor Attack*, 79th Cong., 2d sess., 1945 (New York: DaCapo Press, 1972), pp. 179–180, 262–263, 264, 266A, 405–409.

Chapter 5. Bureaucracy and Centralization

1. Melvyn Leffler, *A Preponderance of Power: National Security, the Truman Administration, and the Cold War* (Stanford: Stanford University Press, 1992) and Robert Beisner, *Dean Acheson: A Life in the Cold War* (New York: Oxford University Press, 2006) thoughtfully survey the evolution of U.S. foreign policy during the early cold war years 1945–1952.

2. *Report of the Joint Committee on the Investigation of the Pearl Harbor Attack*; William Henhoeffer, *The Intelligence War in 1941: A 50th An-*

niversary Perspective (Washington: Center for the Study of Intelligence, 1992), pp. 30–31; Athan Theoharis, "Revisionism," in Alexander DeConde, Richard Burns, and Fredrik Logevall, eds., *Encyclopedia of American Foreign Policy*, 2d ed. (New York: Scribners, 2002), pp. 413–414; Christopher Andrew, *For the President's Eyes Only: Secret Intelligence and the American Presidency from Washington to Bush* (New York: HarperCollins, 1995), pp. 103–122.

3. Senate Select Committee on Intelligence Activities, Book VI, pp. 151–153; Rudgers, *Creating the Secret State*, pp. 19–22; Theoharis and Cox, *The Boss*, p. 189; Arthur Darling, *The Central Intelligence Agency: An Instrument of Government to 1950* (University Park: Pennsylvania State University Press, 1990), pp. 20–28.

4. Rudgers, *Creating the Secret State*, pp. 22–25; Darling, *The Central Intelligence Agency*, pp. 28–31; Riebling, *Wedge*, pp. 58–60; Gentry, *J. Edgar Hoover*, p. 313; Theoharis and Cox, *The Boss*, p. 189; Richard Gid Powers, *Secrecy and Power: The Life of J. Edgar Hoover* (New York: Free Press, 1987), p. 273.

5. Gentry, *J. Edgar Hoover*, pp. 314–315; Rudgers, *Creating the Secret State*, pp. 25–29; Riebling, *Wedge*, pp. 60–61; Senate Select Committee on Intelligence Activities, Book VI, pp. 153–154.

6. Rudgers, *Creating the Secret State*, pp. 29–46; Darling, *The Central Intelligence Agency*, pp. 35–41; Theoharis and Cox, *The Boss*, p. 190; Senate Select Committee on Intelligence Activities, Book VI, pp. 153–156.

7. Letters, Hoover to Vaughan, September 26 and October 8, 1945; January 9, 1946; June 18, 1947; Letter, Clark to Connelly, February 2, 1946, and enclosed Report Re: Developments in the Intelligence Field in Latin America; all in PSF FBI, Truman Presidential Library. Letter, Stefan to Truman, March 1, 1946 and reply, March 7, 1946, Stephen Spingarn Papers, OF 10-B, Truman Presidential Library.

8. Rudgers, *Creating the Secret State*, pp. 43–44, 47–60; Theoharis and Cox, *The Boss*, pp. 199–200n.

9. Memo, Truman re Central Intelligence Service, November 7, 1945, and Letter, Attorney General to President with attached directive, January 19, 1946, OF 892, National Intelligence Authority, Truman Presidential Library; Memo, Souers to Clifford, December 27, 1945, Clark Clifford Papers, National Intelligence Authority, Truman Presidential Library; Rudgers, *Creating the Secret State*, pp. 63–92; Darling, *The Central Intelligence Agency*, pp. 43–74; Michael Warner, ed., *The CIA Under Harry Truman* (Washington, D.C.: Center for the Study of Intelligence, 1994), pp. 17–32.

10. Memo, Elsey for File, July 17, 1946, Clark Clifford Papers, National Intelligence Authority, Truman Presidential Library.

11. Rudgers, *Creating the Secret State*, pp. 63–138; Darling, *The Central Intelligence Agency*, pp. 16–176; Barrett, *CIA and Congress*, pp. 9–22; Warner, *CIA Under Truman*, pp. 105–109, 131–135.

12. U.S. Senate, Select Committee to Study Governmental Operations with Respect to Intelligence Activities, *Final Report, Foreign and Military Intelligence*, Book I, 94th Cong., 2d sess., 1976, pp. 127–131, 492–496; Barrett, *CIA and Congress*, pp. 17–20; Darling, *The Central Intelligence Agency*, pp. 180–183, 186; Rudgers, *Creating the Secret State*, pp. 136–148; Warner, *CIA Under Truman*, pp. 287–294.

13. Barrett, *CIA and Congress*, pp. 15, 23; Senate Select Committee on Intelligence Activities, Book I, pp. 136–138; Darling, *The Central Intelligence Agency*, pp. 177, 184; Rudgers, *Creating the Secret State*, pp. 143–147.

14. Darling, *The Central Intelligence Agency*, pp. 195–218; Riebling, *Wedge*, pp. 73–77; Warner, *CIA Under Truman*, p. 77.

15. Anna Kasten Nelson, "President Truman and the National Security Council," *Journal of American History*, vol. 72, no. 2 (September 1985), pp. 360–378.

16. Warner, *CIA Under Truman*, pp. 141–148, 173–175, 183–188, 191–195, 213–216, 222–239, 347, 437–439; Senate Select Committee on Intelligence Activities, Book I, pp. 22–23, 48–50, 131–135, 485–489; Rudgers, *Creating the Secret State*, pp. 167–179; Darling, *The Central Intelligence Agency*, pp. 246–281, 410–412; John Prados, *Presidents' Secret Wars: CIA and Pentagon Covert Operations from World War II Through the Persian Gulf* (Chicago: Ivan R. Dee, 1996), pp. 26–90; John Prados, *Safe for Democracy: The Secret Wars of the CIA* (Chicago: Ivan R. Dee, 2006), pp. 38–41.

17. Darling, *The Central Intelligence Agency*, pp. 194–421, Rudgers, *Creating the Secret State*, pp. 149–180; Warner, *CIA Under Truman*, pp. 137–138, 169–171, 296–318, 341–345, 457–468.

18. Warner, *CIA Under Truman*, pp. 177–179.

19. Reports, Executive Secretary to NSC, June 28, 1948; August 6, 1948; November 16, 1948; March 22, 1949; NSC Agenda, March 17, 1949; Memo, Souers to NSC, May 4, 1949; all in PSF NSC, Truman Presidential Library. Memo, Spingarn to President, October 15, 1948, Stephen Spingarn Papers, White House Assignment, Truman Presidential Library.

20. Darling, *The Central Intelligence Agency*, pp. 335–336, 357–359, 367–368, 390–391; Memo, Souers to NSC, April 23, 1949 and Letter, Hoover to Souers, August 4, 1949, PSC NSC, Truman Presidential Library.

21. James Bamford, *Puzzle Palace: A Report on America's Most Secret Agency* (New York: Houghton Mifflin, 1982), pp. 68–81; Senate Select Committee on Intelligence Activities, Book I, pp. 325–326.

22. Bamford, *Puzzle Palace*, pp. 302–315; U.S. Senate, Select Committee to Study Governmental Operations with Respect to Intelligence Activities, *Hearings on Intelligence Activities, Vol. 5, The National Security Agency and Fourth Amendment Rights*, 94th Cong., 1st sess., 1975, pp. 57–60; U.S. Senate, Select Committee to Study Governmental Operations with Respect to Intelligence Activities, *Final Report, Supplementary Detailed Staff Re-*

ports on Intelligence Activities and the Rights of Americans, Book III, 94th Cong., 2d sess., 1976, pp. 740–741, 765–776; U.S. House, Subcommittee of the Committee on Government Operations, *Hearings on Nonverbal Communications by Federal Intelligence Agencies*, 94th Cong., 1st and 2d sess., 1975–1976, pp. 209–210, 323–324; Memo, Snyder to Bureau of Budget, June 8, 1948, John Snyder Papers, Bureau of the Budget, Truman Presidential Library; *Congressional Record*, 82d Cong., 1st sess., 1951, vol. 97, Parts 4 and 10, pp. 5390, 5533–5540, 13211, 13549, 13747–13748, 13783, 13784, 13786; U.S. House, Committee on the Judiciary, *Report No. 462, Amending Certain Titles of the U.S. Code, and for Other Purposes, May 15, 1951*, pp. 7–8, 30–31; U.S. Senate, Committee on the Judiciary, *Report No. 1020, Amending Certain Titles of the United States Code, and for Other Purposes*, October 16, 1951, pp. 3, 9, 32–33.

23. Bamford, *Puzzle Palace*, p. 315.

24. Benson and Warner, *Venona*, pp. xii–xv, xxi–xxvii, xxx; John Haynes and Harvey Klehr, *Venona: Decoding Soviet Espionage in America* (New Haven: Yale University Press, 1999), pp. 8–10, 23–39.

25. U.S. Senate, Select Committee to Study Governmental Operations with Respect to Intelligence Activities, *Hearings on Intelligence Activities, Vol. 2, Huston Plan*, 94th Cong., 1st sess., 1975, pp. 23, 53–54, 68–69, 97, 124, 173, 174, 178, 185, 190, 191, 194, 195, 199, 249–253, 268–269, 272, 346–358, 365, 372–386; Senate Select Committee on Intelligence Activities, Book III, pp. 311–312, 355, 519–520, 930–933, 942, 946–948, 971.

26. Harrison Salisbury, *Without Fear or Favor: An Uncompromising Look at The New York Times* (New York: Ballantine Books, 1981), pp. 580–582; Telephone Interview, Theoharis with Bryan, July 18, 1981; Memos, Nichols to Tolson, April 14, 16, and 21, 1953, Joseph Bryan III folder, Nichols O&C; Athan Theoharis, "The CIA and the *New York Times*: An Unanswered Question," *Government Publications Review*, vol. 10 (1983), pp. 257–259.

Chapter 6. Secrecy and the Loss of Accountability

1. Rhodri Jeffreys-Jones, *The CIA and American Democracy* (New Haven: Yale University Press, 1989), pp. 70, 102; Senate Select Committee on Intelligence Activities, Book I, p. 50; Barrett, *CIA and Congress*, pp. 195, 211–214.

2. Senate Select Committee on Intelligence Activities, Book I, pp. 149–150; Jeffreys-Jones, *CIA and American Democracy*, pp. 78–79; Barrett, *CIA and Congress*, pp. 171–176, 210–211, 223–233; Prados, *Safe for Democracy*, p. 151.

3. This personalized oversight is described in detail in Barrett, *CIA and Congress*; see pp. 458–463; for particular episodes, see pp. 4, 27, 30, 101, 117, 163, 205, 276–277, 319–322, 331.

4. Hugh Clegg folder, Nichols O&C; Memos, Hoover to Tolson, Mohr, Bishop, and Callahan, September 24 and 30, 1970, Tolson File; Frank Donner, *The Age of Surveillance: The Aims and Methods of America's Political Intelligence System* (New York: Knopf, 1980), pp. 103–104.

5. Matthew Aid, "'Not So Anonymous': Parting the Veil of Secrecy About the National Security Agency," in Athan Theoharis, ed., *A Culture of Secrecy: The Government Versus the People's Right to Know* (Lawrence: University Press of Kansas, 1998), pp. 60–77; Bamford, *Puzzle Palace*, pp. 82–158, 220, 357; Senate Select Committee on Intelligence Activities, Book VI, p. 268; Senate Select Committee on Intelligence Activities, *Hearings on the National Security Agency*, pp. 1–3, 7; Senate Select Committee on Intelligence Activities, Book I, pp. 327, 331, 334, 354–35, 464; Senate Select Committee on Intelligence Activities, Book III, pp. 736–783; Andrew, *For the President's Eyes Only*, pp. 216–217.

6. Senate Select Committee on Intelligence Activities, Book I, pp. 109–112, 146–147; Jeffreys-Jones, *CIA and American Democracy*, pp. 83, 85, 92; Prados, *Presidents' Secret Wars*, pp. 90–113; Prados, *Safe for Democracy*, pp. 150–151, 160–161.

7. Prados, *Presidents' Secret Wars*, pp. 145–148; Senate Select Committee on Intelligence Activities, Book I, pp. 114–115; Barrett, *CIA and Congress*, pp. 226–227, 275, 314–315.

8. Letters, Soucy to FBI Director, September 7 and December 27, 1943; Letter, Hoover to Soucy, October 18, 1943; Joseph Kennedy folder, Hoover O&C.

9. Memo, Hoover to Tolson, Boardman, Belmont, and Nichols, February 16, 1956, Joseph Kennedy folder, Hoover O&C.

10. U.S. Senate, Select Committee to Study Governmental Operations with Respect to Intelligence Activities, *Hearings on Intelligence Activities, Vol. 4, Mail Opening*, 94th Cong., 1st sess., 1975, pp. 10, 26, 31, 44, 46, 70–73, 84, 175–188, 190–194; Senate Select Committee on Intelligence Activities, Book III, pp. 562, 565–570, 579–582, 585–586, 594.

11. Nigel West, *The Illegals: The Double Lives of the Cold War's Most Secret Agents* (London: Hodder & Stoughton, 1998), pp. 116–126; Robert Lamphere and Tom Shachtman, *The FBI-KGB War: A Special Agent's Story* (New York: Random House, 1986), pp. 273–277; Senate Select Committee on Intelligence Activities, Book III, p. 625; Riebling, *Wedge*, pp. 143–147.

12. Senate Select Committee on Intelligence Activities, vol. 4, pp. 4–10, 15–16, 18–19, 21–23, 113, 153–154, 168, 185, 190–196, 203, 257–258; Senate Select Committee on Intelligence Activities, Book III, pp. 565, 570–579, 625–634; Athan Theoharis, "In-House Cover-up: Researching FBI Files," in Athan Theoharis, ed., *Beyond the Hiss Case: The FBI, Congress, and the Cold War* (Philadelphia: Temple University Press, 1982), pp. 27–29.

13. Senate Select Committee on Intelligence Activities, Book I, pp. 392–409; U.S. Senate, Select Committee on Intelligence and Committee on

Human Resources, Subcommittee on Health and Scientific Research, *Joint Hearings on Project MKULTRA, the CIA's Program in Behavorial Modification*, 95th Cong., 1st sess., 1977, pp. 2–4, 8–15, 21–23, 25, 38, 43, 45–55, 103–107, 134–141; Theoharis, "In-House Cover-up," pp. 40–41, 43.

14. Warner, *CIA Under Truman*, pp. 383–384; Lyman Kirkpatrick, *The U.S. Intelligence Community: Foreign Policy and Domestic Activities* (New York: Hill & Wang, 1973), p. 153; Donner, *Age of Surveillance*, p. 269n; Jeffreys-Jones, *CIA and American Democracy*, pp. 77, 157–158; Victor Marchetti and John Marks, *The CIA and the Cult of Intelligence* (New York: Knopf, 1974), pp. 48, 232; Senate Select Committee on Intelligence Activities, Book I, pp. 181, 184–185, 184n4; Prados, *Safe for Democracy*, pp. 92–93, 369.

15. Kirkpatrick, *The U.S. Intelligence Community*, pp. 151, 153, 156, 187; Senate Select Committee on Intelligence Activities, Book I, pp. 179–184, 188, 189–201; Frances Stonor Saunders, *Who Paid the Piper? The CIA and the Cultural Cold War* (London: Granta Books, 1999), pp. 293–298; Jeffreys-Jones, *CIA and American Democracy*, p. 158; Donner, *Age of Surveillance*, p. 270n; Salisbury, *Without Fear or Favor*, pp. 484–485, 491–509, 569–575, 580–583; Sigmund Diamond, *Compromised Campus: The Collaboration of Universities with the Intelligence Community, 1945–1955* (New York: Oxford University Press, 1992), pp. 52–56, 59–60, 65–110, 298n3, 310n39, 314n41, 328n21; Prados, *Safe for Democracy*, pp. 89, 91–92, 283.

16. Saunders, *Who Paid the Piper?*, pp. 42–43, 62–65, 83–380; Volker Berghahn, *America and the Intellectual Cold War in Europe: Shepard Stone Between Philanthropy, Academy, and Diplomacy* (Princeton: Princeton University Press, 2001), pp. 127–142, 171–172, 176, 214–249; Warner, *CIA Under Truman*, pp. 134–135.

17. Riebling, *Wedge*, pp. 134–135; Prados, *Safe for Democracy*, p. 429.

18. Diamond, *Compromised Campus*, pp. 5–64, 68–70, 81–85.

19. Alexander Charns, *Cloak and Gavel: FBI Wiretaps, Bugs, Informers, and the Supreme Court* (Urbana: University of Illinois Press, 1992), pp. 4–7, 46–47, 63.

20. Mike Forrest Keen, *Stalking the Sociological Imagination: J. Edgar Hoover's FBI Surveillance of American Sociology* (Westport: Greenwood Press, 1999), pp. 1–2, 5–6, 14–26, 36–47, 77–80, 108–118, 125–138, 174–183, 191–199; Jessica Wang, *American Science in an Age of Anxiety: Scientists, Anticommunism, and the Cold War* (Chapel Hill: University of North Carolina Press, 1999), pp. 58–84; Theoharis, *Chasing Spies*, pp. 212, 223–230; Diamond, *Compromised Campus*, pp. 139–140, 142–143, 151–166, 179–203, 205–209, 243–246, 265–266, 269; Ellen Schrecker, *Many Are the Crimes: McCarthyism in America* (Boston: Little, Brown, 1998), pp. 211–212, 221–222; Theoharis and Cox, *The Boss*, pp. 321–322; Sigmund Diamond, "The Arrangement: The FBI and Harvard University in

the McCarthy Period," in Theoharis, *Beyond the Hiss Case*, pp. 343–358, 362–364; Donner, *Age of Surveillance*, pp. 155–160.

21. Senate Select Committee on Intelligence Activities, Book III, p. 430.

22. Senate Select Committee on Intelligence Activities, Book III, pp. 3–77; Theoharis and Cox, *The Boss*, pp. 119–120, 126–128, 131, 134–139, 147–148, 177, 191, 203, 210–211, 216, 247, 262–263, 277–278, 310–311, 322; Theoharis, *Spying on Americans*, pp. 133–134, 164–165; Schrecker, *Many Are the Crimes*, p. 227; Donner, *Age of Surveillance*, 177–184; O'Reilly, *Hoover and the Un-Americans*, pp. 31–33, 78–82, 112, 125, 164–165, 199–20, 211–212, 216; Gentry, *J. Edgar Hoover*, p. 179.

23. Theoharis and Cox, *The Boss*, pp. 165–167, 213–219, 250–256, 261, 261n, 280–300, 308–309, 315–322; Theoharis, *Chasing Spies*, pp. 59, 120, 156–164, 168, 199–220, 241–244; Schrecker, *Many Are the Crimes*, pp. 204, 215–216; Michael Ybarra, *Washington Gone Crazy: Senator Pat McCarran and the Great American Communist Hunt* (Hanover, N.H.: Steerforth Press, 2004), pp. 248, 386, 393, 547–548; O'Reilly, *Hoover and the Un-Americans*, pp. 73–77, 81, 91–100, 115–116, 120–125, 128–129, 137–138, 145–146, 165–166, 169, 174, 193–195, 202–216; Ovid Demaris, *The Director: An Oral Biography* (New York: Harper's, 1975), p. 164; Donner, *Age of Surveillance*, pp. 101–117.

24. Natalie Robins, *Alien Ink: The FBI's War on Freedom of Expression* (New York: William Morrow, 1992), pp. 77, 85, 87, 96–98, 109, 143, 148, 157–164, 199–205, 210–216, 310–315, 330–341; Herbert Mitgang, *Dangerous Dossiers: Exposing the Secret War Against America's Greatest Authors* (New York: Donald Fine, 1988), pp. 43–52, 61, 79, 120–124, 128–131, 153–161, 164–171, 263–269.

25. Senate Select Committee on Intelligence Activities, Book III, p. 447; Memo, Nichols to Tolson, February 27, 1953, FBI 62-88217-943; Memo, Hoover to McGranery, August 25, 1952, FBI 62-88217-Not Recorded; Letter, Hoover to Overstreet, December 7, 1956, FBI 100-114575-70; Memos, Sullivan to Belmont, September 19, October 1, and November 25, 1958, FBI 10-114575-88, 90; Theoharis, *Chasing Spies*, pp. 156–168; Schrecker, *Many Are the Crimes*, pp. 317–334; Theoharis and Cox, *The Boss*, pp. 203–208, 310–311; Gentry, *J. Edgar Hoover*, pp. 446–447.

26. Athan Theoharis and John Cox, "A Tale of Two Authors: J. Edgar Hoover, Political Censor," *Authors Guild Bulletin* (Summer 1989), pp. 9–10.

27. *Milwaukee Sentinel*, May 19, 1986, p. 3.

28. Theoharis, *Chasing Spies*, pp. 191–197.

29. *Washington Post*, April 13, 1995, p. C1; Barrett, *CIA and Congress*, pp. 236, 300, 301, 323, 356, 361, 364, 368.

30. *Report to the President by the Commission on CIA Activities Within the United States* (Washington, D.C.: U.S. Government Printing Office, June 1975), pp. 251–269; U.S. Senate, Select Committee to Study Governmental

Operations with Respect to Intelligence Activities, *Final Report, The Investigation of the Assassination of President John F. Kennedy: Performance of the Intelligence Agencies*, Book V, 94th Cong., 2d sess., 1976; Anna Kasten Nelson, "The John F. Kennedy Assassination Records Review Board," in Theoharis, ed., *A Culture of Secrecy*, pp. 211–214; Gentry, *J. Edgar Hoover*, pp. 541–557; Powers, *Secrecy and Power*, pp. 383–390; Riebling, *Wedge*, pp. 173–176.

31. Senate Select Committee on Intelligence Activities, Book V, pp. 4, 12–13, 32, 56–57, 65–67, 87–97; Riebling, *Wedge*, pp. 173–174.

32. Agreement Between the FBI and the Secret Service Concerning Presidential Protection, February 3, 1965, Hoover O&C.

33. Senate Select Committee on Intelligence Activities, Book V, pp. 4, 59, 65–67; Riebling, *Wedge*, pp. 173–174; Thomas Powers, *The Man Who Kept the Secrets: Richard Helms and the CIA* (New York: Knopf, 1979), pp. 147–150, 155, 346n76; U.S. Senate, Select Committee to Study Governmental Operations with Respect to Intelligence Activities, *Interim Report, Alleged Assassination Plots Involving Foreign Leaders*, 94th Cong., 1st sess., 1975, pp. 74–85, 94–108, 111–121, 125–134; Riebling, *Wedge*, pp. 162–168.

34. Andrew, *For the President's Eyes Only*, pp. 312–313; John Prados, *Lost Crusader: The Secret Wars of CIA Director William Colby* (New York: Oxford University Press, 2003), pp. 192–193, 255–257, 270–272, 297–298; Riebling, *Wedge*, pp. 179–183, 185–196, 209–226, 236–238, 241–245.

35. Nelson, "The Kennedy Assassination Records Review Board," pp. 214–230.

36. Senate Select Committee on Intelligence Activities, *Interim Report on Assassination Plots*, pp. 5–60, 56n2; Prados, *Safe for Democracy*, p. 275.

37. Senate Select Committee on Intelligence Activities, Book III, p. 968.

Chapter 7. The Breakdown of the Cold War Consensus

1. Senate Select Committee on Intelligence Activities, Book II, p. 167.

2. Theoharis, *Spying on Americans*, pp. 140–148, 154–155, 175–176, 187–188; Donner, *Age of Surveillance*, pp. 144–147, 150–151, 157–160, 181–240; O'Reilly, *Racial Matters*, pp. 178–185, 203–214, 272–273; Senate Select Committee on Intelligence Activities, vol. 6, pp. 5–7, 12, 14–34, 73–75, 94–95, 110–115, 119–123, 126, 137–140, 152–156, 361–362, 434–442, 486–489, 579–601, 775–780, 813–817; Senate Select Committee on Intelligence Activities, Book II, pp. 50, 68, 71–77, 86–91, 167, 175–179, 193–195, 232–233, 246, 257; Senate Select Committee on Intelligence Activities, Book III, pp. 4–5, 8, 17–57, 59–61, 450–452, 470–495, 506–541; *New York Times*, March 23, 2004, p. A17, and May 6, 2004, p. A25; Geoffrey Rips, ed., *The Campaign Against the Underground Press* (San Francisco: City Lights, 1981).

3. Informal Memo, Sullivan to Belmont, December 2, 1964, FBI 100-106670-1024; Anonymous Letter to King, undated but November 21, 1964, Martin Luther King folder, Hoover O&C; Senate Select Committee on Intelligence Activities, Book III, pp. 81–84; O'Reilly, *Racial Matters*, pp. 125–155; Donner, *Age of Surveillance*, pp. 214–219; David Garrow, *The FBI and Martin Luther King, Jr.: From "Solo" to Memphis* (New York: Norton, 1981), pp. 21–77, 101–150, 160–172.

4. Theoharis and Cox, *The Boss*, pp. 149, 185–186, 244–245, 269–273, 353, 356–357; Theoharis, *Spying on Americans*, pp. 157–172; Gentry, *J. Edgar Hoover*, pp. 560–561.

5. Theoharis and Cox, *The Boss*, pp. 349–353.

6. Theoharis, *Spying on Americans*, pp. 180–181; Senate Select Committee on Intelligence Activities, vol. 6, pp. 174–180, 189, 495–510.

7. Theoharis, *Spying on Americans*, p. 181; Senate Select Committee on Intelligence Activities, vol. 6, pp. 192, 194–195, 539; Gentry, *J. Edgar Hoover*, pp. 578–580.

8. Theoharis, *Spying on Americans*, pp. 176–179; Donner, *Age of Surveillance*, p. 254n; Senate Select Committee on Intelligence Activities, vol. 6, pp. 479, 639, 683, 720; Senate Select Committee on Intelligence Activities, Book II, pp. 16, 117, 120, 229–230, 238, 248, 251; Senate Select Committee on Intelligence Activities, Book III, pp. 313–314, 483–485, 489.

9. Theoharis, *Spying on Americans*, pp. 181–183, 185–186; Senate Select Committee on Intelligence Activities, vol. 6, pp. 164–165, 193, 195–196, 251–253, 483–484, 732–739, 758–760.

10. Senate Select Committee on Intelligence Activities, vol. 6, pp. 368–369, 642–644.

11. Theoharis, *Spying on Americans*, pp. 187–188, 191–194; Senate Select Committee on Intelligence Activities, Book II, pp. 10, 74, 76, 117, 120–122, 175–176, 200–201, 207–208, 230–232, 238, 257; Senate Select Committee on Intelligence Activities, Book III, pp. 245, 246, 314, 323–337, 343–345, 532, 551; Jon Wiener, *Gimme Some Truth: The John Lennon FBI Files* (Berkeley: University of California Press, 1999), pp. 1–5, 13, 48–51, 91, 110–311.

12. Memos, DeLoach to Tolson, March 3 and 7, 1966, President Lyndon Johnson folder, Hoover O&C. Memos, Hoover to Tolson, Belmont, Sullivan, and DeLoach, July 6 and October 6, 1965; Memo, Hoover to Tolson, DeLoach, Sullivan, and Wick, August 27, 1967; all in Tolson File.

13. Memo, Hoover to Tolson, Sullivan, Mohr, Bishop, Brennan, and Callahan, November 20, 1970, Tolson File. Memo, Felt to Tolson, June 10, 1971; Memo, Wannall to Felt, July 28, 1971; Memo, Ponder to Tolson, September 14, 1971; Letter, Hoover to Nixon, September 20, 1971; all in Expansion of FBI Foreign Intelligence folder, Hoover O&C.

14. Senate Select Committee on Intelligence Activities, Book III, pp. 519–521; Senate Select Committee on Intelligence Activities, Book II, pp. 97–99.

15. Senate Select Committee on Intelligence Activities, Book II, pp. 99–102; Senate Select Committee on Intelligence Activities, Book III, pp. 681–682, 687–707, 711–721. Johnson's action was not atypical. The June 2007 release of the CIA's "family jewels," widely covered by the press, revealed a similar action: President Kennedy's decision to ask the CIA in 1962–1963 to wiretap reporters under a code-named Project Mockingbird program. Because wiretapping was illegal and because the CIA would violate its charter, which prohibited it from engaging in "internal security" functions, the program was clearly beyond the law. It was prompted by the FBI's inability to identify the source of leaks of classified information in 1961 to *Newsweek* correspondent Lloyd Norman and in 1962 to *New York Times* military correspondent Hanson W. Baldwin. The latter failure led President Kennedy, during an August 1962 meeting with CIA Director John McCone and members of the Foreign Intelligence Advisory Board, to authorize the CIA to "develop an expert group that would be available at all times to follow up on security leaks." This idea had been proposed by board member James Killian of MIT, who suggested the value of a "sensitive" group to follow the press and seek evidence of "trends and contacts" between reporters and administration officials with access to classified information. Meeting later with McCone, Kennedy inquired about the progress of the proposed "sensitive" group. He was assured that the agency had established "this task force which would be a continuing investigative group reporting to me."

16. Senate Select Committee on Intelligence Activities, Book III, pp. 682, 721–732.

17. Bamford, *Puzzle Palace*, pp. 317–324; Theoharis, *Spying on Americans*, pp. 121–122; Senate Select Committee on Intelligence Activities, vol. 5, pp. 5–16, 30–34, 36–38, 147–150, 156–157; Senate Select Committee on Intelligence Activities, Book III, pp. 738–740, 743–752, 762–765.

18. U.S. Senate, Committee on the Judiciary, Subcommittee on Administrative Practice and Procedure, *Hearings on Administrative Procedure Act*, 89th Cong., 1st sess., 1965, pp. 195, 198–199, 202–203, 206; *Senate Report No. 119*, p. 7; *Senate Report No. 1053*, p. 4; *Senate Report No. 21*, p. 4; *Senate Report No. 518*, pp. 2–3; *Hearings on Invasion of Privacy (Government Agencies)*, pp. 1–3, 5, 8–12. Senate Select Committee on Intelligence Activities, vol. 6, pp. 830–835; Senate Select Committee on Intelligence Activities, Book II, pp. 286n80; Senate Select Committee on Intelligence Activities, Book III, pp. 307–310, 65–68, 676–677. Memos, Hoover to Tolson, Belmont, Gale, Rosen, Sullivan, and DeLoach, March 1 and 2 and July 14, 1965; Memo, Hoover to Tolson, Belmont, Mohr, DeLoach, Gale, Rosen, and Sullivan, August 24, 1965; Memo, Hoover to Tolson and Belmont, November 15, 1965; all in Tolson File.

19. Senate Select Committee on Intelligence Activities, Book III, pp. 285–286; Theoharis, *From the Secret Files*, pp. 150–176, 268–275; Charns, *Cloak and Gavel*, pp. 36–43, 52–63, 69–75.

20. Theoharis and Cox, *The Boss*, p. 393; Senate Select Committee on Intelligence Activities, vol. 6, pp. 357–359, 830–832; Senate Select Committee on Intelligence Activities, Book III, pp. 302, 668–670; Senate Select Committee on Intelligence Activities, Book II, pp. 109–111.

21. Senate Select Committee on Intelligence Activities, vol. 2, p. 68; Senate Select Committee on Intelligence Activities, Book II, p. 112n537; Senate Select Committee on Intelligence Activities, Book III, pp. 932–933, 946–947.

22. Theoharis and Cox, *The Boss*, pp. 355–356.

23. Senate Select Committee on Intelligence Activities, vol. 4, pp. 187–196, 203–204; Senate Select Committee on Intelligence Activities, Book III, pp. 604–611.

24. Jeffreys-Jones, *CIA and American Democracy*, pp. 155, 157–161; Powers, *The Man Who Kept the Secrets*, p. 277; Salisbury, *Without Fear or Favor*, pp. 514–528; Senate Select Committee on Intelligence Activities, Book I, p. 185; Prados, *Safe for Democracy*, pp. 368–369, 375–376.

25. Saunders, *Who Paid the Piper?*, p. 381; Senate Select Committee on Intelligence Activities, Book I, pp. 185–191; Prados, *Safe for Democracy*, pp. 369–372.

26. Senate Select Committee on Intelligence Activities, Book III, pp. 508–509, 522, 699–700, 924, 928–929; Senate Select Committee on Intelligence Activities, Book II, pp. 112, 172; U.S. Senate, Select Committee to Study Governmental Operations with Respect to Intelligence Activities, *Hearings on Intelligence Activities, Vol. 2, Huston Plan*, 94th Cong., 1st sess., 1975, pp. 10–12, 28–30, 86, 103–105, 128–129, 134–135, 203–206, 287–312, 401–403.

27. Senate Select Committee on Intelligence Activities, vol. 2, p. 3; Senate Select Committee on Intelligence Activities, Book III, pp. 924–925, 928–930.

28. David Wise, *The American Police State: The Government Against the People* (New York: Random House, 1976), pp. 258–269; Senate Select Committee on Intelligence Activities, vol. 2, pp. 283–286, 346; Senate Select Committee on Intelligence Activities, Book III, p. 933.

29. Theoharis, *Spying on Americans*, pp. 19–36. The text of the Huston Plan and the various memoranda relating to its formulation and implementation are reprinted in Senate Select Committee on Intelligence Activities, vol. 2, pp. 141–203, 207–248.

30. Senate Select Committee on Intelligence Activities, vol. 2, pp. 268–272; Senate Select Committee on Intelligence Activities, Book III, pp. 977–978.

31. U.S. House, Subcommittee of the Committee on Government Operations, *Hearings on Inquiry into the Destruction of Former FBI Director Hoover's Files and FBI Recordkeeping*, 94th Cong., 1st sess., 1975, pp. 14, 36–64, 6, 93, 95, 107, 203–208, 218–230.

32. Theoharis, *Spying on Americans*, pp. 148–154.

33. Wise, *American Police State*, pp. 253–254; Commission on CIA Activities, *Report*, pp. 203–204; Senate Select Committee on Intelligence Activities, Book III, p. 404n76; U.S. Senate, Select Committee to Study Government Operations with Respect to Intelligence Activities, *Hearings on Intelligence Activities, Vol. 1, Unauthorized Storage of Toxic Agents*, 94th Cong., 1st sess., 1975, pp. 22–23; Senate Select Committee on Intelligence Activities, Book I, pp. 403–404.

34. Senate Select Committee on Intelligence Activities, vol. 4, pp. 26–28, 72–83; Senate Select Committee on Intelligence Activities, Book III, pp. 566–567, 581, 600–604.

35. Athan Theoharis, "Illegal Surveillance: Will Congress Stop the Snooping?" *The Nation*, February 2, 1976, pp. 140–142; Senate Select Committee on Intelligence Activities, vol. 5, pp. 15–16, 158–163; Senate Select Committee on Intelligence Activities, Book III, pp. 739–740, 739n18, 756–761.

36. *New York Times*, December 22, 1974, p. 1; Press Release, Department of Justice, Statement of Attorney General Edward Levi, February 27, 1975.

37. Senate Select Committee on Intelligence Activities, Book II, pp. 343–354.

38. Loch Johnson, *A Season of Inquiry: The Senate Intelligence Investigation* (Lexington: University Press of Kentucky, 1985); Kathryn Olmsted, *Challenging the Secret Government: The Post-Watergate Investigation of the CIA and FBI* (Chapel Hill: University of North Carolina Press, 1996); Prados, *Safe for Democracy*, pp. 434–439.

39. Senate Select Committee on Intelligence Activities, Book II, pp. 289–341.

40. Theoharis, *Spying on Americans*, p. 235; Johnson, *Season of Inquiry*, pp. 172–249; Olmsted, *Challenging Secret Government*, pp. 174–176.

41. U.S. Senate, Committee on the Judiciary, *Hearings on FBI Statutory Charter*, 95th Cong., 2d sess., 1978, Parts 1, 2, and 3.

42. S. 2525, February 9, 1978; U.S. Senate, Select Committee on Intelligence, *Report No. 95-217, Annual Report of the Senate*, 95th Cong., 1st sess., 1977; Theoharis, *Spying on Americans*, pp. 242–243; Johnson, *Season of Inquiry*, pp. 254–257.

43. Theoharis, *Spying on Americans*, pp. 97–119; Athan Theoharis, "Misleading the Presidents: Thirty Years of Wiretapping," *The Nation*, June 14, 1971, pp. 745–749; Bamford, *Puzzle Palace*, pp. 462–468; U.S. Senate, *Report No. 95-701 Foreign Intelligence Surveillance Act of 1978*, 95th Cong., 2d sess., March 14, 1978.

44. Senate Judiciary Committee, *FBI Statutory Charter*, Part 2, pp. 235–241.

45. Theoharis, *Spying on Americans*, p. 235; Johnson, *Season of Inquiry*, pp. 193, 195–197; Prados, *Safe for Democracy*, p. 457.

46. Theoharis, *Spying on Americans*, pp. 236–237; Johnson, *Season of Inquiry*, pp. 254–255; Prados, *Safe for Democracy*, p. 459.

Chapter 8. Reaffirmation of the National Security State

1. U.S. Senate, Select Committee on Intelligence, *Hearings on S. 2284 National Intelligence Act of 1980*, 96th Cong., 2d sess., 1980.

2. *Ibid.*, p. 1.

3. Johnson, *America's Secret Power*, pp. 254–255, 265; Johnson, *Season of Inquiry*, pp. 256, 263; Jeffreys-Jones, *CIA and American Democracy*, pp. 227–228, 233; Prados, *Safe for Democracy*, p. 496; Andrew, *For the President's Eyes Only*, pp. 454–455, 459, 465–466; Tony Poveda, "Controversies and Issues," in Athan Theoharis, ed., *The FBI: A Comprehensive Reference Guide* (Phoenix: Oryx Press, 1999), pp. 347–348.

4. Rhodri Jeffreys-Jones, *Cloak and Dollar: A History of American Secret Intelligence* (New Haven: Yale University Press, 2002), p. 239; Herbert Mitgang, "Annals of Government: Policing America's Writers," *New Yorker*, October 5, 1987, p. 48.

5. Press Release, Department of Justice, March 7, 1983. For contrasting assessments of FBI domestic surveillance and the Smith Guidelines, see John Elliff, "The Attorney General's Guidelines for FBI Investigations" and Athan Theoharis, "FBI Surveillance: Past and Present," *Cornell Law Review*, Symposium National Security and Civil Liberties, vol. 69, no. 4 (April 1984), pp. 785–815, 883–894.

6. Theoharis, *FBI and American Democracy*, pp. 164, 166; Robins, *Alien Ink*, pp. 375–383; Athan Theoharis, "The FBI and Dissent in the United States," in C. E. S. Franks, ed., *Dissent and the State* (Toronto: Oxford University Press, 1989), p. 107.

7. Theoharis, "The FBI and Dissent," pp. 108–109.

8. *Final Report of the Independent Counsel for Iran/Contra Matters, vol. I, Investigations and Prosecutions* (Washington, D.C.: Report of the Independent Counsel, 1993), p. 255–259.

9. Richard Immerman, "A Brief History of the CIA," and John Prados, "A World of Secrets: Intelligence and Counterintelligence," in Athan Theoharis, ed., *The Central Intelligence Agency: Security Under Scrutiny* (Westport: Greenwood Press, 2006), pp. 59–61, 63, 65–67, 148–149, 215–221. Athan Theoharis, "Introduction," and Scott Armstrong, "The War over Secrecy: Democracy's Most Important Low-Intensity Conflict," in Theoharis, *Culture of Secrecy*, pp. 10, 140–161; Andrew, *For the President's Eyes Only*, pp. 478–494; Prados, *Presidents' Secret Wars*, pp. 359–367, 377–386; Riebling, *Wedge*, pp. 368, 370, 401–405.

10. See, for example, Daniel Patrick Moynihan, *Secrecy: The American Experience* (New Haven: Yale University Press, 1998) and the essays in Theoharis, *A Culture of Secrecy*.

11. David Wise, *The Spy Who Got Away: The Inside Story of Edward Lee Howard, the CIA Agent Who Betrayed His Country's Secrets and Escaped to Moscow* (New York: Random House, 1988); Milt Bearden and James Risen, *The Main Enemy: The Inside Story of the CIA's Final Showdown with the KGB* (New York: Random House, 2003), pp. 70–92, 105, 111–118, 134, 141; Riebling, *Wedge*, pp. 354–358.

12. David Wise, *Nightmover: How Aldrich Ames Sold the CIA to the KGB for $4.6 Million* (New York: HarperCollins, 1995); Tim Weiner, David Johnston, and Neil Lewis, *Betrayal: The Story of Aldrich Ames, an American Spy* (New York: Random House, 1995); Bearden and Risen, *Main Enemy*, pp. 15–16, 79–81, 377–378, 467, 473–474, 521, 526–530.

13. Weiner, Johnston, and Lewis, *Betrayal*, p. 282; David Wise, *Spy: The Inside Story of How the FBI's Robert Hanssen Betrayed America* (New York: Random House, 2002), pp. 171, 176.

14. Wise, *Spy*; Bearden and Risen, *Main Enemy*, pp. 126–133, 319–320, 372–375, 493–494.

15. *9/11 Commission Report*, pp. 47–143, 179–214, 255–277; Joint Committee, *Report*, pp. 20–22; Theoharis, *FBI and American Democracy*, pp. 6–7, 166–167; Tony Poveda, "Notable Cases," in Theoharis, ed., *FBI Reference Guide*, pp. 93–98; Richard Immerman, "A Brief History of the CIA," in Theoharis, ed., *The Central Intelligence Agency*, pp. 67–70.

16. *New York Times*, September 17, 2001, p. A5; September 18, 2001, p. B4; September 20, 2001, p. B6; September 21, 2001, p. B9; September 28, 2001, p. A1; October 1, 2001, p. A1; October 2, 2001, p. A1; October 4, 2001, p. B7; October 12, 2001, p. B13; October 13, 2001, p. B6; October 18, 2001, p. B9; October 25, 2001, p. B9; October 26, 2001, p. A1; October 27, 2001, p. B5.

17. *New York Times*, December 16, 2005, p. A1; December 18, 2005, p. 1; December 21, 2005, p. A1; December 22, 2005, p. A14; December 24, 2005, p. A1; February 7, 2006, p. A1; April 13, 2006, p. A17; May 12, 2006, p. A1; May 13, 2006, p. A1; May 14, 2006, p. A1; May 17, 2006, p. A15; May 18, 2006, p. A23; July 1, 2006, p. A12.

18. *New York Times*, November 9, 2001, p. B1; December 1, 2001, p. A1; May 30, 2002, p. A1; May 31, 2002, p. A18; November 21, 2002, p. A1; November 30, 2002, p. A1; November 12, 2003, p. A14; June 21, 2005, p. A1. *Milwaukee JournalSentinel*, December 14, 2003, p. 7A. The Attorney General's Guidelines on General Crime, Racketeering Enterprise and Terrorist Enterprise Investigations, May 30, 2002, *http://www.usdoj .gov/olp/index,html#agguide.*

19. *9/11 Commission Report*, pp. 261–262.

20. *New York Times*, October 28, 2001, p. A1.

21. *9/11 Commission Report*, pp. 2–4, 8–10, 225–227, 239, 242, 248; *New York Times*, May 4, 2002, p. A10; May 9, 2002, p. A22; June 19, 2002, p. A18; September 25, 2002, p. A12.

22. *New York Times*, January 17, 2006, p. A1.

23. *New York Times*, December 20, 2005, p. A1; December 21, 2005, p. A22; December 21, 2005, p. A22; December 23, 2005, p. A18; January 2, 2006, p. A15; January 7, 2006, p. A1; January 19, 2006, p. A17; February 7, 2006, p. A1; February 8, 2006, p. A10; February 11, 2006, p. A1; February 12, 2006, p. 24; March 3, 2006, p. A17; February 16, 2006, p. A24; February 22, 2006, p. A9; April 7, 2006, p. A20; July 9, 2006, p. 1; July 19, 2006, p. A14; November 10, 2006, p. A25.

24. *New York Times*, October 9, 2001, p. A1; October 13, 2001, p. A1; October 16, 2001, p. B5; October 19, 2001, p. B5; October 20, 2001, p. A1 and B7; October 26, 2001, p. B7; November 3, 2001, p. A1; November 7, 2001, p. A1; November 9, 2001, p. A1; November 10, 2001, p. B1; November 17, 2001, p. A1; November 20, 2001, p. B1; November 21, 2001, p. B1; December 6, 2001, p. B8; December 7, 2001, p. B9; December 13, 2001, p. A1; December 14, 2001, p. B6; December 22, 2001, p. A1; December 31, 2001, p. A1; January 15, 2002, p. A11; February 13, 2002, p. A16; February 26, 2002, p. A1; February 27, 2002, p. A10; March 23, 2002, p. A9; May 7, 2002, p. A1; May 10, 2002, p. A28; June 23, 2002, p.1; June 26, 2002, p. A19; August 2, 2002, p. A14; August 10, 2002, p. A9; August 12, 2002, p. A1; August 14, 2002, p. A21; August 26, 2002, p. A10; August 27, 2002, p. A10; September 4, 2002, p. A15; September 5, 2002, p. A17; September 6, 2002, p. A13; July 2, 2003, p. A1; August 2, 2003, p. A9; August 27, 2003, p. A13; July 21, 2004, p. A17; August 6, 2004, p. A10; August 19, 2004, p. A25; October 3, 2004, p. 31; September 17, 2005, p. A1; September 26, 2006, p. A16; November 18, 2006, p. A10.

25. *New York Times*, October 21, 2001, p. B1; June 17, 2002, p. A13; October 6, 2002, p. 1; February 14, 2003, p. A14; February 22, 2003, p. A10; May 3, 2004, p. A18. *Milwaukee JournalSentinel*, December 3, 2001, p. 6A; June 17, 2002, p. 6A; February 22, 2003, p. 7A; March 3, 2003, p. 7A; September 28, 2003, p. 1A; December 8, 2003, p. 4A; May 2, 2004, p. 4A; October 4, 2005, p. 3A; February 21, 2007, p. 4A. AP wire story, November 6, 2006, *http://news.yahoo.com/s/ap/2006 1106/ap.*

26. *New York Times*, November 1, 2001, p. A1; August 29, 2002, p. A1; March 17, 2003, p. A14; April 12, 2003, p. B11; April 19, 2003, p. B7; May 8, 2003, p. A17; May 20, 2003, p. A15; June 4, 2003, p. A1; December 12, 2003, p. A32; January 29, 2004, p. A14; September 2, 2004, p. A10; September 3, 2004, p. A10; October 7, 2004, p. A1; October 13, 2004, p. A15; May 13, 2005, p. A14; March 30, 2006, p. A16.

27. *New York Times*, September 13, 2002, p. A13; September 14, 2002, p. A1; September 15, 2002, pp. 1 and 12; September 16, 2002, p. A11; September 18, 2002, p. A13; September 19, 2002, p. A18; September 20, 2002, p. A1; September 21, 2002, p. A10; October 4, 2002, p. A15; October 9, 2002, p. A26; October 22, 2002, p. A14; November 10, 2002, p. 15; De-

cember 18, 2002, p. A16; January 11, 2003, p. A9; March 26, 2003, p. B15; March 30, 2003, p. A18; April 9, 2003, p. B13; May 20, 2003, p. A16; May 22, 2003, p. A14; October 12, 2003, p. 1.

28. *New York Times*, June 9, 2005, p. A18; June 11, 2005, p. A9; June 17, 2005, p. A16; April 10, 2006, p. A20; April 27, 2006, p. A17; October 2, 2006, p. A10; October 10, 2006, p. A1. Frontline, "The Enemy Within," October 10, 2006.

29. *New York Times*, May 22, 2004, p. A14; May 25, 2004, p. A16; May 26, 2004, p. A1; June 5, 2004, p. A1; October 5, 2004, p. A21; November 17, 2004, p. A14; July 15, 2005, p. A12; January 7, 2006, p. A8; November 30, 2006, p. A18.

30. *New York Times*, February 10, 2004, p. A12, and February 11, 2004, p. A16.

31. Press release, American Civil Liberties Union, May 4, 2006, *www.aclu.org/spyfiles; Milwaukee JournalSentinel*, April 18, 2003, p. 12A, and March 16, 2006, p. 15A; *New York Times*, November 17, 2002, p. 1; March 25, 2003, p. A9; November 23, 2003, p. 1; December 30, 2003, p. A17; July 5, 2004, p. A1; August 16, 2004, p. A1; August 18, 2004, p. A14; August 25, 2004, p. A1; August 28, 2004, p. A9; August 30, 2004, p. 10; April 7, 2005, p. A23; June 17, 2005, p. A1; July 18, 2005, p. A12; December 20, 2005, p. A1.

32. American Civil Liberties Union, *Unpatriotic Acts: The FBI's Power to Rifle Through Your Records and Personal Belongings Without Telling You* (New York: American Civil Liberties Union, 2003), p. 15. *Milwaukee JournalSentinel*, April 29, 2006, p. 5A, and May 6, 2006, p. 3A. *New York Times*, April 27, 2004, p. A14; May 1, 2004, p. A1; March 9, 2006, p. A17; June 2, 2006, p. A17; March 10, 2007, p. A1; March 21, 2007, p. 3A. *Washington Post*, March 12, 2004, p. A1; March 18, 2007, p. A1. Statement, Inspector General Glenn Fine, House Judiciary Committee, March 20, 2007, *http://www.usdoj.gov/org/testimony/0703*. U.S. Department of Justice, Office of the Inspector General, A Review of the Federal Bureau of Investigation Use of National Security Letters, March 2007, *http://www .usdoj.gov/oig/report/0703*.

33. *New York Times*, March 17, 2004, p. A16; January 14, 2006, p. A8; October 13, 2006, p. A16; November 21, 2006, p. A17; January 14, 2007, p. 1; January 15, 2007, p. A12.

34. *9/11 Commission Report*, pp. 40, 409, 417.

35. *Ibid.*, pp. 155–160, 215–223, 226–227, 229–230, 237, 240, 353–354.

INDEX

A NOTE ON THE AUTHOR

Athan Theoharis is emeritus professor of history at Marquette University and a recognized authority on the history of the Federal Bureau of Investigation. The author or editor of more than twenty books, he has received a lifetime achievement award from the American Civil Liberties Union, the Binkley-Stephenson Award from the Organization of American Historians, and the Gavel Award from the American Bar Association. Mr. Theoharis is a graduate of the University of Chicago and has also taught American history at Texas A&M University, Wayne State University, and the City University of New York at Staten Island. He lives in Fox Point, Wisconsin.